Principles and **Practices** of
Gaming-Simulation

Principles
and
Practices
of
Gaming-Simulation

Cathy Stein Greenblat
Richard D. Duke

SAGE PUBLICATIONS   Beverly Hills   London

Chapters 7, 8, 9, 10, 14, and 15 originally appeared in the journal *Simulation & Games*.

Chapter 13 originally appeared in the journal *Teaching Sociology*.

Chapters 3, 5, and 6 originally appeared in Richard D. Duke, *Gaming: The Future's Language*, New York: Halsted Press, 1974.

Many of the chapters have been revised from Cathy S. Greenblat and Richard D. Duke, *Gaming-Simulation: Rationale, Design, and Applications*, New York: Halsted Press, 1975.

For information address:

SAGE Publications, Inc.
275 South Beverly Drive
Beverly Hills, California 90212

SAGE Publications Ltd
28 Banner Street
London EC1Y 8QE, England

Printed in the United States of America

Library of Congress Cataloging in Publication Data

Greenblat, Cathy S., 1940-
    Principles and practices of gaming-simulation.

    Abridged and rev. ed. of: Gaming-simulation—rationale, design, and applications. [1975]
    Bibliography: p.
    1. Game theory—Addresses, essays, lectures. 2. Social sciences—Simulation methods—Addresses, essays, lectures. I. Duke, Richard D. II. Greenblat, Cathy S., 1940- Gaming-simulation—rationale, design, and applications. III. Title.
H61.25.G732   1981   300'.724   81-18201
ISBN 0-8039-1675-2   AACR2
ISBN 0-8039-1676-0 (pbk.)

FIRST PRINTING

Contents

Introduction

The impetus to put together the original version of this volume emerged from the frustrations we both had experienced in trying to learn about gaming-simulation, to write about it, and to teach about it to our graduate students and others who had developed an interest in the field. Often we needed, or others requested, reading materials, and it was difficult to make recommendations. We found several very good books dealing with selected aspects of the field, but no comprehensive, in-depth treatments. There existed, of course, a growing body of literature in the form of articles; these, however, were widely scattered and inaccessible to potential readers unless they were willing to expend considerable time and effort. Finally, there were a few topics on which very little had been written at all. The potential of gaming-simulation for research and in the area of public policy, for example, had scarcely been addressed in the literature despite increasing numbers of applications in these arenas. Therefore few readings could be found in any source on these topics.

We saw our task, then, as twofold. First, we wanted to develop and present in one volume a set of succinct overview essays on the three major themes of rationale, design, and applications. The "text" part of the original volume, therefore, presented integrative essays that could be read separately by the person desiring a comprehensive overview of the field.

Second, we wished to provide the more serious reader the opportunity for in-depth coverage of topics. Therefore we supplemented our overview with a set of articles, some reprinted and some written especially for the volume. These were utilized either to expand upon ideas presented in the lead articles or to offer examples of points made there. In toto, we believed the volume would offer both the newcomer to gaming and the practicing professional an integrated, comprehensive set of materials which expressed a theoretical base and pragmatic guides for day-to-day usage.

The success of the original volume, viewed from a six-year perspective, suggests that we were accurate in our original perception of need. Not only did the volume receive extremely positive reviews in a wide variety of professional journals, but it continues today to be described in annotated bibliographies from such organizations as the American Political Science Association and the American Sociological Association as "the best and most comprehensive book in the field."

This new volume is not meant to replace the older one, but rather to meet somewhat different demands. While the original version graces the shelves of many libraries, is used by a large number of serious gamers, and has sometimes been employed as a text for graduate students, its length and price have limited its utilization in teaching and in overseas contexts. Indeed, the original idea for this version came from friends and colleagues in Europe who used the book extensively, but lamented not being able to pass it on to their students and colleagues who had less time, less knowledge of English, and could not afford to have students purchase the volume if they were only going to read the main "text" part of the volume. We discussed with them providing a shortened version that would eliminate the readings and that might therefore lend itself to easier translation, paperback format, and no problems of obtaining permissions for translation and foreign publication of the articles by other authors.

In reviewing these possibilities with the publisher, we realized a shortened version would also be of assistance to persons in the United States who wanted a shorter but equally serious introduction to gaming-simulation. Upon further reflection we agreed that it would be worthwhile to include other articles by the two authors which had appeared in the original volume or which we had written subsequent to the book's publication in 1975 and to add some new materials to update findings or broaden the scope of the volume.

This book, then, represents an abridgment of the original volume in that it omits many of the readings by colleagues, and a revision of it in that it includes several of our newer writings. Three sections of the first book required substantial updating to reflect the current state of the field. First, there has been considerable work on the topic of evaluation of games. Mary Bredemeier and Cathy Greenblat have thus prepared an entirely new article for this volume, summarizing the current state of evaluation research.

Second, the section on public policy uses has been expanded with the addition of two new chapters, one by Richard D. Duke and one by Richard Duke and Jan Renee Graf. These essays describe recent applications in this arena, and focus on the use of microcomputers in game design.

Third, a vast amount of written material dealing with gaming has appeared since 1975; thus the bibliography has been substantially updated and expanded. We have abandoned the attempt to categorize the materials by subtopic as so many cross the boundaries originally established. We would like to thank Michele T. Duke for her assistance in this area.

The articles taken from the original version are unchanged with two exceptions. First, the references to the readings which followed them have been eliminated. Second, all articles have been edited to delete sexist language. Game designers, researchers, and users are no longer all referred to by the pronouns "he" and "his," as we lamentably found to be the case in the earlier writings. This change reflects not only newer linguistic usage, but the state of the field historically, as both men and women have been actively involved in all facets of exploration of the nature and potential of gaming-simulations.

Cathy Stein Greenblat
Department of Sociology,
Rutgers University

Richard D. Duke
Department of Urban Planning,
University of Michigan

PART I

THE NATURE AND RATIONALE
OF GAMING-SIMULATION

CHAPTER ONE

SEEING FORESTS AND TREES:

Gaming-Simulation and Contemporary Problems of Learning and Communication

CATHY STEIN GREENBLAT

One spring day last year, I took a visiting friend from another part of the country into New York City. We spent a marvelous afternoon roaming through Greenwich Village and, later, Chinatown. At the conclusion of the day, she commented, "I can't imagine why people speak so disparagingly of Manhattan. It's really very charming."

My friend is an intelligent woman, and she knew that Greenwich Village and Chinatown were not typical of New York, but having seen only these two neighborhoods, she had no idea of where they "fit" into the larger whole called "Manhattan." Were the winding streets and small stores found there unique to those neighborhoods, or could one find many examples of this ambience in the city?

Another few days were spent taking a less intense look at a large number of neighborhoods, getting the feel of one and then going on to another. At the end of the week, confusion still reigned; now there was too much information, and the problem was not knowing how it all fit together. My friend felt a bit like the inchworm who crawled over the Mona Lisa and then tried to understand the painting from the pieces of information it could put together. Again, I was left with the question of how to give someone a good sense of the city.

The answer came to me the other day through a serendipitous occurrence. A plane strike and a busy schedule led me to take a helicopter from Newark Airport to LaGuardia. For the first time I saw Manhattan from the air at a low altitude. As we hovered at about the level of the top of the Empire State Building, moving across the city, I realized I was able to "see" its major dimensions clearly. Of course, much was missing in such a view: I couldn't smell the fresh-cooked foods in the ethnic neighborhoods, or see the results of differential garbage collection facilities, or note the different paces of life on Broadway, Fifth Avenue, the garment district, and 125th St. These flavors were lacking up there. But what I *was* provided with was an *overview*—a framework that gave me a sense of how big the "beast" was, what its major characteristics were, and how they fit together; how typical skyscrapers were as compared to brownstones, and what kind of transportation routes connected the different neighborhoods, making them variously accessible to members of other sections. In short, from this vantage point, the city as a *geographic system* could be seen and comprehended. Of course, I couldn't see or know of the subways, but then any system has an "underground" or "network" or "black box" not easily found, but there to be discovered by the enterprising researcher.

From now on, then, I have a plan for the best of all possible introductory tours: I would first take friends for a helicopter ride over the city, giving them the framework. Then, bit by bit, I'd expose them to the neighborhoods, confident that they could appreciate the charms and horrors of each place, but also that they could place them in the proper context of the city as a whole. And hopefully someone would do the same for me in another city.

If all this seems discursive and irrelevant to the topic of gaming, I suggest that it's not, for my tour plan deals directly with the central thesis of this book regarding the importance of gaming: we need ways of providing comprehension of wholes to overcome provincialism, to counteract the narrow perspectives that derive from specialization, and to provide a mode of retaining detail. As we shall try to show, gaming represents a mode of developing this holistic understanding, and thus is an important communication and learning tool.

COMMUNICATION-LEARNING NEEDS IN TECHNOLOGICALLY ADVANCED SOCIETIES

In those parts of the world in which the "technological revolution" has taken place, people have achieved extraordinary feats, but have also encountered new kinds of problems. The complex of traits associated with the "civilized" end of the folk-civilization continuum includes larger aggregates, multiple communications channels among varied kinds of people, a complex division of labor, deliberate design in personal and collective life, more impersonality in interpersonal relations, and a world outlook that differs significantly from that of typical members of more traditional societies (Redfield, 1962; Tonnies, 1940; Becker, 1950; Lerner, 1958). Each of these characteristics may be looked upon as positive or negative, as a benefit or a cost. For example, weaker kinship ties are related both to greater mobility of the labor force and to rapid change in information creating "generation gaps." Is it thus to be applauded or bemoaned?

It makes little sense to issue lamentations for the passing of a former idyllic state; while the folk society may have provided more positive, warm, meaningful relationships, it also entailed high disease and death rates, considerable illiteracy, and the maintenance of fear and superstition. The transition has thus been complex, and the interpretation of whether the end result is, on balance, "good" or "bad" is dependent upon values (Tumin, 1958).

These changes have brought about a major set of problems and challenges in the communication-learning domain. No longer can the information needed to sustain a rich and meaningful life be carried through oral transmission from members of one generation to members of another. Older people, rather than serving as repositories of learning and skills and being venerated for their wisdom, find that they are quickly "outdated," replaced by younger colleagues who have had more recent exposure to scientific discoveries and developments, and put "out to pasture."

Knowledge has been increasing at a geometric rate, so that it is estimated that, by the mid-1960s, the output of books approached 1000 per day, the number of scientific journals and articles was doubling about every fifteen years, and computers were raising the rate of knowledge production to extraordinary speeds (Toffler, 1970: 30-32). This acceleration was both a product of technological advance and a creator of it.

The "knowledge explosion," combined with bureaucratization and the increasing complexity of the division of labor, has led to the development of cadres of highly trained specialists. Speaking of this crisis in the scientific community, Kenneth Boulding (1968: 4) cautions:

> One wonders sometimes if science will not grind to a stop in an assemblage of walled-in hermits, each mumbling to himself words in a private language that only he can understand. In these days the arts may have beaten the sciences to this desert of mutual unintelligibility, but that may be merely because the swift intuitions of art reach the future faster than the plodding leg work of the scientists. The more science breaks into sub-groups, and the less communication is possible among the disciplines, however, the greater chance there is that the total growth of knowledge is being slowed down by the loss of relevant communications. The spread of specialized deafness means that someone who ought to know something that someone else knows isn't able to find it out for lack of generalized ears.

Within their fields, individuals often must absorb vast quantities of information to develop and maintain their positions. Simultaneously they are urged, as citizens, to develop at least a general comprehension of other aspects of the world in which they live and must operate. If the society is to take advantage of the technological expertise and to flourish, it must find ways to combat the narrow perspectives born of pressures of specialization. *Integrative* modes of learning must be found.

There are, then, two types of communication-learning needs in contemporary societies such as ours: (1) the need for modes of learning large quantities of information; and (2) the need for modes of developing general comprehensions of some domains rather than detailed information about them. In both cases, the need is for an awareness and understanding of elements and relationships—a "systems" awareness. As the world becomes more and more complex, most of us encounter enormous difficulty comprehending those systems in which we operate in our everyday lives. Without time and space being collapsed, elements being reduced to manageable size, and some simplification of the number of variables being effectuated, comprehension of these systems is rendered extremely difficult, if not impossible (Goffman, 1961).

Furthermore, decision makers, be they executives or voters, must develop appreciations of "wholes" in order to judge the general thrust of policy (Michael, 1968). The business executive, the general citizen, and the policy maker must integrate reports with other half-sensed appreciations, for they require "gestalt appreciations rather than explicit knowledge of bits of data" (Rhyne, 1975: 18).

In addition, the need for modes of developing systems awareness is critical because it is a necessary precursor to the development of understanding of details. Without a sense of the whole, detail is rejected. A framework within which ideas can be placed must be developed before those ideas can be integrated. Thus, to approach effectively a new book or article, one should read the introduction, table of contents, skim the chapters, look at the nature of the presentation, and so on. Likewise, to maximize comprehension of a chapter, one should first read the lead paragraph, then read all topic sentences through the chapter, and finally read the concluding paragraph. With this overview established, one is then—and only then—ready to begin the ordinary process of sequential reading of the chapter sentences. This approach is not usually stressed, however.

> For *any* excursion into understanding, we should start first with sweeping comprehensions and then seek to learn, or teach component facts. The route of science, prosaic exposition, and academic specialty has normally been the opposite [Rhyne, 1972: 97].

An approach that stresses bit-by-bit acquisition of information without prior acquisition of a holistic sense carries severe threats of conveying miscomprehensions of the sort that beset the king's blind emissaries who stationed themselves at different parts of an elephant and offered descriptions of the creature they felt. Holistic learning is needed as a first step; hence, my decision concerning the helicopter ride.

There is yet another problem. Many skills, roles, and norms that must be understood cannot be learned by direct experience; *vicarious* learning is required. Attainment of educational goals such as the following, suggested by Edgar Friedenberg (1963: 221-222), must depend to some extent on alternatives to direct experience:

> The highest function, I would maintain, is to help people understand the meaning of their lives, and become more sensitive to the meaning of other peoples' lives and relate to them more fully. Education increases the range and complexity of relationships that make sense to us, to which we can contribute, and on which we can bring to bear competent ethical judgement. If we are to transcend our own immediate environment, we must have access to the record of past and present, learn the skills needed to interpret it, and learn to tell good data from poor, whether it be the empirical data of the sciences or the moral and aesthetic data of the humanities. We must be able to read, and to know where what we read fits into the structure of human experience; and to write with enough subtlety and complexity to convey the special quality of our mind to others. We must explore, and we must have the privacy and authority necessary to protect ourselves from intrusion if we are to use energy for exploration rather than defense.

At this point, two more needs must be added to those offered above. In a society such as ours, in which change is constant and rapid, we must not only teach people to *see* the forests and trees, but we must show them *how to find the woods* and *motivate them to want to make the search*. In nonmetaphoric terms, we must develop ways of building motivation to learn, and then modes of developing people who know how to learn—to explore, conceptualize, inquire, experiment, and critically analyze. This conception of the problem focuses not only on the content of communication-learning needs, but upon processes.

MEETING THE CHALLENGES

How, then, can we meet these challenges? That is, what are the characteristics of the environments and media by means of which the required learning is most likely to transpire?

Educators, of course, have fought over the answers to these questions with no resolution, but many suggest that critical elements include the following: (1) We need to find modes of creating motivation prior to transmitting information; (2) the learner must be an active participant in the learning process, rather than a passive recipient of information; (3) instruction must be individualized such that learning is at the appropriate pace for each learner; (4) there must be prompt feedback on success and error.

Moore and Anderson (1975) develop these ideas into four heuristic principles for the design of learning environments. In summary, they argue the following: First, the learner should be given the opportunity to operate from various *perspectives*. The learner should not just be a recipient of information, but should at times be an agent, a referee, and a reciprocator. Second, activities should contain their own goals and sources of motivation, not just represent means to some end (such as grades). That is, in an effective learning environment, activities are *autotelic*. Third, learners should be freed from a dependence on authority and allowed to reason for themselves; they are thus made more *productive* in the learning process. And fourth, the environment should be responsive to the learners' activity. Not only should they be given feedback, but they should be helped to be *reflexive*, evaluating their own progress.

Those familiar with gaming-simulations will recognize that these principles parallel the major arguments given for the effectiveness of gaming in teaching. Games entail the active involvement of learners with the subject matter in autotelic activities that free them from dependence on authority and offer them feedback and ways of measuring their progress toward a goal.

But there is more to it than that. When we argue that gaming-simulation may be a way to deal with the challenges delineated earlier, it is partly because we see games as *communications* devices, rather than holding to the more narrow conception of them as pedagogic devices. The problems outlined in the beginning of this essay are basically problems of communications: the complexity of the world is something that has to be understood more or less all at once. What is required is a mode of simultaneous rather than sequential presentation of parts of the overall message. Rhyne argues that prose is a poor tool for creating pattern comprehension. It is "sequential, working point-to-point along a chain of assertions or questions. It treats one molecule of meaning at a time" (Rhyne, 1975: 19).

The systems awareness we urge as the contemporary need also requires a holistic language, one able to convey gestalt. That, we believe, is what gaming-simulation is. The chapter by Richard Duke demonstrates the distinctions between gaming-simulation and other forms of communications, and provides the basis for our argument that gaming-simulation is a language for transmitting both specific facts and general principles of social theories.

CHAPTER TWO

BASIC CONCEPTS AND LINKAGES

CATHY STEIN GREENBLAT

Further elaboration of our thesis that games are effective communication devices requires that we spell out more thoroughly what gaming-simulations are and how they relate to social theory.

THEORIES, SYSTEMS, AND TYPES OF MODELS

A theory is a set of logically related propositions about some aspect of reality. Where classical science was concerned mostly with problems involving only a few variables and one-way chains of causality, most of the problems addressed in contemporary social science theory are multivariate. They are problems of "organized complexity"—that is, of the interaction of a large but not infinite number of variables (cf. von Bertalanffy, 1968: 11).

The variables in such theories are organized into a *system;* that is, the conceptualization includes identifiable parts which are mutually interdependent and fit together to make a whole.

> We define a system in general as a complex of elements or components directly or indirectly related in a causal network, such that at least some of the components are related to some others in a more or less stable way *at any one time*. The interrelations may be mutual or unidirectional, linear, non-linear or intermittent, and varying in degrees of causal efficacy or priority. The particular kinds of more or less stable inter-relationships of components that become established at any time constitute the particular *structure* of the system at that time [Buckley, 1968: 493].

The basic problems and questions, then, for the social scientist, are problems of interrelationships.

As scientists work, they often formulate a *model* or models—a representation of their view of reality, showing the major elements and their relationships. These are statements of theory; they indicate definitions, assumptions, and propositions from the larger body of theory, for even where they are tentative and exploratory, they should be built, insofar as possible, "not from ad hoc fragments, but from the available general theories that seem germane and from appropriate portions of the larger body of sociological knowledge" (Riley, 1963: 9). The model, then, is a way of construing and representing a particular set of social phenomena.

But what do such models look like? The most familiar form to most of us is the *verbal model*. These are linear in presentation; we confront one component at a time. For example, we have all read such statements as "Social stratification systems function to distribute favorable self-images unequally throughout a population." Most teaching and publication in the social sciences depends upon verbal models; in lecture halls, small classrooms, and the library we encounter them by the thousands.

Graphic models are used with increasing frequency, for the presentation of complexity is aided by the simultaneity of expression. Note, for example, the difference in the verbal and the visual model of the mutual causal relationships offered in the example in Figure 2.1. Once the graphic symbols are understood, the figure gives a concise summary of the elements and their relationships. Where there are systems of simultaneous changes, graphic models seem to convey more than linear verbal models.

> Mutual causal relationships may be defined between more than two elements. Let us look at the . . . diagram (Figure 2.1). The arrows indicate the direction of influences. + indicates that the changes occur in the same direction, but not necessarily positively. For example, the + between G and B indicates that an increase in the amount of garbage per area causes an increase in the number of bacteria per area. But, at the same time, it indicates that a decrease in the amount of garbage per area causes a decrease in the number of bacteria per area. The − between S and B indicates that an increase in sanitation facilities causes a decrease in the number of bacteria per area. But, at the same time, it indicates that a decrease in sanitation facilities causes an increase in the number of bacteria per area.
>
> As may be noticed, some of the arrows form loops. For example, there is a loop of arrows from P to M, M to C, and C back to M. A loop indicates mutual causal relationships. In a loop, the influence of an element comes back to itself through other elements. For example, in the loop of P-M-C-P, an increase in the number of people causes an increase in modernization, which in turn increases migration to the city, which in turn increases the number of people in the city. In short, an increase in population causes a further increase in population through modernization and migration. On the other hand, a decrease in population causes a decrease in modernization, which in turn causes a decrease in migration, which in turn decreases population. In short, a decrease in population causes a further decrease in population through decreased modern-

ization and decreased migration. Whatever the change, either an increase or a decrease, amplifies itself. This is so when we take population as our criterion. But the same is true if we take modernization as a criterion: an increase in modernization causes a further increase in modernization through migration and population increase; and a decrease in modernization causes a further decrease in modernization through decreased migration and decreased population. The same holds true if we take the migration as the criterion.

In a loop, therefore, each element has an influence on all other elements either directly or indirectly, and each element influences itself through other elements. There is no hierarchical causal priority in any of the elements. It is in this sense that we understand the mutual causal relationships [Maruyama, 1968: 311-312].

Some statements of theory are made in a special type of graphic form: these are *mathematical models*. We learn in the natural sciences that the circumference of a circle is derivable from the formula: $C = r^2$. So, too, we find that desegregation patterns, urban growth, and population expansion are only some of the social phenomena to have been conceptualized in mathematical form. Generally it is argued that the more formal presentation involved in the formulae are clearer than the purely verbal statements. They are neater, and, once having learned the symbols, the learner can "see" all the elements and their relationships.

A fourth, related kind of model is the *physical model*. Watson, describing the DNA molecule as a double helix, reports that he realized this through "playing around" with a tinker-toy model—a physical representation. Some of you may have seen plastic models of the human anatomy created to show students the parts of the human body and how they fit together. By viewing the model, one can gain a more systematic view of relationships of size, place, and form than by listening to a lecture on the neck bone being connected to the shin bone! And the model is three-dimensional, so it can be turned and viewed from many angles, unlike a diagram of the body.

All the above types of models share one characteristic limitation: they show the structure of the referent system, but do not satisfactorily display the functions or dynamic processes. In other words, they are static models. It is on the basis of this characteristic that we distinguish the fifth type of model: the *simulation*. Included in this category are such things as wind tunnels for testing aircraft under varying conditions; representations of automobile panels for teaching driving; and Zorba the Greek's operating model or simulation of the device he would later construct for bringing logs down the mountain.

The critical factor differentiating the simulation from the other types of models is that the simulation is an *operating model*. That is, it demonstrates not simply the state of the system at some given time, but also the way the

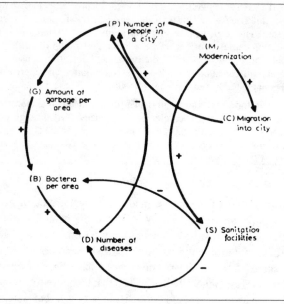

FIGURE 2.1

system changes. Think, for example, of the difference between the type of model a junior high school science student might make to show the sun and the planets, and contrast it with the model found in a planetarium. The latter shows not only the number and relative size of the planets, but also their velocities. Thus, the observer can see the different patterns of relationships which create eclipses, and so on. It is dynamic.

Simulation, then, entails abstraction and representation from a larger system. Central features must be identified and simplified, while less important elements are omitted from the model. It is the very process of highlighting some elements and eliminating others that makes the model useful. A city street map is easier for a driver to use and more helpful to him if it does not show the differences in altitude in different parts of the city; but a map showing the route from Denver to Los Angeles is more helpful if it *does* show mountain ranges and if it eliminates most local streets. So, too, with a simulation, the utility derives from correct selection of elements to emphasize and elements to eliminate. The selection of such features depends upon the purpose the model is to serve.

Most of us are familiar with simulations of technological systems, having seen simulated space maneuvers on TV while real spacecraft were traveling to, orbiting, landing on, or departing from the moon. Likewise, many have seen simulations of the control panels of aircraft used to train future pilots to deal with flying conditions and problems at less expense than would be involved in putting trainees in real planes on missions. *Social systems,* too, can be simulated: marital dyads, organizations, neighborhoods, cities, nations, or groups of nations. The principle is the same: central features are identified and put together such that they operate in a manner similar to the real world system.

SIMULATIONS, GAMES, AND GAMING-SIMULATIONS

Simulation models can be made to operate in one of three ways. First a computer can be used to make decisions and take actions. Other actions and the consequences of the decisions then are yielded by the computer model. Second, a combination of computer and human players can make the model operate. The computer may serve simply as a high-speed calculator, or it may contain a model or set of models within it which are triggered by the actions of the players. Third, all operations may be generated by human players and the consequences calculated by humans. The first of these is a "computer simulation"; the second and third are referred to as "gaming-simulations," "game-simulations," or "simulation games." Some would further distinguish between the two by prefacing them "man-machine" and "all-man," respectively.

The term "game" is applied to those simulations which work wholly or partly on the basis of players' decisions, because the environment and activities of participants have the characteristics of games: players have goals, sets of activities to perform; constraints on what can be done; and payoffs (good and bad) as consequences of the actions. The elements in a gaming-simulation are patterned from real life—that is, the roles, goals, activities, constraints, and consequences and the linkages among them simulate those elements of the real-world system. In the gaming-simulation GHETTO, for example, players are given educational, occupational, and family profiles similar to those found in most ghettos. The choices they are offered in terms of how they will spend their time are similar in character and availability to those offered ghetto dwellers, and the payoffs (such as money for jobs and for illegal enterprises, and possibilities of arrest for the latter) are also realistic.

"Gaming-simulation," then, is a hybrid form, involving the performance of game activities in simulated contexts. (This position, it should be noted, differs somewhat from that taken by some others, notably John Raser [1969], who treats games as models not sufficiently developed to warrant the label simulation.)

Several amplifications of these ideas are recommended. James Coleman (1975) explores in succinct fashion the reasons social scientists are interested in looking at games and game play. R. Garry Shirts (1975) draws some of the distinctions and notes overlaps between "games," "simulations," and "contests." Robert Armstrong and Margaret Hobson (1975) elaborate upon the discussion of gaming-simulation components and operation. The 1978 book *The Grasshopper* by Bernard Suits is highly recommended by many experienced gamers.

CHAPTER THREE

MANAGING COMPLEXITY:

Gaming—A Future's Language

RICHARD D. DUKE

THE PROBLEM

Humankind is a little harried of late. The naked ape barely blinked, only to discover that his animal being has moved from the cave to the moon with precious little time for adjustment, measured in evolutionary terms. It is difficult to derive a valid "alienation index" for a society, perhaps impossible for different points in historical time. Nonetheless, evidence abounds that all is not right with Western civilization as it is currently structured; further, the situation has deteriorated markedly in the past quarter of a century. The tune-out, drop-out, cop-out syndrome is ever apparent although the recurrent waves of enthusiasm (such as populist activity in environmental concerns) give reason to believe all is not lost. But even in such cases where enthusiasms are high and a general sense of urgency and responsibility exists at the level of the individual, there is pervasive frustration. Individuals need to be part of those processes affecting their lives, but are currently devoid of any effective means to alter things or join the dialogue about potential change. This situation reveals some dimensions of life today that were not previously true:

—The problems of today are infinitely more complex, involving systems and interacting subsystems that go beyond normal human ken and which do not yield to conventional jargon or traditional forms of communication.
—The sheer quantity of individuals who want to be effectively part of the dialogue is large and growing rapidly.
—There is a growing personal urgency because the solutions pursued today constitute a more pervasive intrusion in the individual's life. (In earlier times, the king's men may have come periodically for the taxes, but in the interim

period, life was constrained only by the elements and by whatever circumstances might exist within a personalized clan; today, the Internal Revenue Service comes every week and unknown Big Brother, in a thousand ways, constrains the daily actions of our lives.)

This situation, of course, is not new. Without too much difficulty, humanity's struggle for the personalized control of their lives can be traced through the Magna Carta and the decline of the king's power to the Parliament to the Declaration of Independence and resulting constitutional governmental forms (whose painfully won gains are now threatened by a technical aristocracy, the high priests of 1984). Even the great urban political bosses performed a valid personalizing influence buffering the citizen from the emerging systems and technologies that must control this world. (Sadly, only vestiges of this humanizing function remain; witness the light years between the individual and national politics—can it be other than Alice in Wonderland with spy versus spy, body counts from a constitutionally nonexistent war, complexity of domestic programs that boggle the expert mind while dominating, in strict inverse relation, the lives of the least able citizenry?)

At the very moment when individuals seemed to have garnered the power to control their personal destiny by their own hands, they have been caught unaware in the grinding pincers movement of the complexity of societal survival in modern times and the inevitable technological response. This crunch has been on its way since the industrial revolution, but its very rapid progression was precipitated by World War II, in particular by the spinoffs in computer technology and the resultant elaboration of the concept of "systems" and related, evolving technologies. Now the high priests of technology speak only to the high priests of technology; God is dead, and the citizen, no matter how strongly motivated, can hardly get a word in edgewise!

Problems of the management of modern Western society (and in a particular sense, the great urban centers) have generated the modern equivalent of the biblical Tower of Babel. To unravel the present "want structure" in human terms, to harness appropriate technologies, and to manage a successful and continuous response in an ongoing societal context generates a communication net (non-net?) that is truly unimaginable and certainly unmanageable. Society's failure to respond to individual need is, in large part, a communication problem.

The naked ape waved and grunted, and we do little better. He lived in a relatively simple world, and over many centuries developed what have been viewed as sophisticated languages but which in reality are only involved extensions of sequential form (including not only a written and spoken

English, but also the sophisticated artificial languages of mathematics, computer programming, musical notation, and so on) to deal with this noncomplex environment. The naked (now harried) ape of today still employs these simple sequential tongues, but, in a world several magnitudes more complex, it leaves him speechless. The highly constrained and sequential languages of the past and their related technologies (even in their highest forms) fail at conveying gestalt, and so the complexity of today cannot be comprehended or communicated except with the greatest of effort, and then only by a new elite. For example, consider our great urban centers as they exist today, multisystems within multisystems; alternative upon alternative, presenting incomprehensible, many-futured state(s)—the tongues of many human beings, some unborn, in-migrant and out, being daily rearticulated as perceptions of the possible change; a great multifaceted sphere of complexity that cannot be managed, but must be.

Societal response, predictably, has been of four concurrent dimensions: false dichotomies, professional elitism, increasing dependency on technology, and gigantism. The inevitable but false dichotomies appear first: pare out of the total fabric of society some element of great urgency; if we can neither understand nor solve the totality, we can solve some definable part, *no matter that other evils are encountered, the least of which may be inefficiency, the most dangerous irrelevancy* (witness "education" as a system currently practiced in the inner city).

As the bureaucracy (education, transportation, health, housing, ad nauseam) transforms life into disconnected cells, society loses not only in the more obvious negative harvest (the "solution" of urban renewal, originally conceived as a simple-minded clearance problem, now yields to more sophisticated approaches at a cost of two decades, only to be replaced by the "solution" of an "interstate highway system" rather than an "interstate transportation system"); but also in a positive sense, since such dichotomy leaves little room for subtlety of solution.

And with the dichotomy came the armies of the professional elite and with them their empires, and the resulting gigantism dwarfs and smothers the citizen. The fiction of alternatives (witness State Highway Engineering) may seduce the generalized citizen, but the poor beggar in front of the bulldozer soon discovers the moment of truth. And as this individual turns into the jaws of this giant beast trying to locate some isolable component unit that will be responsive, he is put down by the elites—the professionals who quite literally speak another language—and he is put off by a technology that appears antihuman; his only alternative is to join together with fragmentary bands to throw slingshots at the giant. And, occasionally, his aim is true! First one, then another public scheme is beat back not to be replaced with positive alternatives, but to a frustrated stand-off where the great urban administrations survive through nonaction, and the great creaking structure grinds through time, the moans of unresolved needs and of endless counter-productive conflict emanating from the incongruous mass.

And who is to comprehend it all? Or who is to speak of it all? And to whom? Is there any remote possibility of establishing a real dialogue about this multifaceted, dynamic gargantua, even among the elite, substituting future timeframe for future timeframe in advance of reality, permitting positive management to replace a negative reactionary reality? And is there any way to enlarge the dialogue to include the activist citizen or someone who might conceivably be called "representative" in that this person transmits a personal translation of ideas for a limited and personally known constituency?

Of course not, not if we insist on restricting ourselves to the languages of the caveman.

But there is hope that the possibility for a quantum jump exists; that communication can move from its rigid and limiting sequentiality to a gestalt mode, and that this supra-language can be used as a simultaneous translation for our modern Tower of Babel.

ESTABLISHING THE NEED FOR FUTURE'S LANGUAGE

"Future Shock" has become part of the popular lexicon. Alvin Toffler in 1970 introduced the concept in a book by that name in which he stresses the death of permanence and the coming of the age, not of Aquarius, but of transience. The book documents in detail his thesis that the world of tomorrow will be significantly different from the world of yesterday along many dimensions. Toffler quotes from Kenneth Boulding:

> As far as many statistical series related to activities of mankind are concerned the date that divides human history into two equal parts is well within living memory. . . . The world of today . . . is as different from the world in which I was born as that world was from Julius Caesar's. I was born in the middle of human history, to date, roughly. Almost as much has happened since I was born as happened before.

The temptation to document here the proof of this accelerated change and its impact on our lives is strong, but the thesis will either be accepted or rejected without elaboration, since it is a familiar one. To place its significance to gaming in proper perspective, I would like to allude to Figure 3.1, a simple graph. The horizontal axis would represent centuries starting perhaps with the year 1 in our current system of counting; the vertical column would represent an index, however obtained, which would attempt to convey complexity, transcience, and rate of change confronting the typical citizen.

Using a logarithmic scale, a curve is plotted which attempts to illustrate this change (perhaps the number of new things which must be assimilated in the lifetime of a given citizen). The curve would start in the extreme lower lefthand corner and be virtually a straight line which a slight incline upward, barely perceptible, until perhaps 1900; incremental jumps might be noted at the time gunpowder was introduced and certainly as the industrial revolution impacted on society. The curve turns vertically during the period 1900-1940, with a sharp increase during the period of World War II. Subsequent to World War II, the curve would be increasing at a near vertical rate, implying change flowing on change at a totally unprecedented rate. Curiously, a number of authors have independently noted World War II as the approximate time of the pivot from the trend line through antiquity to the modern trend line.

Virtually all our language forms have come from antiquity and have sufficed, in spite of their sequentiality, because they rely heavily on analogy, and the analogies employed are predicated on historic circumstance which is not expected to change, by minor adjustments through time. Note that the curve implies that in the post-World War II period a situation far more involved prevails, particularly in the several dimensions of complexity, future orientation, thoughtful consideration of alternatives, and the inevitable recognition of the nature of systems and interlocking subsystems which are affected.

Necessity is the mother of invention, and the post-World War II period has shown many innovations in communication which attempt to deal with this communications problem; each reflects an attempt to convey gestalt, or at least to escape from the harsh burden of strict sequentiality of the written and spoken language forms. If one were to plot the advent of gaming as indicated by the new games which appear in the various cataloging efforts, the curve mimics rather accurately the curve of accelerated change with perhaps a ten- or 15-year lag. This reflects, in my judgment, a spontaneous solution, "gaming," by many people in many problem situations to the problem of developing a gestalt communication form. In short, we have a new language form, a language form which is "future"-oriented. If this premise holds, to date we have seen no general statement or theory which would explain the wide diversity of materials which appear as games, or which might guide the neophyte in efforts to develop effective games for their own communication purpose.

GAMES IN THE COMMUNICATIONS CONTINUUM

The various modes of communication currently in use rest along a continuum ranging from the primitive to the sophisticated; these are combined here into four major divisions: primitive, advanced, integrated-simulated, and integrated-real. In sense, the two extremes of the continuum can be viewed as being linked, in that two parties fully sharing a reality need no overt communication or suffice with primitive modes. (The stadium crowd watching a football game, veteran foot soldiers engaged in a fire fight, two lovers in ecstasy—each situation relies on the fact of shared reality as the basis for communication.) When the individual does resort to any medium, it is to bridge the gap in the perception of reality between two or more parties. The greater the communications gap and the more involved the reality they wish to confront, the more elaborate and sophisticated their language becomes. Carrying this logic forward, a curious phenomenon is encountered. Attempts to convey elaborate systems emerge as a complex language form (gaming/simulation) approaching reality itself, and, in so doing, the process has gone full circle! The fourth category of communication forms (integrated-real) is included here to emphasize this transition. Because of this circular character of communication media, one is not better than the next. Rather, one may be more appropriate than another.

A quick review of the various communication forms is called for. Primitive forms have been divided into informal (grunts and hand signals) and formal (semaphore or light signals). In situations which are simple and transitory, the former will suffice; but as the communications need becomes more important, more involved, or more consistent, these have been formalized. Both forms are characterized by spontaneity, limited message content,

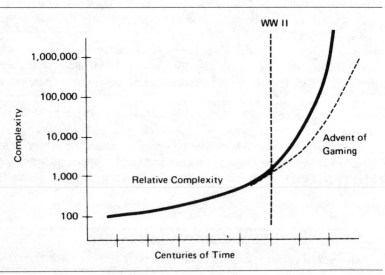

FIGURE 3.1

and immediacy to experience. They are generally used in face-to-face contact. For example, a cry of warning is almost universally understood by people of all cultures. Its function is to alert someone to a danger; it is effective only insofar as the warned person shares the message sender's perception of current reality—that is, in the same place at the same time. Similarly, the standardized international traffic signals used to direct traffic are an example from the primitive-formal category.

Advanced forms of communication include spoken languages, written languages, emotional forms (art, acting, role-playing), and technical forms (such as pictures, mathematic notation, musical notation, schematic diagrams), which are often used as supplements to other advanced forms. It is quite common, of course, to use these in some combination (for example, slides with a lecture), and such uses can be viewed as rudimentary forms of the integrated languages suggested by the final two categories. The first, integrated-simulated, is characterized by deliberate combinations of media (film and television) or by hybrids (gaming/simulation) which employ all prior forms in any combination which best enhances the transmission of some reality. The final category, integrated-real, does not attempt this in an artificial manner, but rather this level of communication inherently recognizes the circular nature of the communication process, and consequently extracts from reality itself. One illustration of this would be apprenticeship programs where the learner (party receiving the message) is placed in a situation of reality but buffered from the consequences of full participation. As he gains "experience" (better perception of reality), these buffers are systematically removed until he becomes fully part of reality.

Table 3.1 identifies six major characteristics associated with the various language forms; and includes a brief interpretation of each of these characteristics relative to the four major types of media. The six characteristics include:

(1) Sequential-gestalt constraints: the inherent ability of the language form to convey gestalt or totality.
(2) Specificity-universality constraints: the degree of flexibility inherent to the language form in adapting the new substantive material.
(3) Spontaneity of use: the ease or relative freedom encountered by the user.
(4) Character of conventions employed: the degree of consistency, the extent of complexity, the relative formality and their general versus special use in a given communications attempt.
(5) Coding-decoding: the extent to which the message must be artificially coded by the initiator and reconstructed by the receiver.
(6) Character of the message that can be conveyed: the success with which a number of message characteristics can be conveyed, including but not limited to complexity, analogy, qualitative thought, quantitative thought, subtlety, permanence (ability to reestablish), precision, intangibles, time constraints, and systems characteristics.

Communication needs (message transmission) can be analyzed by these characteristics, and a medium or communication form is selected which yields the most efficient exchange. When no existing forms are successful, other forms (new or modified) are generated.

Gaming/simulation is the most intricate communication form available and as such its response to these six characteristics is unique.

Because gaming/simulation has emerged spontaneously to convey gestalt considerations, it is not surprising that it excels on this first characteristic. Primitive languages fail completely, although advanced forms can be laboriously employed. The four "integrated" forms are most effective at conveying gestalt with the three artificial media (multimedia, gaming/simulation, and experience) often being more efficient than reality itself.

With regard to the second characteristic used in Table 3.1 (specificity-Table 3.1 universality), the integrated communication forms are the most specific (by reason of their highly particularized and complex construction to convey a single gestalt phenomenon). An example might help: Using a full primitive capability of grunts and hand signals, a traveler might get by temporarily in *any* culture. If he shifts to advanced languages, he is limited to those particular cultures where he is learned (of course, he can participate more fully). If he now selects gaming/simulation, he will be restricted to communication with those who have a particular interest in the single gestalt represented by that gaming/simulation. (This is meant to imply that each gaming/simulation is best viewed as a separate and independent language, at least to the extent that we might view French, Japanese, and English as separate languages.) It is important to examine this premise carefully, for, if it is found acceptable, it then becomes possible to construct general principles to govern the construction of each new gaming/simulation.

The third characteristic of "spontaneity" is intended to convey the relative ease of use of the various modes. Associated with this characteristic are the concepts of "dryness" (defined as the energy required to overcome the resistance to use of a given communication form) and expertise. The advanced forms are often viewed as "dry," and in their more sophisticated use they are almost universally "dry." This inverse relationship becomes a serious constraint when attempting to establish communication about serious and involved problems, and generally results in shared comprehension only among an elite group. Returning to the continuum in Table 3.1, there is an increasing requirement for special expertise as we move from the primitive through the advanced communications forms. This continues through the construction stages of the integrated forms, but is markedly reduced in their use. (Films often present intricate messages successfully to audiences who would not master the same material presented through the advanced languages.) Spontaneity is often constrained in the early stages of using a

TABLE 3.1 The Communications Continuum*

(Examples of Each Communication Form) / Characteristics	PRIMITIVE		ADVANCED				INTEGRATED			
	INFORMAL	FORMAL	SPOKEN	WRITTEN	EMOTIONAL	TECHNICAL	SIMULATED		REAL	
							MULTI-MEDIA	HYBRID	EXPERIENCE	REALITY
	Grunts Hand-Signals	Semiphore Lights Flags	Conversation Lecture Seminar Radio	Telegraph Manuscript Books Text	Acting Art Role-Playing	Math-Notation Musical-Notation Schematics Diagrams	Film Television	Gaming/ Simulation	Apprentice Job Training	(Any Shared Real Time Perception)
SEQUENTIAL-GESTALT (Degree to which the form is constrained)	Most Constrained Because of Sequential Nature		Basic Character is Sequential but Various Devices Employed to Ease Constraint				Highest Gestalt Ability Short of Reality		Fully Gestalt Because Actual Reality	
SPECIFICITY-UNIVERSALITY (Degree of Flexibility of Use)	Employed for All Situations but Limited in Material Conveyed		Standard (universal) Modes Selectively Employed to Meet Specific Communication Need				Mode Specifically Tailored to Communication need		Specific (It is the Reality Encountered)	
SPONTANEITY OF USE (User Resistance, Skill Required, "Dryness" of Form)	Natural, Easy, Convenient		Special Skills Required. Sophistication Often Accompanied by Dryness, Artificiality of Use Inherent				Very Special Effort to Initiate; Then Spontaneous in Use		Natural "Life" Form, Skill Limits Involvement	

(Continued)

33

TABLE 3.1 Continued

Characteristics / (Examples of Each Communication Form)	PRIMITIVE		ADVANCED				INTEGRATED			
	INFORMAL	FORMAL	SPOKEN	WRITTEN	EMOTIONAL	TECHNICAL	SIMULATED		REAL	
							MULTI-MEDIA	HYBRID	EXPERIENCE	REALITY
(Examples of Each Communication Form)	Grunts Hand-Signals	Semiphore Lights Flags	Conversation Lecture Seminar Radio	Telegraph Manuscript Books Text	Acting Art Role Playing	Math-Notation Musical Notation Schematics Diagrams	Film Television	Gaming/Simulation	Apprentice Job Training	(Any Shared Real Time Perception)
CHARACTER OF CONVENTIONS EMPLOYED (Formality, Complexity)	Relatively few Simple, Simple, Informal		Formal and Informal, Simple and Complex, Highly Structured, Many			Highly	Many, *Unique to Each Situation*, Fairly Complex		Many Informal Complex	
CHARACTER OF CODING AND DECODING (Inherent)	None Required or Simple Effort		Essential: May be Elaborate and Highly Specialized				Elaborate Coding to Initiate Simple Effort by User		None Required	
CHARACTER OF THE MESSAGE THAT CAN BE CONVEYED (Complexity, Analogy, Qualitative or Quantative thought, Subtility, Permanance, Precision, Intangibles, Time Constrained, Systems Characteristics)	Only Rudimentary Message		Sophisticated Messages				Gestalt Substitute for Reality		Reality	

*This diagram is only meant to suggest major relationships among the various media to illustrate the character of gaming/simulation. There is no suggestion of the comprehensive review of communication forms or their character.

From: "Gaming Simulation—A New Communication Form," by Richard D. Duke, presented at the Third International Conference on Gaming/Simulation, Birmingham, England, July 1972.

gaming/simulation since the players are literally learning a new and highly specialized language. After several rounds of play, they will master the particulars and now communication advances to a level not previously possible (assuming, of course, that the primary rules of construction have been thoughtfully followed).

The fourth characteristic is "conventions employed." The importance of this is generally not understood by developers of gaming/simulations, with the result frequently being an inferior product. To illustrate convention, consider several examples from the advanced form of communication: grammar for both spoken and written languages; consistency of mathematical notation (also musical notation); the rules governing the use of any given computer language; the symbols employed in flow-charting. Contrast this with several gaming-simulations, all of which employ Lego blocks as a construction device, but, unfortunately, to convey different ideas in each case. Because each gaming/simulation is a separate language, the conventions are frequently invented for that particular instance; there are relatively few conventions universally employed by gaming/simulations except those previously adopted for the communication forms from which the gaming/simulation hybrid is constructed.

The fifth characteristic from Table 3.1 is "coding," by which we mean the artificial and temporary translation of the message to some intermediate form from which it must be decoded before communication takes place. Perhaps the most clear example is semaphore transmission, which requires coding from a given written language into separate and distinct symbolic representations (the flag positions) and subsequent decoding before the message would be understood by its intended receiver. Most media employ coding to some degree; when it is cleverly employed in gaming/simulation, the technique becomes much more powerful—for example, the use of the graphic display "SYMAP" to encode a large data set which can be visually decoded by the player at a more useful level of abstraction. The secret of success in "coding" messages for gaming/simulation is to employ codes which can be readily interpreted by the participants of that particular gaming/simulation.

The final row in Table 3.1 is "message characteristics" and is intended to suggest a large number of particular characteristics, several of which are illustrated (complexity, analogy, and so on). It is essential for the designer of a gaming/simulation to reflect on the character of the message(s) to be conveyed; this will suggest which communications forms are best combined into the hybrid. As a general observation, it seems that there is a direct correlation between the clarity with which the game/simulation designer specifies his communication problem (message, sender[s], receiver[s]) prior to construction, and the quality of the product. (One very good gaming/sim-

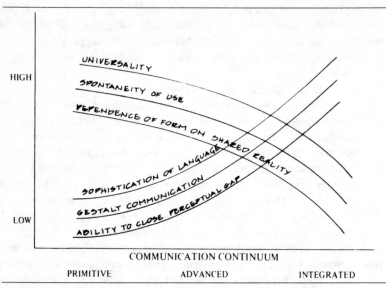

FIGURE 3.2   Message Characteristics and the Communications
             Continuum

ulation had as its objective improved communication among a citizen group
who were constructing a city ordinance to control aesthetics of builders. The
game designer employed art [painting] as one of the component language
forms.)

All along the continuum, the purpose of communication remains the
transmission of perceptions of reality. But as the scope and detail for the
perception to be conveyed increases, becoming more comprehensive, total,
or gestalt-like, a price is always paid in spontaneity of use (see Figure 3.2).

The need for conveying holistic thought, or gestalt, is urgent; the coming
decade will increase this urgency considerably. Perhaps the most trenchant
statement on this need is by R. F. Rhyne (1975). While describing the need
for holistic communication, Rhyne (1975: 16) states, "There is a macro-
problem, an interweaving of adverse conditions that is more extensive, more
richly structured by interior lines of interaction, and more threatening than
any circumstance faced before by all mankind." Rhyne's article was formulated "to stimulate exploration of the means whereby appreciations of complex wholes may be more quickly and more reliably 'told' to others" (Rhyne,
1975: 15). He, too, rejects our ancestral language forms as being inadequate
to the task and argues that new forms must be invented. Arguing that
decision is a gestalt event and not a logically determinable process, he
believes that the citizen or the policy researcher or other decision maker

must first comprehend the whole, the entirety, the gestalt, the system, before the particulars can be dealt with. Rhyne suggests a variety of approaches to this problem and alludes to games as having a particular potential.

We learn through games because, if properly designed, they represent abstract symbolic maps of multidimensional phenomena which serve as a basic reference system for tucking away the bits and pieces of detail which are transmitted and in particular by assisting in the formulation of inquiry from a variety of obtuse angles or perspectives which are meaningful to the individual making the inquiry and which can only be transmitted through an "N"-dimensional, abstract, symbolic-mapping procedure.

If the prior observations on the character of change in the world since World War II are valid, they could perhaps be summarized as follows: prior to World War II, the need for pragmatic information and fact, learned by rote, was imperative; in the new era the need is urgently for the acquisition of heuristics or a flexible set of highly abstract conceptual tools which will let the participant view new and emerging situations, having no precedent, in a way that permits comprehension. We learn through games, then, because it is a relatively safe environment which permits the exploration of many perspectives chosen by the individual, expressed in the jargon of the individual, and subject to fairly prompt feedback in "what-if" contexts. These concepts gain strength when reviewing the work of Moore and Anderson (1975) as they conduct research on learning environments. Curiously enough, they pinpoint the time of change in society as being dramatically correlated with the decade of the 1940s. Properly designed, games have a strong basis in learning theory, which supports their potential as a communication form.

The simultaneous invention of games of a wide diversity of subject matter and technique is a response to a felt need for an improved communication form to deal with problems of gestalt or holistic thought. Just as the folk models alluded to by Moore and Anderson emerged in a societal context as needed, games become a modern equivalent.

WHAT IS A FUTURE'S LANGUAGE?

For the moment, let me identify seven basic requirements that must be met by any future's language:

(1) Ability to convey gestalt or holistic image.
(2) Permit the specification of detail at any appropriate level, in the context of the holistic image.
(3) Structured to permit the pulsing of specific, tangible inquiries or alternatives to permit correlation with the holistic image and any significant detail.

(4) The ability to display, make explicit, or permit the recording of explicit linkages between major segments of the holistic imagery; the creation of an awareness of feedback.

(5) A nonelitist, universal possibility for use; a basic catholicity of design.

(6) A future orientation (implying *any* time frame past or future *other* than the present).

(7) They must be basically transient in format to permit the restructuring or more careful articulation of the problem as viewed by those participating.

Clearly, gaming has not preempted as *the* future's language. However, if certain rules, concepts, or principles are employed consistently, the game product can certainly qualify in a wide variety of situations.

PART II

ELEMENTS OF DESIGN
AND CONSTRUCTION

CHAPTER FOUR

GAMING-SIMULATION AND SOCIAL SCIENCE:

Rewards to the Designer

CATHY STEIN GREENBLAT

"Playing games" has, in recent years, become a popularized expression pointing to actions designed to avoid a host of things, such as reality, "meaning," and each other. Our ideas about games are quite to the contrary; far from thinking of games as ways of hindering communications, we believe that games and gaming-simulations are important learning-communications aids. Some of the argument was presented in the previous section. Here we add the notion that games can be viewed as communication devices in that they are *languages of social theory* to use in "talking" to students, colleagues, and oneself. Where we have previously focused attention upon the more holistic view the *player* can gain from participation, here we urge that social scientists interested in theory construction may find the translation of their ideas into a gaming model to be intellectually exciting and productive. Design of a game—the systematic translation of understandings into an operating model—and subsequent examination of the model through observation of play of it can lead to a refining of theoretical formulations and consequently to a higher level of social scientific understanding.

REASONS AND REWARDS

Raser (1969: 15-19) has suggested four reasons for simulating:

(1) Economy: "It's cheaper to study and experiment with a simulation than with the real thing, and costly mistakes can be avoided by 'running it through in advance.'"

(2) Visibility: "Simulations aid visibility by making certain kinds of phenomena more accessible for observation and measurement, and by introducing clarity into what is otherwise complex, chaotic, or confused."

(3) Reproductibility: "Simulations are valuable because they allow phenomena to be reproduced, and thus enable the experimenter to derive statistical probabilities when the outcome is uncertain, and/or enable him to vary numerous aspects of the system in ways that yield profitable insights into how the system operates. In other words, simulations allow controlled experiments to be made that would otherwise be impossible."

(4) Safety: "Simulations are used for safety purposes, both to protect human beings while they are being trained or studied, and to produce laboratory analogues of dangerous phenomena that we need to study."

Simulation brings with it several kinds of rewards. All focus upon the idea that for a number of kinds of problems, a gaming-simulation may be a more productive way of conceptualizing elements and relationships, whether one's purpose is teaching or refinement of theory. Many people who have worked in several media have found that gaming models represent happy middle grounds between the looseness of verbal tools and the rigidity of mathematical formulae. Thus Feldt (1972: 1) argues that

> the advantages of gaming models over verbal and mathematical models are that a game provides relatively specific designation of concepts and at the same time avoids the semantic problems inherent in most verbal models. Furthermore, the degree of precision required in defining a concept and its relationship to other components of the model is much less than that required in most mathematical models. Thus the game model builder may deal with relationships and components which are not easily quantifiable.

The rewards of building a gaming-simulation model rest upon several crucial features of the process:

(1) The process of design forces greater clarity in thinking about critical elements, and pushes one to think at various levels of abstraction.

(2) The design process forces a search for concreteness; it demands an explication and articulation of theory and of conditions under which relationships hold beyond what is usually demanded of the social scientist.

(3) To make the game work, the social scientist must develop an overall or systemic understanding of the topic; and thus is pushed to synthesize.

(4) The model, once developed, can be experimented with readily, and thus serves as a fruitful tool for exploration of theory.

Let's treat these ideas one by one.

CRITICAL ELEMENTS AND LEVELS OF ABSTRACTION

Like a book, a simulation is an explicit statement of what the designer believes about some aspect of reality. The "referent system" simulated is not "reality" itself, but, rather, a set of theoretical propositions about reality. The design process thus entails delineation of theory, construction of a conceptual model, and translation of this into an operating model or simulation. If the translation is good, the gaming-simulation should operate in much the same way that the real world system operates.

There are two critical points here: first, it is not the whole system that is modeled, but rather selected elements. And second, the model does not need to *look like* the referent system, but should *behave* like it. The decision to simulate thus forces the designer to decide what the essential features of the system are. The designer must abstract from reality, making explicit what has often been implicit, and has likewise to decide upon the appropriate level of abstraction for these purposes. The designer's job is to transform and substitute—to find substitute mechanisms and surrogate functions. The solutions can take quite different forms: some substitutions represent reductions in scale, while others entail the introduction of properties that are different in form but that produce the same *consequences*.

The process of thinking about *what it is* that really is important and how to represent it so the system will "work" may foster new insights, for one must think at different levels of abstraction.

Players in CLUG (the COMMUNITY LAND USE GAME), for example, are asked to bid for land, decide upon the location and extent of public utilities, set tax rates, construct buildings, decide upon renovation of deteriorated buildings, and so on. Of course, they are only "playing" at these things; they do not bring in bulldozers or moving men to displace tenants in urban renewal areas; but the game asks them to make the same decisions and to go through the same steps the real-life developer or planner goes through: it is a *reduction in scale*.

Likewise, in some international relations games, such as INS, DANGEROUS PARALLEL, or CRISIS, "diplomats" confer with their ministers, examine indicators of social, political, and economic states of their countries, meet formally and informally with delegates of other "countries," and so on. Again the parallels between the real-world and simulation behaviors are quite close; the latter are abstracted from the large number of things done by politicians and reduced in scale.

In other games, on the other hand, it is the *function* rather than the *structure* that is considered important. It may be the feelings or attitudes experienced by real-world role players that one wants to simulate in the model, rather than the specific mechanisms that create them. In STARPOWER, for example, players accumulate points through trading and bargaining with little colored chips. Surely this is not a familiar or regular activity for most players, yet the mechanism of trading chips generates the desired outcome variable: differential success in the "marketplace."

In HORATIO ALGER, a simulation of problems of social welfare, some players are allowed to work each round while others are only periodically permitted work roles. To generate the frustration of nonworkers necessary to make the system operate as the real-world poverty-welfare cycle works, the designers have included a "work" element: those who are employed are given tinker toys and told to construct something. It is amazing how alienated players who have no tinker toys to use become—and I'm speaking of college students, faculty, and other adults! Obviously, the verisimilitude of playing with tinker toys vis-à-vis going to work is relatively weak; yet the device makes the simulation operate much like the simulandum. I worked recently with some students designing a game which includes differential work rewards for those with differing amounts of education. They are planning to offer different types of "jobs," and they are borrowing the tinker toy work idea and expanding upon it. Some players each round will be told exactly what to do—their task will entail building units of small parts of a larger whole. Others who acquire more education in the game will be given much more independence and creativity in what they can do with their tinker toy sets. In such a way, we hope to generate some of the different work-related feelings engendered in real-life work situations, and to try to trace their consequences.

In BALDICER, a simulation concerned with population explosion and limited capacities to deal with it, an important variable is differential ability to generate enough produce to feed the nation's people. Each player has responsibility for feeding the population of a country of a specified population. At one point in the round, the player is given a sheet on which to write "PUSH, PULL, DIG, SWEAT" as many times as possible in thirty seconds. The number of completed phrases equals the number of thousands who can be fed that year without obtaining outside assistance. Obviously, this is a far cry from planting, fertilizing, harvesting, but it symbolically represents differential capabilities, generates scarcity for some, and propels players to examine interdependencies.

Finally, in a gerontology game, END OF THE LINE, designer Fred Goodman wanted to simulate the decreasing physical-geographic mobility that comes with increasing age. He rejected mobility "points" to be forfeited and decided to use ropes. Players are tied to their chair legs, with differential lengths of rope representing the amount of mobility they have. Some people then can get around more than others, and, as players age, their ropes are shortened. Homologue, rather than analogue, is employed to communicate the critical elements of restricted mobility.

THE SEARCH FOR CONCRETENESS

The second point made above was that game design demands that one think quite concretely about the system. Constant questions about relationships are generated as the designer works to establish linkages between game elements.

Again, an example will perhaps make this clearer. Some of my students decided to build a "college game" to show the options available to students in deciding how to spend their time, and the short- and long-term consequences of the various alternatives. It was something of a variant of the LIFE CAREER GAME and GHETTO. In the initial process of design, they allowed players to 'invest' time in studying, social life, and so on, and gave them rewards of different types for these activities. But then the question arose of long-term consequences. Was it just the degree, for example, that was important in attaining a job? Or did differential academic success (an A average as opposed to a C average) have differential consequences for obtaining a job as well as for graduate school admission? And what *was* the relationship between grade point average and probability of admission to graduate school? The same kinds of questions arose concerning social life. Soon they started looking in books and journals for data on the relationship between college grades and jobs attained, and salaries, and for the relationship between extent of dating and age of marriage for college graduates. The demand for concreteness stemmed from the demands of game design.

In another such exercise, a group of psychiatric nursing students began design of TERMINEX, a game to sensitize doctors to some of the problems involved in dealing with patients with terminal illnesses. Their thesis was that different "types" of patients should be told of their state in different ways: some should be told outright, others more slowly, and so on. Soon after beginning to construct the conceptual model and the gaming-simulation elements, however, they found it necessary to specify quite directly just what type of strategy was appropriate with what "type" of patient. The general proposition had to be translated into quite specific statements in order to build payoff matrices for strategies employed for each patient type. Again a literature search for data was undertaken.

In the process of design, then, unanswered questions are often unearthed. Again and again one must ask "what happens in this case?"

SYSTEMIC UNDERSTANDING

Closely related to this demand for making critical elements explicit and making conditions and relationships concrete is the third point: in order to make the game work, the designer must develop an *overall* or *systemic* understanding. One has to ask not only about definitions and specific linkages, but also about overall interconnections among roles, goals, resources, and rules. How do they fit together? Coleman (1968), Gamson (1975), and Greenblat (1975c) have described the process of going from theory to operating model, trying to integrate the various elements. The nature of the challenge is conveyed by Gamson (1975: 128) in the following quote:

> I have found the process of continual modification of SIMSOC a peculiarly absorbing and rewarding intellectual experience. It has a concreteness and immediacy which is lacking in much of the intellectual work I do. It I am trying to understand why, for example, a particular social movement developed at one time and not another, I will usually struggle through a sequence of questions until I achieve some vague sense of closure. This suffices until enough questions have been raised about my explanation to give me again a vague sense of uneasiness.
>
> The process is somewhat different with the development of a simulation. It is as if I have a complicated Rube Goldberg device in front of me that will produce certain processes and outcomes. I want it to operate differently in one way or another but it is difficult to know where and how to intervene to achieve this purpose because the apparatus is delicate and highly interconnected. So I walk around it, eyeing it from different angles, and imagine adding a nut here or a bolt there or shutting it off and replacing some more complicated parts.
>
> Each of these interventions must take the extremely specific form of a rule. To intervene, one must play a mental game in which the introduction of every specific change must be weighed in terms of how the whole contraption will operate. Such mental games force one to develop a clear picture of what the apparatus looks like and why it operates as it does. [Each hypothetical alternative must be put in place and imagined in operation.] Finally, an explicit choice has to be made and the game actually run under the altered rules, and one has a chance to discover whether he really understands the contraption or not. When a rule-change has the effect it is supposed to have, the experience can be very exciting—as exciting as predicting a nonobvious outcome in any social situation and having it turn out correctly.

EXPLORATION AND EXPERIMENTATION

Creation of the model, subsequent play with it, and systematic manipulation of parameters may unearth new questions and provide a means of exploration and experimentation. These topics will be explored in greater detail in the chapter on uses of gaming-simulation for research.

The possibilities for experimentation via a simulation are increased if one considers that it is possible to simulate a *proposed* or *hypothetical* system as well as an existing "real" one. A colleague, for example, recently showed me a "Utopian, futuristic" paper he wrote. The two questions it had raised from readers were "But how would we ever get there from here?" and "It sounds good, but would it work?" By incorporating the paper's ideas into a gaming-simulation and manipulating it, he might be able to find some tentative answers to these questions. Gaming-simulations, then, may permit us to hypothesize more realistically about "unreal" but hoped-for states such as nonviolence, absence of war, or recognized interdependence.

CHAPTER FIVE

THE GAME DESIGN PROCESS

RICHARD D. DUKE

INTRODUCTION

The game design process has perhaps been reinvented as frequently as the wheel; combining the two *may* be unique. In any event, the process as presented in Figure 5.1 illustrates at least the major considerations that the game designer must confront.

The game design "wheel" is derived from the perspective of gaming as a communications device. Hence, the emphasis on thoughtful review of alternative modes of presenting the material (should you really use gaming in this instance?); the concern for clear specification of *what* is to be conveyed; and the emphasis on the evaluation of the completed product (whether the players benefit as intended).

The process is iterative in actual practice, although it usually entails some "muddling through" by the designers. Nevertheless, it is important to visualize the process in its entirety, to anticipate each phase from the outset of the process.

There are four distinct phases to game design:

(1) During the *initiation* phase, the designer analyses the communication problem at hand. This requires taking into consideration the nature of the client, intended use of the product, the audience, the subject of the message and exactly what communication purpose is to be served (for example, questionnaire, interdisciplinary dialogue, training). Pragmatic constraints of cost and time must also be considered. On the basis of this analysis, an appropriate medium for communication must be chosen.

(2) If the choice *is* gaming-simulation, the designer continues around the wheel to the *design* stage. A conceptual map must be developed (that is a

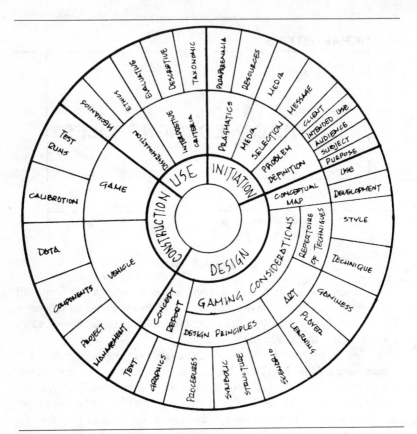

FIGURE 5.1   The Game Design Process

general statement of the ideas to be conveyed through the game). A review
of the state-of-the-art of gaming—that is, of the existing repertoire of gaming techniques—helps determine the nature of the game being designed.
The basic components (scenario, symbolic structure, and procedures) are
developed in a concept report which outlines the form the game will take and
the work that must be done to bring the game to completion.

(3) During *construction,* the gaming vehicle is created and appropriate
data loaded, calibrated, and tested. Finally, the game is reproduced, operators are trained, and the game is put into operation.

(4) The phase of *use* of the game entails a set of responsibilities of
designer to operator, operator to player, and user to designer. Interpretive
criteria for the classification of the game should be provided by the designer.
These four phases are now presented in greater detail.

FOUR PHASES OF GAME DESIGN

Initiation

At the present stage of development in the field of gaming, most if not all games represent "happenings" rather than the products of a deliberate design process. One prominent designer insists that his games convey no "message"; rather, he contends, they are free and ethereal situations which the participant can direct from "inside" the game. The function of a book may well be to establish creative or innovative thought by the reader, thought which may go well beyond the specific content of the book. Nonetheless, the author of the book must intend some message or purpose (such as to inspire creative thought) before a coherent book can be assembled. Similarly, the author of a game must have an express and coherent purpose or "message" to guide the construction of a game. Only the clear articulation of this purpose permits the rational selection of gaming as the appropriate communication mode.

Equally important to the clear expression of message or purpose is the careful definition of the intended audience (surely Dr. Seuss's formal written transmission to other adults would not be recognizable to the children who love his popular books). The game is more occasion-specific than any other form of communication; it is imperative for a game designer to have in mind the intended audience, their motivations for participation, and the typical conditions of use.

The more precisely the designer has articulated the message or purpose of the game, audience characteristics and motivations, and the pragmatic considerations controlling the use of the product, the more effectively various design considerations can be employed to ensure a successful game. This will also give some assurance that gaming is an appropriate media choice.

Design

Game design is a combination of (a) mimicry of existing game formats and styles; (b) an elusive but real "art"; and (c) design principles.

Mimicry of existing games styles. There is a marked tendency for prominent gamers to have an identifiable style. This is so pronounced that it is common parlance among the gaming set to identify and/or quickly explain a game by indicating that it is a typical "Professor Jones game," inserting one of perhaps a dozen well-known names. Unfortunately, the neophyte is likely to ape "Professor Jones" but somehow fail to reflect the sensitivity of the master in its new application. The beginner would do well to have mastered as broad a repertoire of games as possible emphasizing different authors and different subject areas, if the full benefit of the past experience of the profession is to be enjoyed.

The "art" of gaming. The "art" of gaming, like any art, is probably best learned from experience with the medium; nonetheless, one clue can be offered as to its nature. All games are basically iterative in their structure, reinforcing the hunch that this somehow improves learning potential; this is probably achieved by both successively defining the totality of the problem in increasing detail and by positive reinforcement through repetition.

Design principles. Principles of design are categorized here into three general areas:

(1) Use of symbolic structure: A game is really a "language" which entails the integrated use of (an) existing language(s) as well as a "game-specific" language designed for the particular game. (A language is defined as a shared symbol set subject to conventions of use.) These definitions suggest that two levels of skill are required of the game designer; first, the clear articulation of the game-specific language to ensure rapid and effective player use; and, second, careful integration of this new and unique language with each of the other modes of communication employed in this particular game. Any symbolism which is unique to the game represents a hurdle to the players until it has been assimilated. New symbols should only be introduced for specific purposes and players must be trained in their meaning.

(2) Use of scenario: The use of scenario seems to parallel its use in a novel or in the performing arts (legitimate theater, movies, TV). In each case, it becomes an integral part of the technique for conveying the "story" or plot. In gaming, the extent and character of the scenario employed is governed by the considerations indicated above under "initiation." Probably no single failure in game design is more common than an inappropriate use of scenario (too complex or simple, inappropriate to the audience, timing unsuccessful), and this can inevitably be traced to either an initial lack of clarity by the designer relative to purpose, audience, and condition of use or to the insensitive or inappropriate use by the game operator.

(3) Game procedures: There has been an undue emphasis on *rules* in gaming-simulation, perhaps as a result of the strong heritage of game-theoretic applications. A much more productive concept is "procedures," intended as a more flexible term to cover all mechanics of play, including any essential rule structure. Because the game may be viewed as an "environment for learning," it is essential that players be able to interact with the game, often in ways not initially perceived by the designer. In so doing, they may feel it necessary to change the structure of the game. Because of game design considerations, certain conditions may be inviolable (such as the requirement of cycles as iterative experiences or the calculations inherent to a particular model). These may well be called "rules" implying a necessary finality or rigidity. On the contrary, if the players are permitted or encouraged to alter, amend, or enrich procedures within the basic gaming structure (for example, moving from a nonexistent definiton of acceptable player behavior in the game through rudimentary and finally to an advanced articulation in successive cycles of play), we can maximize learning without the labored and unnecessary specification of an elaborate rule structure.

Conceptual mapping and the concept report. Gaming is best understood as a communication form; each game is very specific to some precise communications purpose. The relatively high cost of the technique argues for precision in the design and parsimony in the construction and use of the game. Two powerful tools are available to meet these objectives—conceptual mapping, and its interpreted expression through the gaming technique, the concept report.

Games are most frequently employed for conveying complex systems. It is readily acknowledged that the system may not be understood at the time of game design, and that the basic purpose of the game may be to either extract concepts from a knowledgeable audience, or to assist some research team in the articulation of the system. In each case, the basic objective of the game should be expressed as a conceptual map—an internalized, organized, "gestalt" comprehension of the complex reality being conveyed. Failure to achieve this will most likely lead to an ultimate lack of precision in the game product.

The articulation of the conceptual map permits the systematic review of gaming considerations (repertoire of techniques, art, theory, and principles of design) to achieve the most effective game design for a particular communication purpose. Having achieved this end, it is highly desirable to commit this to writing (text, diagrams) in the form of a concept report before beginning construction. This serves two purposes: (1) it becomes a blueprint to guide the construction process; and (2) more important, it becomes the basis for evaluating the final product. If no documentation of purpose or objective exists, and no coherent review of gaming considerations is presented, the final game will not be subject to intelligent evaluation.

Construction

Many professional gamers like to bypass the first two sectors of game design and jump headlong into construction. As a consequence, there may be a failure to achieve precision of design, the careful engineering of the construct to meet some precise communication need, and almost certainly a loss of parsimony in the construction activities themselves. Nonetheless, there are two reasonable explanations of this tendency to begin in the middle. First, the concept of games as a problem-specific language yielding to orderly rules of design has not been generally recognized; and second, it is hard work to answer all the questions that must be raised to establish detailed game specifications, and the difficulty is compounded by the element of risk inherent in making a written commitment which might later serve as an indictment of the author. The process of constructing a game inevitably forces the designer to confront these questions anyway, although in a less systematic way. Part of the art of good game construction lies in the ability to make a simultaneous solution of many variables. And so, as recognized earlier, we can expect the designer to benefit from an orderly and sequential concept of game design, even though in practice many liberties may be taken.

If a gaming project is of any magnitude, various project management mechanisms may be required. Note that if proper care has been taken in developing the concept report, construction can be a highly organized and efficient process employing standard management practice. If, however, construction is coterminous with an effort at determining objectives and the methodology to be employed, at least marginal chaos is to be expected.

Construction, in either case, entails identifiable components (such as boards, paraphernalia, models), the collection of data required for loading (if necessary) and their joint assembly into an initial (usually rudimentary) game. This must be carefully subjected to calibration and evaluation before release for professional use. Countless hours of participant time have been squandered with immature game products. These often result in the unnecessary aggravation of a captive audience and sometimes bring about the permanent alienation of some players from the gaming technique. This phase, even more than those preceding it, requires that attention be deliberately redirected to the basic game objectives in order to maximize the final fit of the game.

Use

Earlier, many efforts at game design were described as "happenings." If there is a lack of precision in the design of games, it is unfortunately doubly true of many game runs, even though the game itself is cleverly conceived and carefully executed and tested. What is the underlying cause?

If we substitute "book" for "game," we have a clue to this failure. Very sophisticated systems exist and are in routine use which enable "book" to be identified and secured (readily finding the 50 that might be relevant to your problem out of a library of perhaps 1,000,000). Common practices allow reasonably precise evaluation on the grounds of appropriateness, validity of content, level of presentation, and so on, simply by examination of the physical object "book" (this examination may be superficial at first and become more intense as the search narrows to a few books that might be appropriate. At this stage, several passages, even chapters, might be read to complete the evaluation).

Returning to "game," we find no useful parallels—whoever understood the *game* of Monopoly by reading the dreary and endless rules presented in fine print? In short, we have not developed, as a profession, interpretive criteria that are in common usage. Gamers must trust to luck, hoping to improve their batting average through experience and personal contacts.

Three interpretive criteria must be established as routine convention among gamers: (1) a taxonomic system must be employed for filing purposes. This could simply be done by endorsing some existing system currently in use for books, such as the Dewey Decimal System; (2) a brief written abstract in standardized format should be used to reveal design specifications as well as the author's purpose, subject, and intended context of use. Remember, the game is a highly specific communication device—if the author didn't know what the aim was, how do *you* know what you will hit? (3) Finally, standardized procedures for evaluation must be formulated, to assist reviewers, whether for institutional endorsement as in a standard class use of the product, individual selection for one time use, or for game review purposes in journals.

During both the design and construction phases, mechanics and ethics of dissemination must be considered. Mechanics (such as packaging, training operators) are straightforward, but important. Final effective use of the game will, in many cases, be constrained by mechanics and associated costs. These should be thoughtfully anticipated since problems often yield to sophistication of technique.

Of increasing urgency is a sense of ethical responsibility for the product, both in its design and use. Academic tradition and legal precedent are probably adequate for any commercial versions that may be involved (for example, is the product in the public domain, or private property? Has adequate courtesy been given to those whose games were aped?). These are the responsibility of the designer and yield readily to standard convention.

New ethical problems emerge in the *use* of a game, and these are always the responsibility of the operator, although in many cases this responsibility must be shared by the designer. If the designer's conceptual map is a speculation; an alternative to be explored, should it be presented as reality? What are the obligations to the player to avoid injury that occurs beyond the game environment? Ethical questions of gaming are only now beginning to emerge—each designer shares the responsibility for careful thought.

CONCLUSION

Once the game design process is understood as a "gestalt," it can be employed in discontinuous fashion and at various levels of detail. The four phases discussed above are of one fabric, and the art of game design requires their simultaneous solution.

CHAPTER SIX

SPECIFICATIONS FOR GAME DESIGN

RICHARD D. DUKE

The following list is a series of questions for which parameters must be provided *before* game construction begins. The responses, if carefully delineated, provide detailed specifications at the outset of game construction against which the final product can be evaluated.

IS GAMING APPROPRIATE?

Define the Problem

What is the need, conditions, or circumstance that prompted consideration of a game? This statement should be brief and convincing to a neutral observer. The problem statement must be sufficiently detailed to permit evaluation of the success of the game when completed.

(1) Client: Who is the responsible agent? Who is authorized to approve the detailed specifications prior to construction of the game? Who will evaluate for successful completion? *If no client* (as when the game is spontaneous by the designer), an imaginary client should be conjured to ensure thoughtful review of the specifications.

(2) Purpose: What is the primary purpose to be achieved through the game? To transmit information to an audience? As a questionnaire to extract information or opinion from the players? To establish dialogue between players (for example, as a research team)? To motivate players or to prime them for some related experience? To provide an environment in which creative ideas will spontaneously occur? If more than one of these purposes applies, each should be stated explicitly, and they should be clearly placed in order of priority.

(3) Subject matter: The substantive material which is to be dealt with by the game should be defined as explicitly as possible. If no specific subject matter is implied (for example, "frame" games like POLICY NEGOTIATIONS, NEXUS, or IMPASSE?) this should be stated and typical substantive example(s) cited.

(4) Intended audience: For whom is the game intended? Will the players be homogeneous or heterogeneous? What age? Motivation to participate? Sex? Size of group? If several audience profiles are anticipated, define each category. List in order of priority to indicate which group is prime if design considerations require a tradeoff.

(5) Context of use: Under what conditions will the game normally be used? Will it be free-standing or part of a series? Or in conjunction with an academic course or training program? What follow-up circumstances are anticipated? Will the same group run the same exercise repeatedly?

Practical Constraints

What mechanical, political, financial, or other considerations are anticipated relative to constraining the use of the product?

(1) Resources: What financial resources are available for game design, construction, and testing? Is there flexibility to permit alternative designs or cost overruns? How much? Under what circumstances? What financial constraints govern the use of the game? Is the typical cost of play to be within certain limits? What are they? How much time is available for game design? Construction? Testing? Is evidence of productivity to be demanded? At which stages? What evidence? What are the time constraints during the *use* of the game? May it be discontinuous? Will evening or weekend sessions be a normal operational style?

(2) Paraphernalia: Are any constraints to be imposed on materials used by the game? Must it be portable? Under what conditions? Are storage requirements to be specified? What are they? What demands for reproduceability are to be specified? Must the kit use standardized materials? What are they? Is do-it-yourself reproduction permitted? Required? Are instructions for reproducing the kit to be included?

May a computer be used? Which one(s)? What programming language(s) are permitted? Required? Must it be batch-processed? Run on terminals? Are special peripherals permitted (X-Y plotter, C.R.T.)? What are the limits to computer use in dollars or hours? Per cycle? Per run?

Medium Selection

State the reasons for not using other forms of communication (games are generally the most specific and therefore the most costly medium). What are the particular characteristics of the message to be conveyed? May other media be employed with the game? Required? Permitted? Under what constraints (duration, timing, frequency, structured or spontaneous)?

DESIGN

Conceptual Map

Games are a communications medium. What is to be conveyed by this game? Define the system, its components, characteristics, roles, linkages (component to component, role to role, component to role). What considerations are to be emphasized? What themes, issues, or problems are to be stressed?

How is this "message" to be transmitted to the player? Is it to be implicit, buried in the game? Explicit as graphic material or text? Integral in that play of the game requires confrontation with it?

If the message to be transmitted (reality system) is unknown, the purpose of the game being to deduce or extract some perception of reality, system, or message, in what format should the game produce it? Only as a perception retained by the players? As a written record through text and graphics (player-generated)? As a physical representation (iconic model) created by the players? What roles govern the retention, release, or transmission to sponsor of results of play?

Gaming Considerations

Gaming is characterized by an incredibly diverse set of techniques. Which of these are desirable? Required? Prohibited? Are parallels with particular existing games sought? Which ones? Any to be omitted? Why have they been rejected?

(1) Repertoire: What style of game is sought? Emphasis on group dynamics? Or more intellectualized emphasis? Should allocation of scarce resources be central? Or is emphasis to be placed on formulating or conveying a system's gestalt? What basic style or character is desired?

Is the material (message, conceptual map) to be expressed from a particular orientation (field or discipline—psychology, geography and the like) implying both the perspective and jargon?

What level of abstraction is desired? Geographic or social scale? What time frame or horizon? What scale of reduction in time? How are power or finances to be conveyed?

Are game management constraints to be specified? Operator skill, quantity, or training? What level and style of protocols and administrative forms are desired?

How are players to be organized? By group? Individually? Are coalitions to be permitted? Encouraged? Are multiple roles for one player appropriate?

Are particular analogies to be encouraged or omitted by the designer (some known system or concept)?

What structure is to be incorporated for issue generation within game play? Are they to be predetermined or player-generated? Random or preset? Linked? Under what conditions?

Is a physical board to be used? Are constraints of size or complexity required?

(2) Art: "Gaminess" in the final analysis will depend on the skill of the designer. Some consideration, however, may be specified by the client which limit or direct this somewhat elusive characteristic. What degree of player involvement is desired? Large emotional content or emphasis? Or a more deliberate or intellectualized character? Ideally periods of intense involvement will be interspersed with more detached or analytic sessions.

How is the game to be staged? Are particular room arrangements or player configurations to be specified? Are constraints to be placed on pre-game activity? Are warm-up exercises to be considered? Under what conditions are critiques to be held? What duration? Is the style to be free (a "happening") or more controlled?

Are particular learning principles to be emphasized? Is an iterative approach required? How many cycles minimum? Are they to grow more complex? Can level of complexity be stipulated or guided?

Games are best perceived as environments for self-instruction. Are players to have complete freedom of movement within the game or is it to be guided? By the designer? By the operator? By the conscious choice of the players? Are the players to be permitted to invent their own rules? May they alter game procedures? Under what circumstance and frequency?

(3) Design principles: Several elements of design are common to all (or most) games; it may be desirable to specify conditions or characteristics of some of these as design requirements. Is a scenario to be specified? Are alternative scenarios desired? Is the scenario to be explicit, detailed? Highly abstract? To mimic some existing source document? Is it to be capable of modification by the players? The operator? How much resources (time, money) may be permitted for modification during a typical use of the game?

A game is a medium which employs its own distinct "language," and therefore each game requires a unique symbolic structure. The character of this structure should be specified. Is it to be physical? Three-dimensional? Should its complexity be restricted to permit being learned in a specified time by new players? Are symbols to be of a commercial source (such as Lego)? Are they to be presented initially in a codified form? A glossary? A visual aid for continuous display during play? Is a board to be employed? A map or other visual(s)? What degree of complexity is permitted (quantity of new symbols employed, visual details of maps or boards)? Are there any constraints or requirements as to conventional languages or media to be employed (Math? Statistics? Fortran? Flow charting?)?

The character and utility of a game are heavily influenced by the rules and procedures they employ. These may be very rigid (as in games of logic); procedural in that they are specified as requirements to orderly play (as in most social science games); or only partially existent (as in situations mimicking a social dynamic) where players are encouraged to develop their own, or to modify a starting set. What is the character sought in this game? Are circumstances governing the basic accounting system to be treated differently from rules governing player behavior? Is the accounting system to be expressed in a computer language? If not, may it be so complex as to require a calculator? How much operator training for use? Time for routine processing?

Basic complexity of play of any given game is probably best revealed by inspecting the list of "steps of play." Are these, or any subset, to be prespecified (for example, "Prepare a budget," or "Make written estimate of consequence of . . . before viewing next output")? How lengthy or involved is this to be? Can the desired effect be described as advice to the designer? How are they to be presented to the players? Initially? Each cycle?

What information flows are to be provided for? Denied? Emphasized? (Player to player, player to component, component to component.) Are they to be monitored? Recorded? Under what circumstances? By whom? Are they to be preserved beyond the game?

What time scale is to be employed? How is the game to be paced? What duration to a cycle? A game? Is timing to be truncated with successive cycles?

Concept Report

Games are notoriously hard to evaluate. This can be improved upon if a concept report is required of the designer *prior* to game construction. This report should be a synthesis of those considerations reviewed under "Is Gaming Appropriate?" and "Design." It should be a statement of the reality to be conveyed or objectives to be achieved through the game. Is the concept report to be reviewed? By whom? What time intervals for review? What procedures apply to resolve disputes? Is the final product to conform to the concept report? What latitude of difference is acceptable? What penalty(ies) apply in case of failure? Is construction to begin before the detailed concept report is approved by the sponsor?

CONSTRUCTION

If the concept report is carefully prepared and reviewed, construction should be routine and uneventful. However, if the project is large, some particulars may be prespecified by the client.

Pre-Player Activities

Are project management procedures to be specified? Are reports to be prepared which document the various components of the game? If so, how circulated? Must there be client approval? Most games deal with systems that are complex and nonlinear; yet game processing is usually rigidly sequential because of mechanical constraints. The order of processing of various models, components, or decisions must in some sense be artificial. Is it to be prespecified to the designer? In games of any complexity, there are numerous components (roles, models or simulations, paraphernalia, accounting systems) which must be separately designed and/or constructed. These are then assembled and tested. Usually many modifications are necessary to bring a good game together, often necessitating compromise with original specifications or objectives. Are such changes to be reported to the client? Is the concept report to be altered to reflect them? Is approval required? Is data collection, reduction, and loading subject to any quality constraints? Which data items? What degree of accuracy during the assembly and linkage? The entire model must be calibrated to reflect accurate response. Fudge factors (arbitrary values to scale some component up or down) are often used to correct errors. Are those to be reported and appended?

Testing the Game with Players

Most games cannot be claimed as valid unless they have met the "Rule of 10"—at least ten "live" games, the last three of which required no changes (other than perhaps cosmetic or superficial adjustments). Is the game to be tested? With what conditions? Are written evaluations to be required of players? Is the game to be demonstrated for the client?

USE

The game, when complete, is no longer the responsibility of the designer; however, certain considerations incidental to use may be prespecified.

Dissemination

(1) Ethics: Is the product to be private property (client's or designer's) or in the public domain? What are the designer's obligations to the sponsor? To

users? If private property, who holds the copyright or patents, if any? Are royalties to be paid?

What user-related ethics must be considered? Is the design nonmanipulative? Is related literature accurate in describing the game objective and particulars? Are certain debriefing considerations to be mandatory for player protection? Is the game to be used in some larger training context? Are "demonstration" runs potentially a waste of player time of which they must be appraised?

(2) Mechanics: What requirements are to be established for packaging, distribution and operator training? Is the game to be modified and updated? How will these changes be released? Who will distribute the game? Are fees or charges to be permitted for game materials? Are these to be limited to a particular dollar amount? Are they to be waived for certain users? Is the client entitled to multiple sets? How many?

Interpretive Criteria

Games, unlike other media (books, films) are very difficult to judge unless they are actually played. While this may be an inherent difficulty, some steps can be taken to lessen the problem for perspective users.

Is a classification number of some type to be assigned and included in the documentation (such as Dewey Decimal or Library of Congress)? Is a description to be included integrally to the kit which addresses the major points under "Use," or is an abstraction of the concept report required? Is this to be pretested with potential users and reevaluated after they have used the game to ensure accuracy and clarity?

Evaluation

Is the designer-builder required to initiate a formal evaluation of the utility of the product? Is validity to be measured against the reality it purports to address? Against the independent judgment of professionals who know the intended context of use? Against the independent judgment of professional gamers? Against the reaction of players? Other criteria? All of the above? If the game is found wanting, what procedures apply for its modification?

To conclude, these notions are intended to suggest a reasonably comprehensive set of questions a client (and/or designer) may wish to specify before a game is commissioned. Since each game is to fill a specific need, these can only be used to prompt a careful search of conditions appropriate in your particular context.

CHAPTER SEVEN

A PARADIGM FOR GAME DESIGN

RICHARD D. DUKE

During the decade of the 1970s, there was a steady and increasing demand by real-world clients for serious operational gaming/simulation constructs to be used in actual policy formulation situations. These devices are still under increasingly widespread use, both here and abroad. They are usually employed in a predecision context by top administrative personnel in an effort to communicate more effectively with one another about the problem at hand.[1] The problem is typically a very complex real-world situation characterized by

(1) many variables in interaction;
(2) no realistic basis for quantification of variables or their interactions;
(3) no proven conceptual model or precedent on which to base action decisions;
(4) a sociopolitical context of decision-making where actions of the various "players" may be idiosyncratic or arational;
(5) a "futures" context; that is, the decision is irrevocable and the results will not be understood until well into the future.

Each gamer develops an approach or paradigm used to guide the design of these gaming/simulation constructs. While these various approaches share some methodology, they also differ, dependent on both the client's objective and the gamer's philosophy. My own perspective is that games lend themselves particularly to transmitting the character of complex reality;[2] consequently my approach to design is toward achieving that objective.[3] Below are the nine basic steps to game design which I pursue in a disciplined way each time I create a game for a client:

AUTHOR'S NOTE: This article was originally presented as a paper at the Tenth International ISAGA Conference, Leeuwarden, The Netherlands, August 8-11, 1979.

(1) develop written specifications for game design;
(2) develop a comprehensive schematic representation of the problem;
(3) select components of the problem to be gamed;
(4) plan the game with the Systems Component/Gaming Element Matrix;
(5) describe the content of each cell (above, 4) in writing;
(6) search my "repertoire of games" for ideas to represent each cell;
(7) build the game;
(8) evaluate the game (against the criteria of 1, above);
(9) test the game in the field, and modify.

These nine steps have evolved over two decades of using the technique in a wide variety of situations. The steps are described in more detail below.

STEP 1: SPECIFICATIONS FOR GAME DESIGN

This is the specific set of requirements, agreed to in advance by the game builders, describing the expectations and limitations of the game. Before game construction actually begins, the building team needs to determine the game's purpose—the messages to be communicated and the means of conveying it. Game architects need a blueprint composed of carefully delineated, detailed game specifications. At the outset, they need to conform to a plan, providing a clear, concise picture of the product to be created. This prevents unexpected, costly problems from arising later on in the process. There are two resulting advantages:

—*Time-saving*. Agreeing to specifications first tends to speed the design process along. Efficiency is increased, since unforeseen obstacles to progress have been eliminated.

—*Client approval*. The intentions of the client and game designers must correspond. By drawing up game specifications and giving the client something tangible to review, communication can ensue. This permits real differences in message interpretation, purpose, or content to be resolved at the start. These specifications serve, at the conclusion of the field trails of the exercise, as the basis for evaluation of the total effort.

STEP 2: COMPREHENSIVE SCHEMATIC OF SYSTEMS COMPONENTS

This is a specific description of the problem expressed in systems terminology. This is usually achieved through developing "snow cards"[4] by brainstorming, conducting a literature search, and interviewing experts; in turn, these snow cards are then organized into one or more convenient formats (sequential: as in a table of contents, conceptual mapping wheel, three-dimensional construct, flow chart suitable for conversion of the system to a digital computer program, and so on).

STEP 3: SELECTION OF PROBLEM COMPONENTS
TO BE GAMED

The purpose of gaming/simulation is to provide a basis for organized communication about a complex topic. To achieve this objective it is necessary to abstract from the problem set or system those ideas or problem components which require further discussion. This process of abstraction must be guided in the particular by the specifications for game design described earlier. The process itself is quite simple and straightforward. Using one or more of the systems representations above (either the conceptual mapping wheel[5] or the flow chart, for example) and a colored marker pencil, the designer circles those aspects of the system which are considered essential for inclusion in the game.

While this is perhaps one of the most straightforward physical tasks of game design, it becomes one of the most critical in terms of the quality of the final product. There is a strong tendency to put too much detail in the game in recognition of the reality that all things are linked to all things. It is imperative for the team making these decisions to constantly review the "specifications for game design" to ensure a reasonable abstraction process. The specifications for game design serve as the basis or judgmental criteria for making the decision.

STEP 4: PLANNING TO INCLUDE
SYSTEMS COMPONENTS IN THE GAME

Having decided *what* game in step 3, it is now necessary to plan *how* to game these systems components in terms of the basic elements of gaming/ simulations. This step is achieved through the use of a "Systems Component Gaming Element Matrix." This matrix shows the specific way(s) in which a given systems component will be captured in the game design, game element by game element.

A game/simulation consists of twelve basic elements: (1) scenario, (2) pulse, (3) cycle sequence, (4) steps of play, (5) rules, (6) roles, (7) model, (8) decision sequence and linkage, (9) accounting system, (10) indicators, (11) symbology, and (12) paraphernalia. Any problem to be systematically conveyed through game design must specifically represent the problem components through one or another of these twelve gaming elements. (Sometimes a problem component will appear in several of the gaming elements.) This process of "mapping" the problem systematically into a gaming element matrix achieves several results:

(1) First, it provides a record of the decisions that are made.
(2) It is a rigorous methodology which permits a deliberate evaluation of each of

the components of the problem to ensure that it is considered in the game design phase.

(3) It forces consideration, at an early stage, of precisely how, in terms of the twelve gaming elements, each problem might possibly be represented in the game.

(4) Finally, it provides a blueprint for game design as described in step 5 below.

The twelve gaming elements are described below:

1. Scenario. A scenario is simply a text outlining the plot of the game. It outlines starting conditions and describes circumstances leading into play. It deals with all aspects—economic, social, and political—either presented by text or supplemented with diagrams and illustrations. Role descriptions might be considered a part of the scenario, but are normally offered in a separate section of the concept report. Role descriptions will normally establish initial points of reference and discussion for the players.

2. Pulse. A pulse (see note 3) is some event or problem introduced during the course of play to focus the players' attention on a single aspect of the problem. The pulse may be either designer-induced or player-induced. It may be predetermined, random, or triggered by a certain action in the game. A pulse is an organizational device, used to encourage "multilogue" (see note 3) by forcing players to focus on some shared phenomena. One pulse follows another in sequence (or in complex games, several are simultaneously initiated). Each represents an aspect of the conceptual map. During play of the gaming/simulation, these pulses become tangible handles which allow players to grasp the problem in detail and enter into and explore the gestalt of the total problem situation.

3. Cycle Sequence. Cycle sequence is a relatively simple, but very important, part of game design. There are both micro and macro cycle sequences that must be taken into account. The macro sequence takes into account preconditions to the game; the introductory cycle(s); the final cycle; and the evaluation process associated with the total exercise. The micro cycle takes into account the sequence of things that occur within each cycle, including the initiation, policy, action, and evaluation of each cycle.

4. Steps of Play. Steps of play are the explicit progression of activity in the game. There is a macro cycle in each cycle which includes the four steps, initiation, policy, action, and evaluation. During the initiation, the players read the scenario, take into a cycle any pulses/events/issues that have occurred, and consider any new data available to them as a result of the prevous cycle. During the action cycle, players make specific decisions according to a given order. During the evaluation phase of the cycle, all play stops and an intellectual discussion ensues, under the direction of the game operator, which addresses two questions: (1) What are the results of the cycle just completed? (2) How does this experience relate to the real-world problem? The next step is always recycling, which proves especially critical—the success of gaming/simulation in conveying problem gestalt (see note 3) is largely derived from the interactive or cyclical nature of these exercises. Learning takes place through repetition of experience. Each cycle, then, reinforces the knowledge gained previously while additional details are introduced.

Steps of play provide the game basic guidelines of progress. Each sequence denotes another set of instructions, which signals some action(s) to occur. Player participation is directed, expected, and stimulated. Players move through the game one step at a time. This makes it easier for the player and the operator. The ultimate goal of the "steps of play" is to increase learning and to enrich knowledge of the system or problem being represented. During the design of a game, it is likely that these steps will be reevaluated and redesigned several times.

5. Rules. There are a variety of circumstances that might develop in a game, which go beyond the scope of the exercise. If these are anticipated, the designer can present rules that govern these cases. These should be made clear to the players at the outset, and any changes during play should be posted in a conspicuous way.

6. Roles. Roles are characters assigned to players with prescribed patterns of behavior. They are predicted on known real-world counterparts. Participants may play a role similar to their own "real-world" role, but generally it is better to permit the player to experience the game problem system from a position unknown to the person in reality. Roles are always limited in number to those most central to the problem being studied. There are basically three kinds of roles that can be included within the game design—pseudo, gamed, or simulated.

—*Pseudo roles* are invented frequently on the spot to serve some immediate function. (Examples include judges and technical experts.) When the right situation arises, special participants with unique skills are employed on the spot. Pseudo roles remain unlinked to the basic rule structure, nor are they processed formally through the game's accounting system.

—*Gamed roles* are built into the gaming situation framework and played by real players whose decisions are processed by the game's accounting system.

—*Simulated roles* exist in the accounting system but not physically in the gameroom itself. Often they represent broad classes or categories of people (as in voting models and demographic models). It is often useful to have simulated roles in the gaming/simulation to generate output useful to the gamed or pseudo roles.

7. Models. Models are devices derived from the accounting system to keep track of logical processes. They may be simple or complex. They may be expressed in mathematical terms or illustrated graphically. Examples might include the representation of economic process or demographic reality. There are basically three types of models: (1) The heuristic, or homologue, model is the least sophisticated and used most often. (2) Iconic models given the physical appearance of reality (they need not act like reality); board games serve as an example. (3) Analogue models parallel the real-world phenomena and correspond to the real-world counterparts they represent at least at some level of abstraction. Sophisticated simulation models are an example of the latter.

8. Decision Sequence and Linkages. The sequence of decisions and linkage between players' actions must be understood before the game is built. These represent the typical sequence of decisions that players can make during a normal cycle of play. Often these are developed through the use of a matrix: Across the top of the matrix are all of the gamed roles; down the left side are the steps of play. This schematic is intended to answer the question: *Who* is doing *what, when,* and *how*? It also provides data on information flows and feedbacks, role-to-role and role-to-accounting system. Generally, this matrix depicts the activity and intellectual process of each role during consecutive steps of play.

The purpose of this matrix is to assist the game designer in visualizing the sequence of play when the game is finished. The matrix helps to identify role linkages within the game framework, to chart the foreseen reactions of the participants to events during play, and to provide an initial analysis of all gamed, pseudo, and simulated role results before play begins.

When completed, this matrix gives some early insight into the totality of the game during play. In evaluating the contents of the matrix, the need will arise to adapt or change roles for one of several reasons. Players must be more or less equally loaded so that they are all more or less evenly occupied during the presentation. It is also necessary during an analysis of this chart to ensure that decisions are sequenced properly, one behind the other, so that necessary feedback takes place. Finally, the matrix can be used as an aid in explaining to others the sequence of events occurring during a typical game run.

9. Accounting System. The accounting system is a set of fixed procedures incorporated directly into the game to deal consistently with player decisions. These decisions—outcomes of steps of play—are processed, acted upon, and forwarded to some other game component, feeding back either into an indicator, model, role, or some combination of the above. An infinite variety of accounting systems exist. Game designers must develop a system suitable to the particular exercise. In the final analysis, the accounting system must be devised to deal in a rigorous and consistent way with all of the information contained in the cells of the Systems Component/Gaming Element Matrix described earlier in this article.

Having selected and defined the gaming elements from the Systems Component/Gaming Element Matrix, a procedure for their activation must be devised and implemented as an accounting system in the gaming/

simulation. This accounting system may be simple or complex, it may maneuver players' responses through models, simulations, or very simple algorithms, and it may or may not use a computer. It will always be reported out to the players through various indicators which will be displayed on forms, wall charts, and playing boards. Whenever possible, it is desirable to have the players individually keep the accounting system. This gives them a better understanding of the problem being considered and saves a great deal of work for the operator.

Regardless of the format or the combinations employed, the accounting system will inevitably be sequential. This requires very sophisticated judgment by the builders of the exercise to ensure that the sequence of decisions, as represented by the systems of accounts, at least integrates into a larger system or gestalt experience.

10. Indicators. Indicators are those aspects of the accounting system that the operator chooses to emphasize for the participants. They report on the game's progress—the interaction of player's decisions as filtered through the accounting system and linked to the models.

11. Symbology. Symbology is the physical representation of indicators. These are visual aids comprising a set of characteristics about some gamed phenomenon. Symbology is game-specific in that the materials lose meaning outside of the playing arena. They are comprised of extemporaneous material like cardboard chips or wooden blocks, and are integrated into the game to portray some reality such as the land-use or building pattern. Symbology may be any tangible replication incorporated into play to embellish, as well as convey, meaning. Players are asked to focus their attention on these items to address and manipulate them according to procedures.

During this stage of the design process, experimentation with the symbolic structure occurs. It must be the goal of the game builders to gain maximum clarity for the players. To minimize confusion during play, it is necessary to be parsimonious in the selection of these gamed materials.

12. Paraphernalia. Paraphernalia includes everything else required to successfully run the simulation exercise. The material ranges from the decision forms to the wall charts to colored pens and the game board itself.

STEP 5: SUMMARIZING THE CONTENT OF EACH GAMING ELEMENT

To build a gaming/simulation, then, it is necessary to define each gaming element along two dimensions: (1) its substantive content, and (2) the gaming mechanisms that are thought to be appropriate for representing this content in the game. To describe the *content* of each game element, one summarizes the notations from all cells for each column of the Systems Component/Game Element Matrix.

To obtain the first information—that is, the content which must be included under each of the indicated game elements—the game-building team simply makes a summary notation of all of the notations of each cell of the appropriate column for the Systems Component/Game Element Matrix developed under step 4. For example, under the column, "roles," the sundry rows of the matrix describing the problem in a systematic way will reveal those decision makers that have to be included. By listing all of those (going down the column) a complete list of roles that must be represented can then be included.

STEP 6: SELECTING GAMING MECHANISMS FROM ONE'S REPERTOIRE OF TECHNIQUES

Next, using ideas from a personal "repertoire of games," the game builder describes ideas about how each of the gaming elements will be represented. This is best done by going down the game element listing, point by point, as one lists the gaming technique which seems most effective.

STEP 7: GAME CONSTRUCTION AND TESTING

Game construction is an iterative process.[6] The experienced game designer will first attempt the design of the game at a very rudimentary level. These preliminary efforts are used primarily to help the game design team conceptualize the problem as it might be converted into gaming/simulation format. It is important to capture the design blueprint in a written concept report before game design begins in earnest. The concept report achieves three major objectives:

(1) It ensures that the game designers go through a deliberate process which takes into account the several steps noted above. This is more efficient and results in better game design than does a random process.
(2) It provides a very sharply delineated and documented basis for the client to review the expected product in its conceptualized stage. Gaming/simulation is a client-oriented tool and the concept report helps to ensure that the final product is useful to the client.
(3) Finally, the concept report serves as a blueprint or working document for the design team during the construction phase.

Actual construction is a trial-and-error process which progresses as follows: Each game element is built (designed, written, conceptualized). As the team progresses down the list of gaming elements, these are continually checked, one against the other, to ensure that they dovetail or "fit." When all gaming elements have been completed as initial, rudimentary, or trial efforts, a series of gaming "walkthroughs" are attempted. At this point, the "rule of ten" comes into play. The game builders must recognize that the early cycles or game runs will be full of difficulties. They will be pleasantly surprised, however, to discover that by the second, third, or fourth run, the form of the game will clearly emerge. To ensure that the final gaming/simulation product is reasonable, testing must be governed by the "rule of ten." That is, a game should be presented as complete only after it has been tested with appropriate audiences on ten separate occasions, the final three of which should require no further significant adjustment or modification to the gaming/simulation. The "rule of ten" goes through three more or less distinct phases:

—Trial construction or testing as an iterative process. In this, the design team "talks through" the game, considering various mock-ups and carrying the process through its logical processes.

—Pretesting corresponds to a "dress rehearsal." The entire product is tested with a small group of participants. Participants include the design team and a few colleagues and interested volunteers.

—Formal testing ensues after most "bugs" have been eliminated. This entails more rigorous evaluation of the finalized version before it is turned over to the client.

The client, participants, and game designers must all recognize that many different runs may be required before the game is finally calibrated. In fact, there may never be a time when a "final" game exists. More likely, the users will find that continuous modification of the game is productive throughout the lifetime of its use.

STEP 8: GAME EVALUATION

After the game has been completed and turned over to the client for field use, it is necessary for the client to evaluate the product. The only logical basis for evaluation of the gaming/simulation is the original "specifications for game design" described earlier. There were the guidelines approved by the sponsor in advance, and they must serve as the basis for evaluating the product. At this point it becomes clear to both the game builders and the client that the more specific and plausible the original "specifications," the more clear-cut becomes the final game evaluation.

STEP 9: FIELD USE OF THE GAMING/SIMULATION

Once the gaming/simulation has been designed, tested, modified, and evaluated, it is time to put it into field use. Field use will normally require the training of appropriate game operators. This can be accomplished through holding workshops for those who intend to use the game, or by sending trained game operators into the field to assist in the actual use of the exercise. While the operation of the game may seem formidable to the neophyte, field experience with complex games like the F.A.O. gaming/simulation SNUS (Simulated Nutrition System; see Duke and Cary, 1975) indicates that it is not difficult to achieve adequate field use.

Finally, a distribution plan for the gaming/simulation is essential. Responsibility for distributing the game must rest clearly with an existing institution or commercial firm. This institution or firm should be authorized to duplicate the materials, train operators, and arrange for field use and demonstrations.

NOTES

1. A recent example is CONRAIL, the Consolidated Rail Corporation, which used a gaming/simulation to explore the probable impact of railroad deregulation on its operations. Participation in this exercise ranged from the various vice-presidents in charge of the several corporate function areas, to the board. Subsequently it has been used throughout the corporation, as well as with most competition and the regulatory agencies, to illustrate CONRAIL's thinking on the issue. The exercise, of course, changed considerably over the original six months of intensive use (see Duke and Cary, 1979).

2. *Complex reality:* a complex, interactive, and/or dynamic system, either abstract or concrete.

3. *Gaming/simulation:* a gestalt communication mode which contains a game-specific language, appropriate communication technologies, and the multilogue interaction pattern.

Gestalt: "a structure or configuration of physical, biological, or psychological phenomena so integrated as to constitute a functional unit with properties not derivable from its part in summation" (Webster's *Third New International Dictionary*).

Communication mode: a form of communication composed of a language, a pattern of interaction, and a communication technology.

Game-specific language: a symbol set and its conventions of use, unique to a given game.

Communication technology: a device for encoding, transmitting, and decoding a message.

Multilogue: multiple, simultaneous dialogue organized by pulse.

Pulse: a problem, issue, alternative, or information presented to the players through the game, used to trigger an exchange of messages between players.

These preceding definitions are derived from Duke (1974). Section two of that work explains the communications approach to gaming in detail.

4. *Snow cards:* Small scraps of paper used to capture a single idea, concept subject, or concern of the participants trying to capture an image of a "complex reality" (see note 2, above).

5. For a complete description of the conceptual mapping technique, see Duke and Greenblat (1979).

6. For a more complete description of the game design process, see Greenblat and Duke (1975: Part II).

CHAPTER EIGHT

FORMAT FOR THE GAME—
LOGIC OR INTUITION?

RICHARD D. DUKE

In Chapter 7, I put forth "nine steps" for game design. Alternatively, perhaps, the chapter could have been called "Game Design Made Easy" or "Even You Can Build a Game!"

My "nine steps" are:

(1) Develop written specifications for game design.
(2) Develop a comprehensive schematic representation of the problem.
(3) Select components of the problem to be gamed.
(4) Plan the game with the Systems Component/Game Element Matrix.
(5) Describe the content of each cell in writing.
(6) Search your "Repertoire of Games" for ideas to represent each cell.
(7) Build the game.
(8) Game evaluation (against the criteria of Step 1).
(9) Field use and modification.

Similar documents abound in the literature; every major gamer has solved this problem not once but several times, and my list of steps—simple instructions for "How To Do It"—is quite good (as are the lists of my colleagues). Nevertheless, my list of instructions resorts to magic with Step 7: "Now, go build the game!"

Of course, I'm prepared to defend my "nine steps" as being carefully thought through and useful. And, of course, I can describe in great length why the first six steps will almost automatically solve Step 7. But the simple, eloquent truth seems to be that no matter who describes the problem, sooner or later it boils down to "Go build the game," at which point the designer is forced to resort to personal intuition and/or to the format of some other game that might suggest itself from previous experience.

In reviewing past games that I have built and in talking with many other gamers about their various experiences in game design, I have not received much help on this point. They do often make one or more of these three comments:

"I just keep 'playing around' with it 'til it works."

"It just seemed like the same kind of problem as the 'X' game dealt with."

"I don't really know where I got the idea for the game—it just seemed to come out of the blue."

In each case, they were quite familiar with their client, their objectives, and the subject matter. In many cases, they had been quite methodical about their game-building activity. In all cases, they are hard-pressed to describe their reasons for selecting the game format which they finally chose.

In developing this chapter, I decided to select several games that I have contracted for and completed in the recent past. These experiences all share the following criteria:

(1) They were all developed for a paying client; the clients knew what their "problem" was; and the clients made the final judgment as to how well the exercise met their objectives.
(2) All five games have dealt with serious real-world problems which involved complex subject matter.
(3) All these exercises were developed from the philosophy of games as a mode of communication (as contrasted with a teaching tool, a "happening", and so on; see Duke, 1974).
(4) Each of the exercises was developed in a disciplined sequence (see the "nine steps" above).
(5) Each met the objectives of the client.

The following five games have each used different formats (see Table 8.1). Each is unique in its application and, to my knowledge, original in its design. This chapter will address the question, "Why were these particular formats used for these particular applications?" Here in five iterations, is the answer:

(1) The CONRAIL Railroad Deregulation Game dealt with a policy question that represents national policy affecting a major corporation. The situation is little short of desperate, with CONRAIL requiring an enormous public subsidy each year to survive. Energy concerns require that efficient transport be developed (and competition and the free enterprise system are the presumed answer); inflation fears are of great concern (will deregulation feed the flames?).

The management of CONRAIL wanted to develop a more complete understanding of deregulation (as it was shaping up in a particular legislative bill) to gain some perspective on the in-house options available if it came to pass, and to convey their understanding to members of Congress, their competitors, the regulatory agencies, and the public.

The subject matter is complex, technical, and "dry." The main "actors" have a serious interest in the subject. If any insight is to be gained, they must be pulled far enough away from their day-to-day interests so that they might distinguish the "forest from the trees." The concept of the cone of abstraction becomes the guiding criteria.

TABLE 8.1   Five Games—Objectives and Formats

Client	Game	Objective	Format
1. CONRAIL	Railroad Deregulation Game	To allow top management to evaluate the impact on CONRAIL of deregulation of the rail industry.	Rate-setting problem(s) using form with a microprocessor back-up; wall graphics for "eyewash."
2. Chase Manhatten Bank	The Montauk Exercise	To allow C.M.B. executives to evaluate development strategies for the International Division in a 1985-1990 window.	A matrix game to establish a logical referent for voluminous data where each cell defines the next more detailed matrix.
3. UNESCO	HEX—The Human Settlement Management Exercise	To encourage conferees to "let down their hair" for a candid discussion of the problems of communication, horizontal and vertical, in national planning.	Three games, each part of a hexagonal pattern, on stilts. Interactions required, both vertically and horizontally.
4. FAO	SNUS— Simulated Nutrition System	To familiarize national planning teams of Third World countries with the impact of various policies, both manufacturing and non-manufacturing sectors, on national nutrition planning.	A large board of (4′ × 4′) with movable chips representing a stylized flow chart of the processes involved.
5. JPL	Geothermal Energy Game	To force an engineering team to design an "Executive Summary" of a lengthy technical report which was suitable for congressional review.	A large wheel (3′ dia.) divided into many rings and sectors; scenarios of major options.

In response to these observations, the game design team first tried to mimic a CONRAIL "war room" located in Philadelphia. This took the form of a railroad route map which underwent a series of simplifications. The original 4,000+ terminals became 7; the 1,000+ competing transport lines became 3; the 10,000 shipments became 11; and the 7 distinct car-types evolved into 1. In turn, the process of rate-setting became more central than these omitted details. The accounting system was relegated to a microprocessor; and the final exercises became very much like a "live" case study, with the arguments and processes of rate-setting being highlighted after the technical detail had been presented in the original exercise.

(2) The Montauk Exercise. Chase Manhattan Bank was concerned that its position in the international market remain competitive over the next decade. Toward that end, a major study had been undertaken to collect data from its various world markets about its present and possible future states. A meeting was planned for the presentation of this data to management, with the objective of consolidating the enormous data files into some meaningful and hopefully manageable propositions for management to respond to. The original plan to present the data as format on a live computer hook-up had to be abandoned—the volume was too overwhelming (several millions of discrete data items were available; a logical presentation would entail several thousand matrices, each of approximately 100 cells); and the data was too "soft" (much of it was speculation about some future condition) to permit rigorous quantitative manipulation. To make matters more difficult, there was only a month available in which to develop, test, and present the final game!

The answer was to develop a role-playing exercise with two major innovations: (1) specialists on the staff were to serve as "human computers" and give the best answers possible, based on the data available *and* their human judgment, and (2) a series of nested matrices was employed as a very visible logical construct to keep the participants from becoming lost in the data.

The resulting exercise permitted the participants to guide the discussion in any direction while keeping a road map through the nested matrices. If a particular thrust was not successful, the format permitted a fresh beginning with relative ease.

(3) Geothermal Energy Game. The Jet Propulsion Laboratory has evolved into a major contract research group for the federal government. One of its contracts entailed an evaluation of geothermal energy as a potential alternative to fossil fuels. A major study of several years' duration was completed, except for one very important detail—the government required a brief (50-page) executive summary of the technical report (several thousand pages) expressed in terms which would be meaningful to Congress.

Several attempts to develop this document failed for two reasons: (1) it was always too long (none of the staff of engineers was willing to see *his* work eliminated from the final document; (2) it was always too technical (well-head pressures, pipe size, details of environmental impact, and so on; nothing about international energy prospects, major options available to Congress, or the like).

JPL asked for a game to be used to organize a two-day conference to focus on the problem. The objective was to evolve an outline for the executive summary which would list the content of the final document and the length of each anticipated section. Only three weeks were available.

The design team developed a game with three components: (1) 10 scenarios, each describing one of the major policy options available to Congress (for example, develop national corporation, leave development to private industry); (2) 30 role descriptions, one for each of the engineering teams and each describing a U.S. Congressman or Senator thought to be pivotal to the final decision; and (3) a wheel (conceptual map) that organized about 1000 variables, technical and nontechnical, which were central to an understanding of the problem (Duke and Greenblat, 1979).

The staff was then asked to form 10 teams of 3 each. Each team evaluated the conceptual maps from the standpoint of their respective roles and scenarios; their decisions were placed on the conceptual mapping wheel in color. The 10 wheels were later consolidated into one large wheel. Each wheel had blank spaces to allow new items to be added.

The results, as you will suspect, were that the engineers, in the role of politicians, were disinterested in technical data and more interested in social, political, economic, and environmental data. With the marked wheels as a guide, they were able to construct and agree to an outline in one afternoon; the report was successfully completed soon after.

(4) SNUS: Simulated Nutrition System. The Nutrition Division of the Food and Agricultural Organization of the United Nations has as one of its objectives the training of national planning teams of Third World nations concerned with nutrition at the level of national policy. This is a complex subject which involves the production, transport, marketing, and final distribution of agricultural products; completion of industrial products; and the various decisions in the public and private sectors which affect the flow of food to human beings. The primary objective of the training was to familiarize the participants with the totality of the process and to sensitize them to the impact on nutrition among the poor.

Preliminary discussion with the staff in Rome and with other nutrition experts suggested that the topic was complex; that agricultural and industrial processes had to be included; that a flow of goods was an essential characteristic; and that policy actors *and* production actors had to be represented. Discussions further suggested that the best way to illustrate the process would be in a simulated hypothetical country.

My own explorations into a general theory of game design had suggested that games were of three types: (1) implicit, (2) explicit, and (3) integral. Of these, the third type lent itself best to areas of science because it required a deliberate representation or model to be reconstructed; it permitted the game to be evolved directly by interaction of the player and the model.

A flow chart was developed and approved by the client. This was converted into an actual board game on which the participants would move physically through the logic of the flow chart. This was later blended with a map representing the geography of a small nation; and the result, SNUS, has been quite effective for its purpose.

(5) HEX–The Human Settlement Game. The Human Settlement Division of UNESCO holds conferences for the purpose of training midmanagement public officials at locations throughout the world. These focus on human problems such as housing, education, public facilities, utilities. The conferees speak a great variety of languages from conference to conference.

UNESCO sought to develop a game which could serve as an introduction to these meetings—to serve as an ice-breaker. Because these meetings were frequently attended by local, provincial, and regional officials, there was often an initial period in which the participants were uncomfortable and less than candid in describing where they felt the problem lay (each level of government, of course, felt that some other level of government was responsible). Further discussions with U.N. staff and various experts suggested that the greatest concern was with management problems, particularly problems in vertical communication.

The result was the development of three games played simultaneously. They were placed on stilts, one above the other. Participants are told to solve the game on their own "level" and are left to discover in practice that this can only be done if all three games are solved simultaneously; this, in turn, requires vertical communication. The game begins quite quickly; and as it winds down, the critique leads into an in-depth discussion of the real-world problems of communication in the actual country where the game is being played.

These five examples attempt to suggest a process of game design which is in part (1) adherence to discipline, (2) the development of a logic for each case, (3) a reference to a repertoire of techniques, (4) intuition and inspiration, and (5) finally, luck. Nonetheless, the author believes that of all these factors' adherence to discipline is the most important and effective. The others will follow.

CHAPTER NINE

SOCIOLOGICAL THEORY AND THE "MULTIPLE REALITY" GAME

CATHY STEIN GREENBLAT

Social simulation games have been described as languages of theory, explicit statements about what the designers believe about reality, and operating models of central features of systems or processes. All these definitions point to the intimate relationship between simulation games and social theory: the games are dynamic representations of theory. Simulation design demands a high level of explication and articulation of theory, for to develop a simulation we have to define the essential features of the referent system, abstract from reality, and develop a mode of presentation of both structural and functional relationships. Through the process of gaming or simulating, therefore, we refine our theoretical formulations (see Raser, 1969; Coleman, 1969; Stoll and Inbar, 1972).

Many of us also use simulations to teach theories to our students. We have our student-players operate a model, observe and analyze the way the system functions, and assess the extent to which it resembles the real-world correlates. We do this in the belief that this process makes it easier for them to grasp and assimilate systemic relationships which are difficult to comprehend through lectures or other linear presentations, and that it makes social science subject matter more real and vivid (see Boocock and Schild, 1968; Greenblat, 1975e, 1971b).

It is incumbent upon us, then, as designers and users, to examine the theories built into simulation games to see how accurate and inclusive such

AUTHOR'S NOTE: I am very much in debt to Richard D. Duke for his encouragement and comments as I began work on this paper. Harry C. Bredemeier and Allan Feldt also provided helpful criticisms of earlier formulations. A grant from the Rutgers Research Council permitted me to deliver this paper at the Third Annual Symposium of the International Simulation and Gaming Association in Birmingham, England, July 5-9, 1972.

models are. My perusal of a number of games that are useful for teaching sociology recently led me to the belief that many social simulations have omitted a critical concept of sociological theory: the concept of differing definitions of reality or "multiple realities." The present chapter is an attempt to review this aspect of theory and to show how it might be included in game models.

DIFFERING DEFINITIONS OF REALITY

People go through their daily lives trying to make sense of the world in which they live. Through the process of defining situations and constructing realities from shreds and patches of experience and memory, they impute meaning to persons and objects (see Berger and Luckmann, 1966; McHugh, 1968; Lyman and Scott, 1970; Cicourel, 1969; Douglass, 1971). The same events, persons, or objects, however, take on different meanings for different people, who thus create varying interpretations, or "multiple realities."[1] Literature and drama abound with examples—*Rashomon* (Kanin and Kanin, 1959) and *$100 Misunderstanding* (Gover, 1961)—and all of us have seen personal examples or social science accounts of husbands' and wives', representatives of labor and management, or inmates' and guards' highly conflicting accounts of the same happenings (see Manocchio and Dunn, 1970).

These definitions of reality tend not to be totally unique and individual. There are several sources of commonality and difference in people's perceptions and definitions, including (1) positions in the social structure, (2) goals which direct attention and order priorities, and (3) personal biographies. First, members of society are born into groups which have social heritages with preformulated systems of relevances and typifications, their own argots, and sets of values. Through the process of socialization, newborns, like newcomers to any group, are given a picture of reality as seen by their group. This picture includes definitions of themselves, their group, and others, and of the appropriate degrees of contact with various others who have contrary or conflicting information or ideas. Hence, as their view of the world is developed, it tends to become somewhat insulated from challenges (see Allport, 1954). Position in the social structure accounts, then, not only for the extent of available resources, but for the rules, norms, and definitions one receives, for the degree of cross-group communication, and for the extent of challenge to certainty one encounters and accepts.

Multiple realities also stem from variability of goals. Different goals are salient for different people at any given time, and to the same person at varying points in his life. Depending upon one's goals, various aspects of a situation or event will be seen as relevant. Where individuals have different goals, we can at least expect that they will have different evaluations of things, if not different interpretations.

In addition, any social actor has a history, and, hence, definitions of a situation are partly biographically determined, affected by the individual's unique stock of previous experiences and recollections. Individual combinations of contacts and socialization experiences thus render differences between the definitions that might otherwise be expected of those with similar roles and goals (see Heeren, 1970). Thus, multiple realities often arise among those variously situated in the social structure with respect to the threats, dangers, or liabilities they are exposed or vulnerable to, as well as the opportunities and action alternatives open to them.

These multiple realities are more than just objects of curiosity for the analyst of social life, for differences in the meanings of events and persons produce differences in behavior. W. I. Thomas's famous aphorism (1928: 584), "If men define situations as real, they are real in their consequences" offers the link between the social construction of reality and the encounters between people. To understand social behavior, one must understand not simply the social structure, but the images of reality that members carry and which make certain kinds of behavior appropriate and, more than appropriate, typical. Constraints and opportunities exists not simply as objective characteristics of social systems, but in the heads of participants. To understand a person's behavior, then, you have to understand what that person *thinks* exists, not what "really or objectively exists." It is not, for example, the number of actual job opportunities that you must inquire about to comprehend the behavior of the ex-convict who feels pushed to return to crime as the "only way." It is not just the "real power" of a student body you must assess to understand the dynamics of campus politics at many colleges, but the students' *felt* powerlessness to alter existing conditions. Sociological literature contains increasing data attesting to the ways in which one belief may lead to another, affect later observations and behaviors, and thus create self-fulfilling prophesies (Merton, 1968; Lemert, 1962; Becker, 1964). Some of the ways in which our *expectations* may create what seem to be scientific findings have also been documented (Rosenthal, 1966).

For the sociologist, then, an important step in trying to comprehend a social system is to learn how the actors define their situations and the events that transpire. If, as game designers, we wish to create models that operate like these real systems, we must simulate both the structural elements and the differential perceptions of system participants.

Have we done this? Generally, I think not. Most games I have seen include two of the sources of differential definitions: different roles and different goals for players. Thus, over the course of play, participants may develop alternative perceptions of the same things and events. In most games, however, the constraints carried in the heads of the real-world system-participants—constraints developed through their prior socialization—are not given to the players. Hence, the multiple realities, conflicting views, and barriers to challenge of these views which are of critical importance *from the first moment of interaction* between the real-world system participants are absent. This frequently leads to game behavior quite different from behavior in the system simulated. We cannot and should not rely on game players who have not lived within the referent system to come to the interaction with the stereotypes, blinders, and prior ideas which affect the perceptions, attitudes, and behavior of their real-world counterparts. Yet this is what we have generally done.

What I am arguing, then, is that players should be given different and conflicting information, corresponding to the different and conflicting perceptions held by their real-world counterparts. All should not be presented with the same manual for play. It is not enough to provide *missing* information; we must provide *mis*information. We have to allow different views of reality, if not "corrected," to create differential opportunities and restrictions, and thus to provide the potentials for self-fulfilling prophesies.

Let me offer an example, utilizing a college setting, since that is presumably a familiar system to most of us. At hypothetical College X, if you asked the junior faculty about the distribution of influence among junior faculty, senior faculty, and administration, they might tell you that, of every ten "units" of influence, junior faculty have one unit, senior faculty have two units, and the administration has seven units. Further interviewing at College X might reveal that the senior faculty believe that junior faculty have three units, senior faculty have four units, and the administration has three units. The administrators, you might find, see the distribution yet a third way: junior faculty, two; senior faculty, five; and administration, three. A social scientist, coming to do a study of power and influence at College X, and thus assessing the relative influence of the three constituencies, might conclude that the distribution is really junior faculty, one unit; senior faculty, four units; and administration, three units.

Now we decide to build a simulation of the system. If we follow the usual procedure, we are likely to turn to the social scientist's "objective" description and write a game manual in which all players are informed that the junior faculty has one influence point, senior faculty has four influence points, and the administration has three influence points to allocate. Then we will give them the task of making decisions, voting on policies, negotiating, and so on. What we have thereby done, I believe, is to act as if the reality that motivates each real-world group and underlies their actions is the scientific reality rather than its own individual reality. But remember W.I. Thomas's statement, quoted earlier: "If men define situations as real, they are real in their consequences." College X operates as it does because of the separate realities that are brought together through the interaction of the constituencies; thus, the simulation must include the three realities. Rather than creating a shared reality that is nonexistent in the real-world college, we must tell each group of game players that the distribution is as their real-world counterparts see it. Each group should thus be given misconceptions about the influence possessed by other groups and about the proportion of influence each group—including itself—has, as shown in Table 9.1. Thus, we should tell junior faculty role players that the distribution is as the real junior faculty perceives it: one, four, five, and then give them their one point of influence. We should tell the senior faculty role players that the distribution of power is as senior faculty described it to us: three, four, three, and then give them their four influence points. Finally, we should tell the administration role players that the distribution is two, five, three, and give them three points. Each group would thus have the number of influence points they think should have—that is, one, four, and three, respectively—but they would be operating in terms of multiple realities. Under these conditions, I believe the behavior of the role-players would bear considerably more resemblance to the behavior of the real-world counterparts at College X than if the game were created as most seem to be, with all participants starting play with a shared reality. As in the real world, with this kind of model, players might think they are playing the same game, but in fact they are playing different versions of a game with the same name!

TABLE 9.1   Differences Between Perceived and Actual Influence at College X and in Simulation of College X

	Perceived influence	Perceived proportion of total influence	Actual influence	Actual proportion of total influence
Junior faculty beliefs:				
About junior faculty	1	1/10	1	1/8
About senior faculty	2	2/10	4	4/8
About administration	7	7/10	3	3/8
Senior faculty beliefs:				
About junior faculty	3	3/10	1	1/8
About senior faculty	4	4/10	4	4/8
About administration	3	3/10	3	3/8
Administration beliefs:				
About junior faculty	2	2/10	1	1/8
About senior faculty	5	5/10	4	4/8
About administration	3	3/10	3	3/8

METHODOLOGY

How, then, does the designer go about introducing a "multiple reality" component into games? The methodology will vary depending upon the element or elements the designer wants to develop in this way: role definitions, resources, or rules of play.

The general procedure in constructing role profiles for a multiple reality game involves asking not, "What are the groups (constituencies) and how can they be characterized?" but rather, "What are the groups and how do they characterize themselves and one another?" Instead of deriving a linear set of "objective role definitions," the designer thus generates a matrix of the sort shown in Figure 9.1.

The cells of the matrix that are marked with an asterisk (*) contain data of *self-perceptions*. Row blocks indicate the multiple realities with respect to each group. For example, the row marked ///// contains data on different ways in which the As are defined—by the As themselves, by the Bs, and by the Cs. The column blocks present the specific, individual views of reality of each particular group. Hence, the column marked \\\\\, for

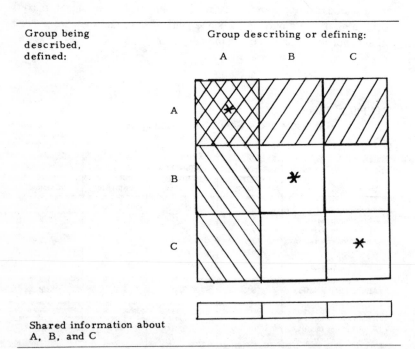

FIGURE 9.1   Role Definition Matrix for a Multiple Reality Game

example, contains the data on how the As view themselves, the Bs, and the Cs. The information in the total matrix offers the multiple realities of role definitions as of the beginning of the simulation.

A matrix such as this serves as the basis for role definition in the players' manuals. The As would receive, in prose form, the information in column A; the Bs, the information in column B; the Cs the information in column C; all would receive the "shared information." Table 9.2 shows a hypothetical example of a filled-in matrix and Table 9.3 offers the corresponding manual pages.

Notice that only the game director is aware that each of the groups actually possesses the same amount of influence: medium. Each group misperceives the others and is in turn misperceived by them. While the Oranges, for example, see themselves as Liberal, they are seen by the Greens as Radical; likewise, while the Greens see themselves as Moderate-Conservative, the Oranges see them as Ultra-Conservative.

From this point, the design process is similar to the "regular" design

TABLE 9.2   Role Definition for COLOR WAR AND PEACE

Group Being Defined:	Group Defining:		
	ORANGE	BLUE	GREEN
Aspect:			
ORANGE:	*		
Sociopolitical orientation	Liberal	Liberal-Radical	Radical
Power or influence	Medium	Low	Low
Definition of present situation	Terrible	Very bad	Bad
BLUE:		*	
Sociopolitical orientation	Moderate to Conservative	Moderate	Liberal
Power of influence	Low	Medium	High
Definition of present situation	Poor	Bad	Very Unpleasant
GREEN:			*
Sociopolitical orientation	Ultra-Conservative	Conservative	Conservative-Moderate
Power or influence	High	High	Medium
Definition of present situation	Good	OK	OK with some strains

*SHARED INFORMATION: (i.e., all three groups know the following) Oranges see Blues as sympathetic to them but not very understanding, and see Greens as hostile and rigid. Blues see Oranges as unappreciative of their support, and see Greens as patronizing and suspicious. Greens see Oranges as highly aggressive and immature, and see Blues as sympathetic but not very understanding.

TABLE 9.3   Role Profiles for COLOR WAR AND PEACE

As given to ORANGES:

"There are three groups in the game, as described below: Each player will be assigned to one of these groups, so read the descriptions carefully.

   (1) ORANGES
      The Oranges' sociopolitical position can be characterized as Liberal. They wield a medium amount of influence, and define the present situation as terrible.

   (2) BLUES
      The Blues' sociopolitical orientation is Moderate to Conservative. They wield a low amount of influence, and define the present situation as poor.

   (3) GREENS
      The Greens' sociopolitical orientation is Ultra-Conservative. They wield a high amount of influence, and see the present situation as good.

Past relations among the three groups have been strained. The Oranges feel the Blues have been sympathetic but not very understanding, and that the Greens have been hostile and rigid. The Blues feel the Oranges have been unappreciative of their support, and feel the Greens have acted in a patronizing and suspicious manner. Finally, the Greens feel the Oranges have been highly aggressive and immature, and that the Blues have been sympathetic but not very understanding."

As given to the BLUES:

"There are three groups in the game, as described below. Each player will be assigned to one of these groups, so read the descriptions carefully.

   (1) ORANGES
      The Oranges' sociopolitical orientation can be described as Liberal to Radical. They wield a low amount of influence, and they define the present situation as very bad.

   (2) BLUES
      The Blues' sociopolitical orientation is Moderate. They wield a medium amount of power and view the present situation as bad.

   (3) GREENS
      The Greens' sociopolitical orientation is Conservative. They wield a high amount of infiuence and see the present situation as OK.

Past relations among the three groups have been strained. The Oranges. . . . (CONTINUES SAME AS FOR ORANGES)

As given to the GREENS:

"There are three groups in the game, as described below. Each player will be assigned to one of these groups, so read the descriptions carefully.

   (1) ORANGES
      The Oranges' sociopolitical orientation can be described as Radical. At the present time they wield a low amount of influence and define the present situation is very poor.

   (2) BLUES
      The Blues' sociopolitical position is Liberal. They wield a high amount of influence, and define the present situation as very unpleasant.

   (3) GREENS
      The Greens' sociopolitical position is Conservative to Moderate. They view the present situation as unpleasant, and wield a medium amount of influence.

Past relations among the three. . . . (CONTINUES SAME AS FOR ORANGES) process: goals must be spelled out, a scenario created, and rules of play determined.

The multiple reality game need not, as in the preceding example, contain homogeneous subgroups. The matrix in Table 9.4 shows how the designer could set up differential resources based upon varying beliefs and expectations within and across groups. Note that this is quite different from saying that the groups have different *values,* which is commonly noted in games. Table 9.5 then offers a sample filled-in matrix.

Individual role profiles would then be constructed. So, for example, one Yellow player might be given beliefs 1b, 2a, and 3b: another might get 1c, 2b, and 3c; and so forth. The Purples' theory would also be given out. Distribution could be either through deliberate or random combination, depending upon the designer's beliefs about whether the beliefs tend to cluster.

Note also that, in this sample, the *actual* distribution is such that both groups have equal objective access to the resources. Yet differing proportions of the two groups perceive their resources as equal to those of the other group; some see their group as disadvantaged, and others see it as "advan-

TABLE 9.4   Matrix for Creating Differential Resources Based upon Differential Beliefs and Expectations in a Multiple Reality Game

Belief sets and specific beliefs:	Group A	Group B	Designer's actual set-up
Set X:			
1 ⎧ Exhaustive,	____ %	____ %	
2 ⎨ mutually	____ %	____ %	
3 ⎩ exclusive	____ %	____ %	
beliefs			
	100%	100%	
Set Y;			
1 ⎧ Exhaustive,	____ %	____ %	
2 ⎨ mutually	____ %	____ %	
3 ⎩ exclusive	____ %	____ %	
beliefs			
	100%	100%	
Set Z:			
1 ⎧ Exhaustive,	____ %	____ %	
2 ⎨ mutually	____ %	____ %	
3 ⎩ exclusive	____ %	____ %	
beliefs			
	100%	100%	

taged." I believe that, as in the real world, these perceptions would be likely to persist and color the participants' views and interpretations of events that transpire. So, for example, to determine any player's grades for a given round, the game coordinator might ask how many hours had been invested in studies, ask players to roll a die, and, using something like the chart in Figure 2, reveal their grades. As was noted in Table 9.5, the same probabilities prevail for Yellows, and Purples; several, however, are not likely to believe this and will make decisions accordingly.

TABLE 9.5   Resource Distribution in COLOR WAR AND PEACE

Belief sets and Specific beliefs:	% of YELLOWS with this belief	% of PURPLES with this belief	Actual distribution
1. Academic resources			
a. Yellows get preferential treatment from professors	20	25	
b. Yellows and purples get equal treatment from professors	20	50	Given equal time invested in studies, yellows and purples have equal proba-
c. Purples get preferential treatment from profes- sors	60	25	bilities of good grades
2. Money resources (scholarships)			
a. Yellows have most of the scholarship funds, though purples have as much need	0	20	
b. In general, purples are from wealthier backgrounds than yellows; they have less need for scholarships and fewer have such funds	80	80	Scholarship funds are distributed on the basis of need. 40% of the Yellows have scholarships, and 20% of the purples have scholarships
c. Although purples are generally wealthy and have no need for assistance, they have most of the scholarship funds	20	0	
3. Potentialities for intergroup relations			
a. Yellows don't want to have relationships with purples (although they may pretend to)	0	40	100% of each group are told that inter- group relationships are desirable, but
b. Yellows and purples gener- ally desire good relations with one another and can have them with a little effort	60	60	60% of each group are told this is possible, and 40% of each are told it is impossible be- cause the other
c. Purples don't want to have relationships with yellows (though they may pretend to)	40	0	group doesn't want relationships

Time	Die	Grades	Time	Die	Grades	Time	Die	Grades
Low	1 ——	F	Medium	1 ——	D	High	1 ——	C
	2 ⟩	D		2 ⟩	C		2 ⟩	B
	3			3			3	
	4 ⟩	C		4 ⟩	B		4	
	5			5			5 ⟩	A
	6 ——	B		6 ——	A		6	

FIGURE 9.2   Grades in COLLEGE COLOR WAR AND PEACE Game,
Based upon Time Spent and Roll of Die

CONCLUSION: PROPOSALS FOR DEVELOPMENT AND
USE OF THE CONCEPT

I am NOT, I wish to emphasize, urging that all games designed from now on include a multiple-reality component. Promising as I think the idea is, it carries with it a number of costs that must always be weighed against the benefits. I would like, then, to conclude by reviewing some of these factors, both negative and positive.

The costs include, first, the need for secrecy and careful planning to prevent players from immediately learning of the differential materials. All versions of the manual or other multiple-reality materials must be made to look the same to players, but be like a deck of "marked cards" so that the game director can distribute them easily and accurately. Ballotting or other procedures must be secret, so players cannot see that the actual number of votes cast in the resource distribution has been differentially defined. But these are not brand new problems: in CRISIS, the director must be careful in the distribution of the two newspapers; in PLANS and METROPOLITICS, votes must be privately turned in to the coordinator, albeit for different reasons than those in the procedure advocated here.

A second cost is closely related to this: such materials would be more expensive to produce, as several manuals must be provided, and the packaging is more complex.

A third cost also derives from the need for secrecy: the game would only "work" with players who did not know of the built-in differences in perceptions. Thus, the game director would have to urge those who have played, at the conclusion of the postgame discussion, not to reveal the "secret" of the game. Much as theatre producers of plays such as *Sleuth* enjoin such silence on the part of members of the audience, so game directors would have to urge players to say nothing. To the extent that the game was enjoyable and worthwhile, and players understood the functions of the not-to-be-revealed components, their cooperation could probably reasonably be expected. Again, this is not a totally new demand on the game director, who has already made such pleas with such games as STARPOWER. The problem, however, would be vastly compounded if a high proportion of new games were to incorporate my multiple-reality suggestions, for now we would have the problem of players who had heard nothing about the *specific* game they were about to play, but suspected the multiple-reality "fix" because they had encountered it in several other games. How much of a problem versus a gain this is depends upon whether such "game sophistication" is paralleled by the sociological sophistication of realization that the "trick" is really not a "trick," but rather a simulation of a critical dimension of each of the systems.

This leads me to the fourth potential "cost" of the multiple-reality game: the chance that participants may become hostile to the game director on discovering the existence of different manuals with different information. I firmly believe that the game designer bears responsibility for presenting the compound information in a way that minimizes such reactions, preparing the game director for this possibility, and providing the background information and rationale for the multiple-reality inclusions so that the experience can be made a fruitful one (even for those who react adversely) by accurately explaining them in the postplay discussion.

Fifth, and finally, I believe that the benefits will often not outweigh the costs where the game is designed to simulate a social system or process in a very abstract way. For example, in SIMSOC, players begin with minimal structural arrangements and confront the need to develop a social organization. The seven basic groups and four regions have no direct, exact counterparts in any real-world society. Hence, no "prehistory" vis-à-vis one another is necessary to avoid artificial and often deceptively facile early interactions although it is desirable, as I have argued, in games that purport to simulate more specific systems or processes, such as negotiations between school board members or between city residents confronted with referenda on government reform. Whereas I believe that the latter game is strengthened by my inclusion, the former, highly abstract game, I believe, teaches better by allowing the multiple realities to be emergent rather than supplied.

What, then, are the benefits to be weighed against these increased costs to both the designer and the user? The discussion in the body of this chapter has offered simply the embryonic formulations of my idea. A wide variety of elaborations is possible, from the simple to the highly complex. For example, one could vary not simply the agreement-disagreement dimension of consensus, as was done in the examples, but also could vary the knowledge or understanding of this disagreement, and even the realization of the understanding or misunderstanding (see Scheff, 1967). Many of the complexities of differential perceptions, as they affect social behavior, therefore, could be built into simulations by the ambitious designer. Such enterprises should bring the rewards indicated at the beginning of the chapter: higher verisimilitude of participant-real-world behavior, and, hence, a better teaching tool or research device. Rather than hoping some player will come up with a bluff, that another will spread rumors or scandalous reports, and that yet another, like Hamlet, will feign madness, we build in the bluffs, rumors, scandalous reports, and charges of madness that we know play a significant part. Rather than waiting for the "equiprobability through ignorance" principle to operate to lead players to reduce ambiguity through creating interpretations, we provide the definitions known to characterize system participants (Brim, 1955). Particularly where players are naive about the nature of the system and the types of attitudes and behaviors characteristic of those whose roles they are playing, or where the backgrounds of participants are quite different from those system members or are generally homogenous, the supplying of those perceptions, stereotypes, and blinders that guide and influence the real-world system participants should contribute to simulation activity and attitude closer to actual behavior. Hence, observation and analysis are likely to generate better data for testing of the model versus real world, and thus to provide a more fruitful learning experience for students and for those of us who hope to utilize simulations for the construction and refinement of theory.

CHAPTER TEN

FURTHER EXPLORATIONS ON THE MULTIPLE REALITY GAME

CATHY STEIN GREENBLAT
JOHN H. GAGNON

The initial explicit discussions of the utility of a multiple reality perspective in gaming can be found in the previous chapter. The goal in that chapter was to discuss a theoretical point of view in sociology on the diverse realities of persons participating in common social arrangements and to suggest how this perspective might be used to increase the reality content of gaming simulations. On its initial publication in *Simulation and Games* (Greenblat, 1975d), the paper had a positive reception and some modest influence in others' writings and in some game designs. Since the authors and others have tried to use this perspective in further game design and have found it to be fruitful, we decided to reflect again on the enhancement of reality in game design for both teaching and research.

The connection between reality which is modeled and the games which are created from these models—a connection which seemed so straightforward initially—now seems more problematic. The original notion was that what designers wanted to do was to maximize the reality of the game. That this is the goal of game designers now seems more questionable—as does the implicit assumption which underlies that goal, that is, that the designer would possess some view of reality which was somehow either higher or better or more inclusive or more objective than the reality possessed by any single set of participants.

We have now come to the conclusion that both the question of how much reality the game designer wants to put into the game and the assumption that

AUTHORS' NOTE: This is a revised version of a paper presented at the seventh annual meetings of the International Simulation and Gaming Association, Caracas, Venezuela, October 7-9, 1976. This paper was prepared and delivered at the invitation of the association conference committee.

the designer possesses an objective view of the reality that is being modeled need to be addressed more carefully—and in reverse order. Usually the scientist constructs a version of the reality "out there" which is commonly viewed as objective, complete, or scientific. This is contrasted to versions held by the participants in the "out there" reality which are viewed as subjective, partial, or naive. Further, the gaming-simulation that is created from the scientists' version is also thought to be, in some sense, more correct than the views of those who participate in the game. Thus the question is not only how much reality but the selective process by which elements of what is out there are included in the game. The process involves two separate steps: what version of reality does the designer construct from the world and what elements of this version are put into the game for the players to learn. The neutrality of the designer is in question both in terms of building of the model as well as in what goals of play are provided for those who participate in the game.

THE GAME DESIGNER AS SOCIOLOGIST

In the previous chapter, it was argued that members of the same society have different views of reality, depending upon their position in the social structure, their goals, and their biographies. Their differing views of reality lead them to different explanations for the things they and others do and say (including the explanations themselves). In real world interactions, different perceptions and different explanations of the same event emerge from the daily life of the participants, with some degree of overlap. Thus police, criminals, victims, prosecutors, probation officers, and "ordinary citizens" tend to experience some common and some different elements of the law enforcement system; hence they share and differ in their views of it. Similarly, doctors, patients, researchers, and executives of Blue Cross-Blue Shield have both common and disparate conceptions of the health care delivery system.

When the interactions include representatives of two different cultures (or two different historical moments), there are more bases for differential understanding of the meaning of an event, as an experience of the novelist E. M. Forster suggests. Forster was travelling for pleasure with an Indian friend and when their holiday was over his friend was downcast beyond what Forster thought appropriate for a separation that would last only a short time. When Forster and his friend met again Forster (1964: 6-7) chided him on his excessive emotion:

> I began by scolding my friend. I told him that he had been wrong to feel and display so much emotion upon so slight an occasion: that it was inappropriate.

The word "inappropriate" roused him to fury. "What?" he cried. "Do you measure out your emotions as if they were potatoes?" I did not like the simile of the potatoes, but after a moment's reflection I said, "Yes, I do; and what's more, I think I ought to. A small occasion demands a little emotion, just as a large occasion demands a great one. I would like my emotions to be appropriate. This may be measuring them like potatoes, but it is better than slopping them about like water from a pail, which is what you did." He did not like the simile of the pail. "If those are your opinions, they part us forever," he cried, and left the room. Returning immediately, he added: "No—but your whole attitude toward emotion is wrong. Emotion has nothing to do with appropriateness. It matters only that it shall be sincere. I happened to feel deeply. I showed it. It doesn't matter whether I ought to have felt deeply or not."

This remark impressed me very much. Yet I could not agree with it, and said that I valued emotion as much as he did, but used it differently; if I poured it out on small occasions I was afraid of having none left for the great ones, and of being bankrupt at the crises of life. Note the word "bankrupt." I spoke as a member of a prudent middle-class nation, always anxious to meet my liabilities. But my friend spoke as an Oriental, and the Oriental has behind him a tradition, not of middle-class prudence, but of kingly munificence and splendour. He feels his resources are endless, just as John Bull feels his are finite. As regards material resources, the Oriental is clearly unwise. Money isn't endless. If we spend or give away all the money we have, we haven't any more, and must take the consequences, which are frequently unpleasant. But, as regards the resources of the spirit, he may be right. The emotions may be endless. The more we express them, the more we may have to express.

This exchange suggests depths of difference in realities that persons experience, including the way they express emotions. It should be noted that even Forster's distinction between a Ben Franklin view of material possessions ("waste not, want not") and a Keynesian view of the emotions ("the more you spend the more you have") is itself an example of differing realities.

The previous chapter argued that as game designers we often fail to reflect the profundity of these differences in experiencing and explanation in our games. That is, we model from the perspective of the social scientist, viewing the system as a whole. Then we give people different positions in the game structure and different purposes, and wait for different perspectives to emerge from the interaction. But this is not enough, for our players are usually unfamiliar with the real-world situations simulated in the games. They lack the positional or cultural or biographical bases for the possession (or development) of different views of the same situation which affect their real-world counterparts from the first moment of interaction.

Thus it was argued that reality in the games could be increased if more attention was paid to the allocation of information and misinformation to the players at the start of the game. By withholding information from some players or by giving false information and beliefs which would correspond to the different beliefs of the real-world persons, we would allow play to begin with a greater concordance between the multiple realities in the world and the realities in the game. One example offered was a simulation of decision-making in colleges in which junior faculty, senior faculty, and administrators would be given different amounts of information and information differing in content about their perceived and actual power. Thus junior faculty (and other players) would be provided with not only their own justifications for actions and estimates of power but with false views of others' justifications and estimates.[2] The inclusion of this multiple reality component could compensate for the homogeneity and inexperience of the players and make the game play more like real-world behavior. Thus the game would be a vehicle for players to learn about the various perspectives and the role that these have in shaping the outcome of the game; later, players would be introduced to the supra- or more inclusive perspective. The players would think and act more like the real-world participants and then the critique session would show them the overall game design from the sociologist's perspective.

The use of a multiple reality perspective was suggested not to turn game designers into sociologists who study the realities of the social world and then present their findings to an audience of other academics. The concern was with teaching, with making players more like "the natives" and then telling them what it was *really* like, what they failed to understand because of their preexisting blinders and because of the limits of viewing the situation from one limited stance. The game design would incorporate the separate realities; and the critique would reveal them, giving players a new understanding, a new explanation. The game and critique would show not only what each participant felt but a supraview: this is *really* why doctors charge high fees; this is *really* why police view things this way and criminals view them that way. Following play, then, participants would become converted to an objective and more realistic view of the world.

REALITY ACCORDING TO
PRACTITIONERS OR PARTICIPANTS

In reflecting on these goals it became clearer that too simple a view of the reality of the game designer and the realities of the participants had been held. When sociologists study social situations, they develop their own explanations of why actors do various kinds of things, in contrast to those held by the actors. Anthropologists make this distinction between what they label as *emic* and *etic* explanations. The emic refers to the way the natives explain such things as the increase in pigs, the growth of crops, why their daughters are married to members of the turtle clan. The etic refers to the way the anthropologist explains the same phenomena. Thus for example, the natives explain that they marry their daughters to members of the turtle clan to satisfy the gods; the anthropologist explains that the women are married to the turtle clan to achieve social and economic integration. This is a competing explanation to that of the natives; that is, it competes with the natives' versions of reality by utilizing the social position of the sociologist and the anthropologist and the social right which is given them to create "objective" and inclusive reality.[3]

Such explanations are not simple neutral statements, particularly in the context of a gaming or educational situation. Such higher level explanations are instructions for how to understand how you and others behave, and thus to control your behavior in accordance with such understandings. Through them people have alternative courses of action open to them, and supposedly higher levels of understanding that may lead to different purposes in their conduct. Thus games are used to offer new systematic explanations and in the hope that they will affect the way people behave because now they "know better."

In this sense, the game, like much of education, is meant to be a vehicle for consciousness-raising, attitudinal, and behavioral change. It is designed and used in hopes that the "limited" realities will be exposed and the consciousness of the players raised. A further desire is that the players will come to new understandings and take new courses of action as the game learning becomes part of life. *In so doing, the game designer does not simply highlight reality but constructs a new reality for the players.* Since the game embodies a social theory which includes or replaces disparate naive or folk explanations, it offers a competitive explanation for what is going on in the world. If this scientific explanation were offered to and accepted by those whose daughters are to marry into the turtle clan, "social integration" would be substituted for "satisfying the gods" as the reason for clan exogamy. Thus, even the existence of competitive explanations is not a neutral situation unless the alternatives are kept from the natives. If the natives accept the view that their marriage practices are clan exogamy and it is for the purpose of social integration, they may modify their conduct. We take advantage of the cultural status of the social sciences and their objective-scientific perspective to offer a new version of reality to the game players and/or the natives (they may be the same persons) which they can use as a new basis on which to control their behavior and predict the behavior of others.

It is important to point out that all social science explanations embody certain kinds of interests or purposes rather than being purely neutral constructions. Even in the cultural relativism that guides such constructions (such as seeing everyone's point of view) there already implicitly exists a set of democratic, libertarian, problem-solving-by-reform values. Furthermore, such explanations substitute the fact-finding procedures of modern social science for other forms of knowing. Regardless of whether social science explanations have some claim to higher levels of objectivity, inclusiveness, and reality, it is clear that they themselves are additional components in the multiple realities of social life.

THE GAME DESIGNER AS ADVOCATE

Game design for the purposes of raising consciousness, contributing to understanding, helping people see better why they and others act as they do is very attractive. It has the ring of objectivity—the game designer is the scientist who "tells it like it is," the professor who does not advocate one position or another, but exposes all views for perusal and more informed choice. It is a role designers feel comfortable and happy playing, and so they seek ways to build more and more realistic games to teach players more and more about what the world is "really" like. Critiques of games praise or condemn them in terms of how well they simulate reality. For example, the game BLACKS AND WHITES and WOMEN'S LIB have been attacked as poor games because they seem to distort reality significantly, thus teaching things that are not so.

Having recognized that the suprareality of the game may be a competing reality in the world, it is possible to see that even this "objective" suprareality may be selected from as it is modelled from to create a playable game. In several games by Fred Goodman (such as MARBLES), the game operator is called the "Game Overall Director." The operator sports a name tag with the first letters of the role—G.O.D.—written in large letters, and players joke about their conversations with GOD. This label has probably caught more of the truth than is usually admitted, but perhaps the label should be applied more readily to the game designer than to the director. The designer *is* the Game Overall Designer or GOD, for designers do not simply give players views of reality that are objective and overarching but rather they are constantly making value decisions and selecting pieces of reality in terms of those values as they build their products. Further, the GOD is generally a liberal, both as a result of a commitment to scientific objectivity and in terms of the politics of everyday life. The models of reality that are built are usually liberal in character and the games designed exclude illiberal strategies, proscriptions, and solutions.

It is not simply that games are designed to inform but that they are created to serve as bases for action. Thus a game is not criticized only on whether it is a "good" or a "bad" game in an efficiency sense—that is, does it model accurately and teach how things "really" are. Designers also think about whether the game teaches "good" or "bad" things. The point is that the features of "reality" that are put into or highlighted in our games are those that point to the courses of action that designers believe that players should take outside of the gaming situations. The designer examines situations and models them *for some purpose* and hopefully the player draws lessons from them in a purposive way, learning only some aspects of the overall reality.

These value issues appear in the explanation of *why* games are built, *why* simulated experiences are good for students. Some phenomena are modeled because they are "bad." The game allows them a way to understand the plight of those who unfortunately have to experience the bad things in real life. For example, hemophilia is a bad thing and those who have it are unfortunate, but the healthy should understand the reality of the hemophiliac so they will, for example, treat them nicer, give blood donations, create more efficient blood and care delivery systems; BLOOD MONEY appears to be a way to give them such understandings without having to give them the disease. Thus it is often argued that it would be efficacious for students to experience such negative phenomena briefly to appreciate their costs. Since that is impossible, the vicarious experience of a game is the next best thing.

This stance toward what we define as "bad things" can be seen if we consider the phenomenon of war. The social science GODs generally urge that war is a bad thing, and they do not want people to engage in real wars in order to learn that. Thus people play international relations games in which they learn the costs of war in hopes that they will become committed to its avoidance. At the same time there is a disavowal of the military's war games, for these are designed and played to improve the real-world modes of engaging in war. If the liberal social scientist GOD's designed war games, they would emphasize the casualties, the pain, and telling parents that their sons have died, rather than the strategies of strike and counterstrike.

In other instances there are the good things in the world that unfortunately people cannot experience firsthand, at least not at the moment. The argument then is that a game is better than a lecture or reading to teach people how to do these good things better. "Play the game"—so that you can learn how to do the real thing better. "Play THE MARRIAGE GAME"—so you can select a mate more wisely and be a more understanding spouse. "Play METROPOLIS"—so you can learn how to be a better politician. "Play BAFA-BAFA"—so you can learn about not jumping to conclusions about motives when dealing with members of a different culture, but can realize that they view the world differently because of their different values.

What players should learn from our games and what they should not learn from them is part of the design. Games, because of the social realities of those who construct them, tend to support conventional, ameliorative, middle-class morality. The good aspects of a system are modeled to teach its virtues and its style. The bad aspects of a system are modeled in order to correct them, and it is known *how* they should be corrected. Two examples can be given here.

In BLOOD MONEY, players *are* to learn that the health care system should be restructured so that there is more medical care and blood available to hemophiliacs; players are *not* to learn that medical personnel should engage in triage or that hemophiliacs should engage in mass suicide to make the ratio between available resources and demand more equal, although these are possible solutions. The game was designed and it has been run in such a way that it endorses those positions in which the designer/operators believe.[4]

In STARPOWER, one group, the Squares, gain monetary resources and then power over the less well-off Circles and Triangles. The Squares then tend to engage in further capital accumulation partly by exploiting the others. But STARPOWER is neither designed nor run to teach capitalistic accumulation and techniques of exploitation on the part of the Squares nor revolutionary terrorism on the part of the Circles and Triangles. It models a traditional class-layered society for the purpose of teaching why the ruling class should be nicer. Players "see" through the game that if people do not have equal opportunity, the advantaged change the rules and the disadvantaged cheat and/or become apathetic, or unruly. Therefore, the message goes, people should work to have equal opportunity in the world. Enthusiasts of the game—and there are many of them—laud it for its effectiveness in demonstrating this to players; they do not laud it for teaching the Squares how to wield power more effectively, nor for teaching Circles and Triangles how to cheat and lie and be violent to get a piece of the action, though these are possible lessons to be drawn from play. Why not? Because both GODs— the Game Overall Designer and the Game Overall Director—believe in the liberal morality.

To test this general thesis is easy. Try using METRO-APEX as a vehicle for teaching politicians how to cheat the public and for teaching industrialists how to avoid compliance with air pollution ordinances and see if the designer (Richard Duke) responds the same way as when it is used to teach air pollution control officers about the difficulties they will have to face if they are to be successful in policing the environment and making the air safer to breathe. A deviant run of METRO-APEX was reported at the 1975 North American Simulation and Gaming Association meetings—a run in which the players' realities erupted into the suprareality of the game.

Here is the situation. During the introduction of the game a retired military officer, who was one of the students, pointed out that the simulation wasn't complete if organized crime wasn't represented in it. Some students and one of the faculty advisors took care of that. An elaborate system was devised in which funds were transferred to a role being played by the computer and after this 'laundering' back for use in buying political and economic advantage. This organized group through devious means secured the cooperation of the key punch operator and even surreptitiously gained access to the computer terminal.

When the news media began reporting information leaked to it, the following sequence of events occurred. An attempt to buy off the media failed. A grand jury was reluctantly called by the judge (role played by the faculty advisor who was part of the criminal organization), and a special prosecutor was appointed. Meanwhile the press was reporting more and more about questionable and criminal activity of people in various roles. The prosecutor subpoenaed previous computer printouts and developed substantial cases against several players. Before I describe the "Triumph of Justice" or "How the Good Guy in the Role of Justice Lost His Credibility" let us look at the conflicting ethical systems at work in the game. This analysis was really forced by a person playing the role of a city planner who shouted out "All this game is doing is teaching us to be smart crooks! It's teaching all the wrong behavior! . . . It's only teaching how to make it with the establishment!"

The game was stopped immediately and a group analysis-discussion began which revealed a confused network of ethical systems.

But three orientations became clear: role ethics, distributive ethics, and absolute ethics [Fisher, 1975: 145-146].

Such a stance toward deviant runs is typical. Either it is urged that players ought not be allowed to do the "bad things"—the unethical, the exploitative—or that if they are so permitted, these "learnings" are to be expunged through discussion, in which, as in the movies, the good guy must triumph. That is, the players must be shown that crime does not pay, or if it pays in money, it does not pay in terms of contribution to the world and should be defined as immoral. The game provides methods to police deviance more effectively, to prevent graft and bribery—hence corruption is not designed in, or when it is, it is used as an object lesson during the critique.

In addition, then, to the problems of reality constructions implicit in the value neutral or nonjudgmental methods for creating a suprareality that have already been discussed, the game designer in choosing purposes for the game further changes the game from a description of what "really is." If the business world operates by business executives and boards of directors constantly circumventing the law, engaging in bribery, and getting contracts by providing prostitutes for potential clients, these are rarely modeled in games or they exist in failed enterprises. Even if we could solve the earlier question of the relation between participants' reality and the designer's reality (which is "more real"), we do not accurately and dispassionately incorporate certain real-world elements of which we disapprove in the games.

GAMES AND CONSEQUENCES

There is another sense in which the claim should be evaluated that what designers wish is to make their games as realistic as possible. There are two dimensions to this point, and both can be seen by shifting to thinking of the game designer as experimenter (rather than as a scientist or teacher). Generally, games are built not simply as intellectual exercises but with the intent that they will be played—that is, that real people will be put into the role and that they will make the game operate.

When people are urged to be actors in games, it is done partly by saying that they can learn from the experience because there are no real-world consequences. The airplane pilot who learns in a flight simulator how to fly his plane in varying conditions, but learns slowly, does not destroy valuable equipment and sacrifice his life by his mistakes. The person who plays a corporate executive badly does not really bankrupt a company and have to live with a stigmatized reputation in the business community as a result of the experience. The person who creates a bad marriage in THE MARRIAGE GAME does not have to spend years with a husband or wife who is neither respected nor loved, paying a monthly mortgage and orthodontic bills and daily psychic costs for decisions made in the throes of youthful passion and ignorance of what marriage and parenthood were really like.

But the very fact that it is a game, that it is *by definition* unserious and nonconsequential in the real world, limits the efficacy of the experience. One dimension of reality is the consequentiality of the actions—that it really *does* matter what people choose to do. In games this dimension is dramatically reduced. Thus some persons will not play games because games are not serious, and those persons who *do* play bring differing levels of commitment to consequentiality to the play experience. But the very commitment to the value of games contains a commitment to the absence of a salient piece of reality. Often when players infuse that reality into the game by taking it very seriously, designers and operators become disturbed with them. There are players who forget that it is "only a game" or do not treat the experience as inconsequential. Some of them play hard to win, just as some people play to win in tennis; to them winning is not the best thing, it is the *only* thing. In pursuit of that goal, some feel "anything goes," and others play as best they can and nonetheless lose, and become very upset. What do the GODs do then? The players are reminded that it was not real, that they were taking it all too seriously.

Designers are caught in a bind because they recognize that by having students play their games they are creating something more like a laboratory experience in psychology than the experience of listening to a lecture. Thus designers (experimenters) must be concerned with the ethics of the game (experiment) and what the players (subjects) can morally be asked to do or have done to them. Designers worry about creating experiments similar to Milgram's (1963) in which subjects were told to push buttons to give electric shocks to other "subjects."

While designers want the reality of participating in the experience including having the feelings, they do not want to create too much anguish, anger, or frustration, or at least those feelings must be readily relieved if they are generated. The doctors in BLOOD MONEY are to feel misunderstood and the patients to feel that they have been deprived of what they need. The Triangles in STARPOWER should feel that they have been mercilessly taken advantage of by the Squares, and to feel angry about that so that they can convey the depth of anger to the Squares so they in turn will realize how unfair they have been. But then they should feel better right away. The feelings must be rapidly assuaged, so the designer can feel better about having generated them. The players should take the designer's distant stance right away, or after only a few moments of catharsis. If that is difficult or impossible, the game was *too* real. To achieve the aims of the sociologist-teacher, then, we *deliberately* make the reality (both in a consequential and social psychological sense) in the game lower.

CONCLUSION

It was the original intent of this chapter to try to point out the ways in which the multiple reality perspective has been used in recent game design and to suggest ways in which this strategy for increasing the reality of games could be further enhanced. Instead, as often happens in such enterprises, something other than what was intended has resulted—this chapter might be considered another example of a deviant run.

The problems with enhancing the reality of games are more complex than simply increasing the number of reality components that are present in the original design. However, it still seems a good practice to increase the social psychological reality of the roles that players assume by increasing the fit between the information and perceptions that the players have and the usual occupants of such positions. The manipulation of information and misinformation and creating a fertile ground for differential constructions of reality on the part of players still seems a useful strategy. Most games remain relatively simple in that they do not provide any opportunity for the multiple realities that characterize everyday life to emerge even during play. Even when these possibilities are embedded in the game or emerge in play, the degree of success in providing overall systematic understanding to players is unknown.

Underlying the practical problem of increasing game reality there is the metaproblem of the relation between the everyday realities of participants and the suprareality that the game designer creates. There are serious epistemological questions about the claims of suprarealities to be more objective, more real, more inclusive than the folk or naive realities held by participants in daily life. At the very least, it must be admitted these suprarealities are created for particular purposes and are often competitive with other versions of reality.

A more immediate problem is that the consequences of providing such social science explanations of social life to participants is unclear. It is unknown how people use such explanation or to what purposes they are put outside of the gaming circumstances. Some persons may come to explain their marriages by appeals to exchange theory or some city planners may explain the behavior of politicians or business persons on the basis of interest theory derived from simple economic models. In this way social science reality may become part of the day-to-day life of participants. But does it happen and in what ways?

There is no research data on whether different persons with different biographies create selective realities from the common model of the game. Do all players in fact emerge with the understanding even when it has been brought out in discussion? And do the continuing interests of the participants lead to reorganization or reshaping of what appears to be the objective reality of the social scientist?

Other problems with enhancing reality are those that grow out of the liberal and culturally relativistic stance of social scientists themselves. The goals of the game are those that support a liberal democratic and reformist stance toward social problems. Most games are conflict-reducing rather than conflict-increasing—and when conflict is generated its purpose is to show that an ameliorative strategy would prevent conflict in the future. In this sense the game designer's reality provides the experience for the player of the game.

However, the game designer as advocate or GOD may also not be successful. It is not known whether people who play games learn the morality desired or whether they emerge with different ideas. The subsequent behavior of players when they have returned to situations similar to those they have played has rarely been investigated.

Finally, there are issues associated with the social psychological reality of the game. In this case the element of consequentiality is immediately removed, which already eliminates at least one dimension of reality in many situations in the nongame world. However, it is not at all sure that we have removed the effects of participation or those of role-playing which can make a significant claim on a player's emotion and commitments. The game reality often involves a designer's wish to generate commitment but not passion.

There is a lack of data on the effects of game play on players' personal feelings when in the experimentlike situation. Where is a study which asked players to describe how they felt about *themselves* after play, whether they were at peace or troubled?

So the deviant run ends with caveats, confusion, and hopefully, challenges. The question has turned from the simple one of "How can we build more realistic games?" to "How much success do we have in building realistic games?" and "How much success do we *want* in building realistic games?"

NOTES

1. The use of the word *explicit* should make clear that a multiple realities perspective was implicitly involved in many game designs and indeed it was the use of such games by the first author that made the connection manifest.

2. Recently the differential perceptions of faculty of differing rank, gender, and institutional character on issues of institutional policy making has been explored empirically; the impact of these differing definitions of the situation on institutional change has been directly considered (Kenen and Kenen, 1978). The findings from this study provide a basis for differential weights that could be assigned in the matrix of perceptions in the original paper (Greenblat, 1975).

3. Often this right is opposed or explanations are rejected by powerful others (such as religious leaders or politicians) who compete for the right to explain conduct or by natives who do not like the explanations (see the quote from Forster above from this perspective).

4. In one run of BLOOD MONEY a group of nurses created a triage system by not treating those most handicapped by the disease and by concentrating resources on the rehabilitation of those least handicapped. This "deviant run" was one in which the players' reality as health care professionals created a different outcome. Designers should keep track of deviant runs—they may tell us more than we want to know.

PART III

GAMING-SIMULATION FOR TEACHING, TRAINING, AND RESEARCH

CHAPTER ELEVEN

GAMING-SIMULATIONS FOR TEACHING AND TRAINING:
An Overview

CATHY STEIN GREENBLAT

By and large, however, teachers do not think in terms of how a group can be organized and utilized so that as a group it plays a role in relation to the issues and problems that confront the group. . . . In their training teachers have been exposed, almost exclusively, to a psychology of learning that has one past and one present characteristic: the latter is its emphasis on how an individual organism learns, and the former is that the major learning theories were based on studies of the individual Norway rat. If instead of putting one rat in the maze they had put two or more in the maze, the history of American psychology would have been quite different. Conceivably, the social nature of learning might not need to be rediscovered.

Seymour Sarason (1971: 190).

THE RANGE OF EDUCATIONAL APPLICATIONS

In a number of elementary schools in the Detroit area, elementary school children are learning and practicing mathematics by competing in tournaments based on Layman Allen's EQUATIONS game. Based on prior math knowledge, students are put into teams of three competitors. They play a tournament, practicing the manipulation of numbers and signs in an

EQUATIONS game as challenging as their abilities warrant (see Allen, 1972). The winner of each such three-person tournament "moves up" a table to tougher competition; the player with the middle score stays at the table, and the player with the lowest score "moves down" a table. In such a fashion, each student is always matched with those at a similar learning level, and has fun while developing math skills.

"What did you think their culture was like? How did they seem to you when you saw them in their *own* territory? What did they seem like when they came to visit your area? How did *you* feel as a visitor to a strange culture? Which of the two cultures—yours or the other—would you prefer to live in if you had a choice?" I listened as these and other questions were discussed at length and with considerable vehemence by a group of high school students last week. Their common experience was a one and a half hour play of BAFÁ BAFÁ, Garry Shirts' newest game, which, like his earlier STARPOWER, is a huge success with high school and college students and adults as well. We videotaped this class, and the expressions on their faces as they entered the "other culture" and felt frustrated at not being able to figure out what was going on, or as they hosted visitors from the other culture and found themselves amused at the difficulties the others had in coping with their culture showed the effectiveness of the game. Through the game, students gained new insights into the feelings, anxieties, misperceptions, and counterproductive attitudes of people who, by choice or circumstance, interact with members of another culture, and into the meaning and significance of "culture" as an explanatory factor in behavioral analysis.

At the University of Maryland; California State College, Stanislaus; California State College, San Bernardino; the University of California (Santa Barbara); the University of Wisconsin; and Rutgers University last fall, teams of four to twelve undergraduate students participated in the same foreign policy exercise (Noel, 1971). It was the *same* exercise in the sense that each class represented a different nation in the same "world"—a world coordinated by Robert Noel and his staff at the POLIS Laboratory of the University of California (Santa Barbara). According to director Noel, in a personal letter to the author:

> Our experience thus far encourages us to believe that network gaming and simulation has great potential in several aspects of instruction: the opportunity for an instructor to incorporate into a course complex exercises without having to assume the heavy administrative burden such exercises entail; the ability to focus on international relations and foreign policies of a particular nation or subset of nations, without having to form locally the number of nation-teams necessary for an entire game; high student motivation and involvement produced by the inter-campus aspect of the games; and a cost-per-student that promises to decline as our experience increases and as hardware and communications costs continue to decrease.

Plans for 1974 called for participation from students in England and Japan as well.

At Virginia Commonwealth University, 109 graduate students—the entire first-year class of the Graduate School of Social Work—and about 10 faculty members spent the first two days of their first semester participating in one of two simultaneous SIMSOC games. The enterprise was designed to expose them to problems of social organization, conflict, and control; and to give them a set of provocative questions as they began their course in "Community Study." Following the game and some regular course work, groups of twelve to fifteen received field assignments to neighborhoods in Richmond, where they had to cope with problems of social organization, conflict, and control. The simulated experience thus served as an initial "laboratory" to sensitize them to questions and issues and to help them develop a general view of community problems.

A group of five adults who regularly work as a team sat around a desk one day, moving little pieces of colored wood in a plastic tray. The game was . . . ET ALIA . . . , and the required paraphernalia consisted of a "nine-piece puzzle" available for about $.79, and a set of rules by Bob Armstrong, Margaret Hobson, and Jim Hunter. Each player was represented by a color, and the rules regarding "moves," "winning," "authority," and communications were deliberately ambiguous. When I halted play after a half hour or so, we began talking together about how they had dealt with problems that arose in the play session. Suddenly one person said, "Yes, but I think that's something we do *all the time*—we don't talk about goals in advance and see where there are conflicts between the things the five of us are trying to achieve. Remember the time that . . . " A new sense of the nature and value of the game emerged as the rest of the discussion centered on parallels between game problems and real-world problems of small group dynamics. Through this training exercise, the group gained insights into patterns of behavior that aided and impeded their successful functioning.

SIMULATIONS, GAMES, AND TEACHING TECHNIQUES

As the above examples may begin to indicate, the teaching and training uses of gaming-simulations are legion, and the newcomer to the field may well feel inundated by the vast quantity of games and the wide range of applications. In addition, the new user will encounter in early explorations a morass of terms, often, but not always, used interchangeably: "simulation games," "game-simulations," "gaming simulations," "games with simulated environments," "teaching games," "learning games," "instructional games," "educational games."

How can these be sorted out? Some preliminary answers have already been given in our discussion of the terms "simulation," "game," and "gaming-simulation." Now another distinction must be offered as we introduce the idea of teaching or training. Figure 11.1 represents the different combinations and types that emerge when these three ideas are put together.

(A) In Category A are all sorts of teaching-training techniques and materials with which we are familiar: lectures, case studies, discussions, films, audio-visual materials, field study. These are included here to indicate the broad range of other teaching devices.

(B) Sometimes simulations are used for teaching. In category B are those non-game simulations such as flight simulators for pilots and programs in which disasters are simulated to teach or train medical and paramedical personnel to deal with real-world disasters when they happen.

(C) Other simulations, as indicated earlier, are designed for research purposes. In category C we find these nongame, nonteaching simulations, such as the Simulmatics project, undertaken to attempt to predict the outcome of the 1960 presidential election via computer simulation techniques (Pool et al., 1965).

(D) There are some game-simulations played and enjoyed by many people at home, but generally unused for teaching purposes. These are in category D, represented by DIPLOMACY and GETTYSBURG, two gaming-simulations of military operations.

(E) Some games (category E) do not simulate a social system or process, and are played for amusement, fun, to pass the time, develop strategy, develop critical thinking, or any of a number of purposes. Though some are quite intellectually challenging, they generally have not been adopted for teaching purposes. Included here in Category E are such games as Scrabble, Go, and Monopoly. (Monopoly is not clearly in Category E. Some argue, for example, that it is a gaming-simulation of the real estate system and hence belongs in D. My position is that having a social *setting* is not enough to qualify a game to be counted as a gaming-simulation; it must also contain a reasonably accurate representation of the goals, resources, constraints, and consequences of the real-world system. As such, I don't believe Monopoly can be counted as a gaming-simulation.)

(F) Recent years have witnessed the tremendous growth of games for teaching purposes. Some of the former, shown in Category F, include WFF 'N PROOF, EQUATIONS, ON-WORDS, and others in that series; IMPASSE?, a paper and pencil game for individual or group assessment of impacts of policies; and such group dynamics games as . . . ET ALIA . . .

(G) Finally, in Category G, we find those gaming-simulations employed for teaching and training (and sometimes for research and public policy) including METRO-APEX; CLUG; the COMMUNITY LAND USE GAME; THE MARRIAGE GAME: UNDERSTANDING MARITAL DECISION-MAKING; GHETTO; STARPOWER; POLICY NEGOTIATIONS; SITTE; and many others.

When we speak of games, simulations, and gaming-simulations for teaching and training, then, we are speaking of subgroups of games, simulations, and teaching techniques.

GAMING-SIMULATION AND ROLE-PLAYING

Despite some obvious similarities, gaming-simulations differ from role-playing exercises and from such endeavors as mock congresses, mock United Nations, and so forth.

Role-playing is an element of gaming-simulations, but gaming-simulations also include other components. In gaming-simulations, roles are defined in interacting systems; that is, emphasis is on the role as it interacts

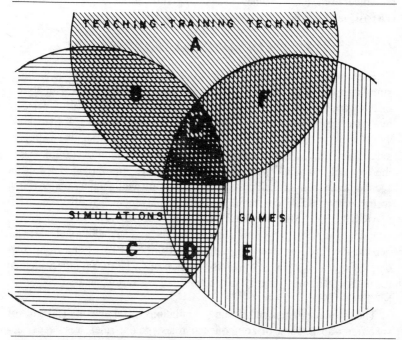

FIGURE 11.1 Simulations, Games, and Teaching Techniques

with other roles, and the model creates the dynamic interaction, the constraints, rewards, and punishments. In most role-playing exercises, on the other hand, the participant is assigned a role and given only the general outline of a situation. From there, the action is freewheeling. In gaming-simulations there is little "second-guessing" in terms of personalities of particular people or positions; in addition to the roles and the scenario, participants are given goals to orient their behavior, resources to attempt to meet their goals, rules to govern the actions they may and may not take, the order of play, the consequences of violations, and the environmental responses—that is, the probable response of parts of the environment that are relevant to the structure or process being simulated but are not incorporated into the roles or the actions taken by the players. Thus the consequences of actions in terms of goal attainment or inhibition are built into the model and can be known in advance or discovered by the player (for elaboration, see Coleman, 1968).

Gaming-simulations thus differ from role-playing exercises in the degree of structure or formalization they entail and in their emphasis on interaction processes rather than on the playing of individual roles. Further, in many instances of classroom role-playing, several students participate while the remainder of the class watches. In a gaming-simulation, all participate; none is a passive observer.

DIVERSITY OF MATERIALS FOR TEACHING

Even the reduction or limitation of our discussion to games and gaming-simulations used for teaching and training purposes leaves us with a great deal of variation. The several thousand teaching-training games known to be available (Horn and Cleaves, 1980; Belch, 1973; Gibbs, 1974; Stadsklev, 1979) vary first of all in the form and complexity of their paraphernalia, the subsequent time, money, and personnel required for their operation, and in the types of learning for which they are therefore appropriate. They differ second in the form of their publication. Some are available in standard book format with manuals to be purchased by each player (such as SIMSOC, THE MARRIAGE GAME, METROPOLIS, CLUG). Others come in boxed kits containing reusable sets of instructions, forms, and any additional materials needed for play (for example, the games from SIMILE II and from Academic Games Associates; the boxed version of CLUG). Yet others include manuals, programs, lengthy instructions for operation, and so on. (e.g., METRO-APEX).

The available games and gaming-simulations differ also in the degree of specificity-abstraction of components: roles, goals, rules, resources, accounting system, and so on and in whether they are externally parameterized (that is, by the designer) or internally parametered (by the participants). Some of the differences this entails are indicated by Brent Ruben in Table 11.1.

Additionally, games and gaming-simulations used in teaching embody different types of models: resource allocation, group dynamics, and system specification. Resource allocation models are structured around concepts of competition for scarce resources (such as limited availability of municipal funds, competition by family members for budget, competitive bidding for land ownership). Group dynamics models emphasize role-playing and/or interpersonal relationships. System specification models entail the explicit expression of a complex system, its roles, components, and linkages. Most gaming-simulations reflect all three of these considerations; however, typically one theme will be dominant. This does not mean to suggest that other types of models cannot be discerned in the broad array of gaming-simulations now available. These three types, however, encompass most.

An overview of the range of differences in gaming-simulations used for teaching can be derived from a review of articles by Heap (1971), Degnan and Haar (1975), and Cohen and Rhenman (1975).

TABLE 11.1 Structural Elements and Design Characteristics of Experience-Based Systems

	Externally Parametered	Internally Parametered
Roles	assigned	emergent
	rigid	flexible
	low ambiguity	high ambiguity
	simple	complex
Interactions	channels specified	channels emerge
	patterns prescribed	patterns emerge
	low ambiguity	high ambiguity
	few channels available	multiple channels available
	predictable	unpredictable
Rules	prescriptive	prescriptive
	fixed	flexible
	constant	changing
	low ambiguity	high ambiguity
	specified	emergent
Goals	imposed	emergent
	uniform	individual
	single	multiple
	clearly defined	ambiguously defined
Criteria	predictable	unpredictable
	uniform	individual
	single	multiple
	likely to involve "winning"	unlikely to involve "winning"
	clearly defined	ambiguously defined

SOURCE: Brent Ruben (1973).

THEORETICAL SUPPORTS

How can we account for the current popularity of games in the academic arena? Despite rises and falls in user enthusiasm (Boocock and Schild, 1968: 13-18), games have been in the schools since the early 1960s, and there is evidence of their continuing and even growing foothold there (Coleman, 1971). There seem to be several theoretical bases upon which such usage rests.

First, as Moore and Anderson (1975) indicate, games and play have long served as modes of socialization. Jerome Bruner, in his *Toward a Theory of Instruction,* remarks (1966: 134-134):

> It was a standard line of nineteenth-century evolutionary thinking that the function of play was to permit the organism to try out his repertory of response in preparation for the later serious business of surviving against the pressures of his habitat. It can be argued equally well that, for human beings at least, play serves the function of reducing the pressures of impulse and incentive and making it possible thereby for intrinsic learning to begin; for if ever there is self-reward in process it is in the sphere of 'doing things for merriment', particularly things that might otherwise be too serious in Niels Bohr's sense ("But there are some things so important that we can only joke about them.").

A second set of theoretical ideas conducive to the enlargement of the role of gaming in the schools embodies notions of the importance of group dynamics, peer learning, and peer pressure in the learning process. Much of this seems to have gained impetus and added credence from the findings of the study by James Coleman and associates *The Adolescent Society* (1961) and the now famous "Coleman Report" on the consequences of inequality of educational opportunities (1966). In the former document, Coleman urged the development of competitive games to be used as a learning method and as a means of improving adolescent regard for learning. It is this idea of the importance of paying attention to and capitalizing upon our understanding of the potentials of interaction between students that Sarason affirms in the quote at the start of this chapter.

Several theories that stress the importance of *activity* in the learning process have been brought to bear on the question of why games have potential educative powers, but fundamental questions remain to be answered about the relationship between cognition and action in learning. In our "ordinary teaching," we transmit information, hope it will be integrated, and that eventually it will be applied to shape action. We "test" after the information transmission, but often discover later that the succeeding stages of the process do not transpire.

Teaching via gaming-simulations entails quite a different sequence. As Coleman (1971) notes, here we use action and hope it will lead to cognition and then to generalization to other actions as it is applied. Early evidence indicates that the end result may in fact come about—but without the middle one. Further research on the process is surely needed.

EVALUATION

What happens when students are taught with games? Game designers and teachers have posed the question or offered speculative answers far more frequently than educational researchers have tried to answer it. The files of anyone who has taught extensively with games are likely to be filled with notes such as the following three letters, attesting to the intensity and duration of excitement generated in some student participants:

> Because your course in Simulations of Social Relations was so enjoyable and educationally profitable, I have strongly advocated that method of teaching. Last year I ran "STARPOWER" in an undergraduate class, which I believe was beneficial to the class, the professor and myself. This semester I plan to run it in a graduate class concerning minorities and power structure. I am writing to you in hopes that you might be able to give me some tips.

> I find myself in medical school taking a course called "The Patient, the Physician, and Society" and the last element of course brings you to mind. The course is a real bore and so I've decided to take it upon myself to liven it up a little. So I am writing you this letter to ask a favor. I would like to introduce my colleagues to the concept of learning through games. Two games come to mind as particularly applicable in this course: they are the Values Games, and the Doctor Game which your graduate students created last spring. I was hoping that you could xerox a copy of the questions in the Values Game and send along the instructions on how to play the Doctor Game. I would really appreciate this and my classmates will too.

> Well, in two months, I will have completed my first year of medical school. . . . The responses to the Values Game and the Doctor Game were outstanding. With the Values Game I rewrote about 10 vignettes which were more applicable to value judgements which doctors face. The group just loved it. They found the idea of gaming an intriguing one and the vignettes most thought provoking. The Doctor Game was a game on Death and Dying, and the principles of the game came practically from the book of the same title by Kubler Ross. We have all read that book. So I modified that game so it dealt with Doctor-Patient communications more generally. Once again the response was fantastic. Young prospective doctors like to be put in their future roles and this game provided that opportunity, consequently they just couldn't praise it enough. Congratulations to the authors of these games; they certainly have a place in the medical school curriculum if properly modified.

"Heightened motivation and interest" are not the only outcomes suggested by aficionados, nor, happily, are anecdotal reports the only type of data extant (though anecdotes are offered as evidence far more frequently than one would hope). The major types of claims about what happens when one teaches with games are outlined in the chapter in this volume entitled "Teaching with Simulation Games: A Review of Claims and Evidence." The claims are there organized into six major categories:

(1) motivation and interest;
(2) cognitive learning;
(3) changes in the character of later course work;
(4) affective learning re: subject matter;
(5) general affective learning; and
(6) changes in classroom structure and relations.

The available evidence as of September 1971 is summarized in that paper, and is brought up to date in the summary of newer evidence by Bredemeier and Greenblat in the succeeding chapter. Data on evaluation is therefore not dealt with in the present chapter. Several ideas, however, warrant highlighting here:

(1) There is an increasing amount of positive data on the effects of teaching with games;
(2) where the evidence does not reveal benefits of gaming techniques over other modes of teaching, neither does it show the reverse; that is, those taught with games do not prove to have learned *less* than those taught in traditional ways;
(3) the time dimension continues to be inadequately dealt with; that is, questions of retention and application have received scanty attention;
(4) results from studies with particular games cannot be generalized to "learning with games in general";
(5) the quality of evaluative research seems to be improving as researchers become more sensitive to the methodological conditions that yield valid and reliable results. Nonetheless, problems persist by virtue of the nature of the games and the conditions of their operation. As Taylor notes, for example, "It should be pointed out that many users of simulation would not wish to evaluate its learning possibilities separately from the other strategies which make up the teaching UNIT in which it is included. They would argue that the simulation acts as a stimulus to subsequent learning and that this spin-off interest can properly be considered as part of the benefit of the technique, even though it may be developed through more traditional methods of learning" (Taylor and Walford, 1972: 39). Fruitful suggestions for those interested in research can be found in Jerry Fletcher's paper, "The Effectiveness of Simulation Games as Learning Environments: A Proposed Program of Research" (1971a).

UNANSWERED QUESTIONS

Articles on gaming seem to have been written almost exclusively by those who are "believers"; surely critics and skeptics exist, but they tend not to have taken to paper with their doubts and criticisms. I, too, obviously am in the camp of those favorable to gaming, but I believe there are some important questions and reservations that the gaming community must confront in future research and conferences—questions that have not been publicly raised or adequately addressed. Some of these are outlined above and in the end of the review of claims and evidence; in addition are those following.

What Harm Is Done by Bad Simulations?

In Marshall McLuhan's book *The Medium is the Massage* there is a cartoon in which a man and a woman sit in front of the TV and one says to the other "When you consider TV's awesome power to educate, aren't you glad it doesn't?" Laments about the paucity of data showing students learning from gaming-simulations are predicated upon the belief that the games have something worthwhile to teach. The hope rests on the belief that the models are valid. But what if the model *distorts* reality?

Unfortunately, there are a number of *bad* simulations, and many of them are at least as seductive as the good ones. Though a simulation distorts, it may be very believable, especially to those unfamiliar with the subject. Such gaming-simulations may not only be bad, but may be dangerous, for they convey misinformation and perpetuate ignorance, stereotypes, and so forth. As a sociologist I have serious reservations, for example, about the BLACKS AND WHITES game. It is based upon a model which includes extremely high mobility for Blacks despite initial handicaps, very high probabilities of problems for whites, and allows Blacks and whites equal chances to "win" or "make it," though by different routes. The student player who "learns" that Blacks have equal chances to win if only they learn to play right may generalize this to the "real world" and conclude that since they're obviously *not* winning it's because they don't play right—(that is, their failure is due to their ignorance rather than to a system in which equal roles and resources are not allocated to those with stigmatized identities (See Schild, 1971, for further comments on this model).

Garry Shirts (1970) has discussed the same type of problem in terms of war games and some games dealing with social problems:

Games are vulnerable in a way that textbooks aren't. Because the interaction between participants is genuine, there is a temptation to conclude that the model, the facts, and everything about the game are also genuine . . . there is a real danger that games about the black community, which are written generally by persons from the suburbs are based on a series of unfounded cliches about what it is like to be black, not only encourage stereotyping but create an attitude of condescension towards blacks. More importantly, they can give the students a false feeling that they actually know what it is like to be discriminated against or what it is like to be black. Such games should not be played unless there is extensive input from the black community through talks, films, literature, personal confrontations and discussion.

What Harm Is Done by Bad Games?

A gaming-simulation may be bad because the simulation is bad (as described above) or because the *gaming* elements are poorly designed. How can these problems be recognized and dealt with? This problem is perhaps less serious than the one above, since poor gaming components will probably lead at worst to *no* learning rather than *mis*learning, but the problem is nonetheless one to be reckoned with. Absence of feedback to players, high role-playing leading to overinvolvement and limitation of analytic abilities, high "win-focus" leading to limited discussion, and other such factors may substantially reduce the efficacy of the experience. While factual information about gaming-simulations is now available, there is still little in the way of carefully done, widely disseminated evaluations of the quality of various games, and users are highly dependent upon word of mouth.

How Do Variations in Teacher Behavior and Attitude Affect Game Operation and Learning from the Experience?

Supposing that we have a *good* gaming-simulation to work with, a critical set of questions deals with the role of the teacher. We know that the teacher is an important variable in the game process, but it is unclear what elements of teacher behavior affect the success or failure of the game run. There are guidelines to successful game operation (see, for example, the next chapter), but these are not always followed. What are the things that teachers do or fail to do that affect what happens and what is learned?

The role of the teacher is described in some of the literature as one of a "coach." Boocock and Coleman (1966) suggest that games teach because the teacher drops the role of judge and jury, but what if the teacher *does* interfere and criticize and suggest? I have heard stories of teachers running international relations games such as CRISIS and, because they felt the pace was too slow, precipitating a war. If the students are not aware that the resultant war was not a consequence of their decisions, what does this do to the learning of cause and effect in international relations? And if they *are* aware of the teacher's intervention and manipulation what attitudes does this lead to in terms of war, authority, manipulation, and so on?

What Kind of Game Is Useful for What Kind of Learning?

We know that games vary in their complexity, in their length, in their degree of abstraction, in the type of model employed, and so forth. But what are the consequences of these differences for learning? What are the relevant differences in parameters which would allow us to talk about *types* of games? And what hypotheses can be generated and tested about the impact of these differences in parameters for different types of learning and different types of learners? An example of such hypotheses is found in Brent Ruben's paper (1973: 14), but research to test these and similar propositions has scarcely begun.

> The relative appropriateness of internal versus external parameters likewise would seem to depend upon the particular learning goals involved. External parameter simulations seem generally better suited for teaching specific content, while internal parameter games and simulations appear more appropriate for the learning of problem-solving processes.

> Where the learning goals suggest that what is to be learned is specific, prescribable, predictable, specifiable and determinant, external parameter environments are appropriate in that the designer or implementing instructor wants all students to learn the target facts, strategies and procedures in the same way. The structural elements of the game or simulation will therefore need to be controlled and manipulated intentionally, to insure that participants deal with specific issues, using specific interactional channels, according to prescribed rules, in order to achieve the designer's predetermined goals.

> External parameter activities are generally appropriate when the learning desired is in the form of answers or decisions which are fixed, constant over time and tend to be technical in nature.

> Internal parameters, on the other hand, are generally better suited than external parameters in instances where the learning is to be structural, general, not prescribable, unpredictable and indeterminant.

How Can We Understand the Asymmetrical Learning Experiences of Students Who Participate in the Same Game?

Discussions of the experience of being a player seem to treat participation as a constant factor. Yet in most gaming-simulations, students are cast in very different simulated roles (such as poor person, city administrator, clergyman) with different goals, constraints, resources, attached to them. By internal definition, then, the experiences are different, and it could be anticipated that the nature and extent of learning by those in different roles would differ. In good postgame discussions there is of course a sharing of experiences and perceptions, but it is unlikely that this vicarious experiencing can fully equalize the differential learning. Attention thus must be directed to understanding and dealing with asymmetrical learning from the same gaming-simulation.

The problem of differential learning is compounded when we consider that the participant is really in three simultaneous roles: in addition to playing the *simulated role,* students are players in a game and students in a class. Those writing about games often ignore the latter two or assume that they are of no importance. Yet either of these may be dominant at any particular time and may seriously affect the learning that transpires. Add to this the effects of peer pressure, and the complications in understanding what is happening are magnified further. Teachers and researchers can ill afford to ignore the "treble role" of players and must try to understand the factors contributing to dominance of one or the other at any given time.

Who *Doesn't* Like Games?
Who *Doesn't* Learn From Them?

Just as there are students who become very excited and involved, so too there are some who recoil from game play, refusing to take part or participating passively. Little attention has been given to trying to understand the characteristics of these students, to knowing the conditions under which games should NOT be employed, or, if they are used, what resistances might be expected.

How Many Games Can Be Used Effectively with a Given Group?

We talk about using gaming-simulations in teaching and mention the good ones we know, but do we *really* mean to recommend unlimited utilization? How many games are "enough?" "Too much?" Aren't there lessons that could be offered about numbers, sequencing, carryover effects, that would help teachers maximize the teaching potential of games?

A friend asked me several years ago whether I thought that the involvement and interest generated in classes by gaming-simulations and the subsequent learning from them derived primarily from their novelty. "What if we used *only* games in teaching," he asked, "and then someone came along with a new innovation called 'the lecture.' Would students show the same improvement in interest, motivation, learning, etc., that they now do when a game is used in lieu of a lecture?" We must seriously confront such questions.

There are, of course, many additional questions that could be raised. Charles Elder (1975) deals with some of these and alerts us to the dangers of uncritical adoption of the technique.

CONCLUSION

These last sections should not be taken as negative depictions of gaming, but rather as urgings to caution. Gaming *is* serious, and it is too important a pedagogical tool to be treated as a fad or allowed to grow like Topsy, to be unchecked, uncriticized, and unevaluated by its proponents and those interested in maximizing its promise.

The costs of using gaming-simulations in classes and training programs are high: they include not only money, but the time and energy to find a suitable gaming-simulation, obtain it, integrate it into the curriculum, learn to operate it, run it, and lead the postgame discussion. Often additional space and personnel must be found, department chairmen or deans persuaded to endorse if not support the endeavor, and so on. These costs must be carefully weighed against a clear set of objectives if wise decisions are to be made. Findings regarding success are often elusive, particularly when the goals entail modification of future behavior in situations such as the one simulated (for example, consumer credit purchasing, marital decision-making, wise public policy decisions and votes). Those of us who believe in the power of gaming-simulations to effectuate learning must strive to create better techniques for differentiating between good and bad games and work relentlessly on developing a better understanding of the dynamics of the positive learning experience with a gaming-simulation.

CHAPTER TWELVE

RUNNING GAMES:

A Guide for Game Operators

RICHARD D. DUKE
CATHY STEIN GREENBLAT

The specific steps to follow to run a game vary, of course, from one game to another. There are, however, four major elements of administration common to all games: (a) preparation; (b) introduction of the game; (c) operation or management of the game; and (d) postgame discussion or critique. Each of these consists of a series of steps that should be followed, and experienced game operators do these quite regularly. In the following pages, we shall attempt to outline the critical elements of game administration and to offer suggestions on how to make your run a smooth and successful one.

PREPARATION

(1) Know what your intentions, aims or pedagogical purposes are; review the available games; and select one that seems appropriate. This may sound like a very obvious piece of advice, but all too often someone runs a game in a class not because it seems appropriate for what they want to present but because someone spoke enthusiastically about it. A game that works well with one group may not work with a group of different ages, backgrounds, and so on; what is successful for one purpose may be a disaster for another. Therefore, the first step is to understand whether the game you have chosen is one that is appropriate to the learning aims that you have in mind, or rather, to have a clear understanding of what you want to teach and to select a game in accordance with those goals.

(2) Having selected the game, integrate it with other materials. If the game is to be used in a class, then it should be tied in to the larger perspective of the course outline. If it is to be used in a nonacademic setting, it should be tied in to other materials, topics, and activities of the group. A game that is

just "stuck in" as a random event without thought to the ways in which it relates to the rest of the curriculum or endeavor will be less successful than one which is meshed with other tools and topics.

(3) Become familiar enough with the game that you can run it well. In some instances, it may be possible to familiarize yourself through prior experience. If you know someone else who is going to run the game, perhaps you can arrange to participate in their run. This provides a familiarity with the mechanics not possible to obtain by simply reading the materials and will give you a player's perspective on the game. Other times it may be feasible to become familiar with the game by running it with a group of friends or a small group of students prior to using it with your "real audience." If it does not require too much time or too many people, this may be a viable and fruitful way to learn the game under conditions in which problems you encounter or slowness of your response is less a problem than in the classroom or with a group that has come together at greater difficulty and expense and may give you greater confidence when you run it later.

If neither of these alternatives seems possible, then the familiarization preparation should take the form of "walking through" a typical round or rounds: go through the material, read the rules from the perspective of a player as well as the perspective of an operator, and be sure that you understand what players are to do at each point. If you know someone who has run the game, ask them for hints to more effective administration.

(4) Be sure you have adequate personnel to run the game. Having gone through the material and become familiar with the game, you should now understand (whether the manual specified it or not) whether you will be able to run the game alone or will require assistance. If the latter, you should now obtain aides in advance and prepare them. It may be that you can use one of the students or other participants to be an assistant for you and that such a person can be selected at the last moment. But do not count on having them capable of performing difficult or complicated operations. Likewise, do not count on preparing an assistant at the same time that you are trying to keep the game running; it simply is too much.

(5) Make up a time schedule for the game. First, this involves being sure that enough time is available for a successful run; a good game squeezed into too little time will become a bad game. Some games can be divided; that is, they can be played one day, stopped, and then continued another day or several additional days. Others require continuous play and even require that initial postgame discussion or critique begin the same day that play takes place. STARPOWER, for example, cannot be started one day, continued into a class period the following day, and then discussed the third day; in order to be used successfully, it must be run in at least an hour and a half of

consecutive time. This kind of time block, of course, is not possible in some circumstances and at those times the game *should not be* employed.

If you are running the game in several time periods rather than in one continuous period, you will have to be sure to allow enough time for players to get "recharged" each time. That is, they lose momentum by going out of the game and into their real life world and then coming back, and thus require additional time each round to get back into the swing of things. This sequencing does, however, permit more time for reflection and planning.

If the time schedule you arrange involves one long play period, be sure you recognize the potential fatigue that will take place and allow for breaks if possible or at least for some kind of stretch period during which the players can move around. Coffee and/or other refreshments are also required in this type of time frame. These breaks should fit in with the 'natural rhythm' of the game. The first such break, for example, should not come until players have had a positive experience after initial confusion. If it comes right after an introductory cycle, some will leave if they can. Breaks taken at times of anticipation of something good to come will be easier to end when you want play to resume.

(6) Prepare all the materials. This obvious step always takes longer than anticipated. Whatever the requirement—whether it be to cut out SIM-BUCKS and tickets in SIMSOC or to arrange the cards in BAFÁ BAFÁ— the mechanical chores of preparation must be done, and far enough in advance that you do not find yourself hustling through cards and sorting them into piles as the players arrive. Such last-minute preparation always entails a psychic cost even if it does not delay the actual commencement of play.

Separation of materials also means careful checking to be sure all things that should be there are in fact there. When games have been run a number of times, little pieces often get lost. A check before you go to the game site will reveal whether things have been moved within your supplies (that is, from one game to another) or perhaps have been lost or broken in a previous run. It should be obvious that such preparation of materials should be done far enough in advance to obtain new ones in case any are missing. Once everything is there and in usable form, arrange the materials so that they can be rapidly put in place at the game site.

(7) Decide whether to give out materials in advance. If the group does not meet regularly but is coming together for a special occasion to play the game, it would not be easy to give out materials for even a complex game. One might, of course, wish to send a mailing to those participants, but this will involve an expense which must be carefully considered to decide whether it is worthwhile. With a class or other group that meets on a regular

basis, the option of giving out materials in advance is, of course, open to the operator. For many games, this would be unnecessary and, in fact, undesirable. The games are simple and can be easily introduced at the time of play. Other games will not operate successfully *unless* players have seen something in advance. For example, the players in SIMSOC should review the basic rules before they start to play. Players of THE MARRIAGE GAME must read a section describing the designers' view of marriage as a social system prior to play or they will not understand the rationale behind the moves and choices they are asked to make, and thus will not learn as much about marital decision-making.

With other games, the operator must decide when to distribute materials. With a few it may be advisable to give out some material in advance so the players can begin to think about what they wish to do. This may be most appropriate where the materials contain fairly factual accounts that must be reviewed carefully. For example, we have found it fruitful to give out the players' manuals for METROPOLITICS the day before play. Participants can then review the six options open to them for support and see the pro and con arguments for each of the positions. The material will remain dry, however, until they begin to use it in play of the game. It is as if they were given a straight reading assignment on the materials, and it is difficult to get very excited or enthused about them. Such distribution of materials, however, may make exciting things happen earlier in the play period. In general, prior distribution does not prove as fruitful as one wishes. At the end of the first round, participants in METRO-APEX always urge that they should have been given the materials to review in advance to prevent the confusion they felt at the start. Experience with the game, however, has revealed that the rules do not become clear until players begin to use them; sending out manuals in advance then may do more harm than good, for players may read them and be confused *alone*, thus developing a negative set before they come to the actual play period. It may be better to have them begin together, where at least they can commiserate with one another about the enormity of the task before them! They will soon discover that the confusion is dispelled as they begin to play and to use the instructions they have been given.

If materials are sent out or given out in advance, then there are three main things to keep in mind: (1) keep the amount limited so as not to overwhelm players; (2) send or give out a chronology of events—that is, the overall sequences and the steps in a given round; (3) do not rely on players' remembering to bring materials with them; have duplicates available for them.

(8) Decide on various dimensions of role assignment. First, you must decide *when* roles are to be assigned or given out. If materials are to be given out in advance, perhaps you wish to also allow players to know what roles they will play. With games such as METRO-APEX or DANGEROUS PARALLEL, the manuals for each player are different; therefore if materials are

to be given out in advance, players must be informed of the role they will play when given the appropriate manual. In a game such as METROPO-LITICS, these two decisions need not go hand in hand; that is, materials could be given out early but the players need not be informed of their roles until they actually meet for play of the game. In games such as this, where the manuals are common to all players irrespective of role, it may, in fact, be wise to separate the two things—that is, to have players read through the materials in toto, unaware of their game roles. In that way they may pay more attention to elements not critical for them, but central to the model as a whole. Thus, for example, in using THE MARRIAGE GAME it may be wise not to tell players in advance whether they will be playing males or females; in that way they are more likely to read both sets of charts presented for jobs, marital status, parental status, and so on and to become aware of the disparities built into the game.

A related decision is that of *how* roles should be distributed. Should they be assigned by the game operator? Should they be given at random? Or should players be allowed to choose their roles? The specific game manual may offer some advice on this, and it is hard to advise in general terms.

If the decision is made to assign roles, the next question becomes "how should they be assigned?" Should aggressive students or players be given leadership positions? Alternatively, should quiet people be given leadership positions in hopes that they will emerge from their shells? It is, of course, tempting to give the roles to those you know will play them in an active manner. Sometimes, however, the most potent leaders are those one would not recognize as such on the basis of the ordinary classroom experiences preceding use of the game. Assigning some leadership roles to those who have not displayed outspoken traits may provide those students with the opportunity to show themselves in a very new light.

Finally you must give thought to the *number* of players per role. Perhaps this should have been mentioned earlier, for often a game operator will look at a game and decide that it cannot be used with his group since his group is too large. This decision is reached on the basis of the number of roles vis-á-vis the number of participants. What should be kept in mind, however, is that the best learning experience may emerge if several people play a role together. Our "rule of three" suggests that the best learning takes place when there are three players per role. The mental lethargy which may emerge from one person playing a role is negated by the presence of the second; the two must discuss the strategies they will pursue. The presence of the third person creates an inherent instability and means that more active discussion is likely to take place. In some games, of course, such doubling or trebling on a role may be impossible; in THE MARRIAGE GAME, for example, only one person can play a role. In many others, however, role teams of three can be created.

(9) Prepare the space and the furniture arrangement. This is not simply a physical aspect, for the arrangement of furniture and the arrangement of groups in the room may very strategically affect the interaction that takes place. Of course, the basic problem is to be sure that there is enough space. If you are running SIMSOC, for example, you should try to have four rooms so each region can be in a separate room. For BAFÁ BAFÁ, you must have two rooms. For most other games, the spatial needs are not for multiple rooms but for sufficient space for players to move around as play progresses. Such space, of course, is greater than the space required for an equivalent number of people if they were to be sitting still for a lecture; games with high interaction require more space. Most game manuals will inform you of the amount of space desirable for a run of the game.

Having run games in a number of unfamiliar places, we have discovered the utility of going, *as soon as you arrive on site,* to check out the rooms that have been assigned to you. They may not be suitable and changes may need to be made. Rooms that are too large or rooms with stationary furniture also provide a problem. If you cannot avoid the former, something can be used to set off a part of the room as a "no man's land," and it should be made clear to players that they are to play only in the section marked off for them.

The arrangement of furniture and the location of groups within the room will also prove to be important. Groups or roles that are centrally located are more likely to play central roles than are those located on the periphery. In METRO-APEX, for example, the role of the Air Pollution Control Officers will be quite different if they are placed in the center of the room than if they are placed in a corner; likewise, the role the politicians play will be different if county and city politicians are placed near one another than if they are placed on opposite sides of the room where communication is impeded between them.

Additionally, the nature of the role or the perception of it may depend upon such subtle cues as the degree of crowdedness or the degree of comfort provided by the furniture or furniture arrangement. In running SIMSOC, for example, try to give the largest, most spacious, airiest, sunniest room with the most plush furniture to the region with major resources of the society as a whole. Correlatively, assign a small, dark, bare, unaesthetic room to the impoverished region. Such physical arrangements often will lend support and drama to those very disparities one hopes will be felt by players. In one run, for example, a player from the Green Region had gone to visit the Red Region. As he emerged from their room, he said in an aside to no one in particular, "Boy, I'm not going back there again—it's too crowded and dirty and unpleasant. I like my room much better." How much that reminded us of the feelings of the rich as they drive through poverty areas, closing their windows and promising themselves to take another route another time! It was good food for discussion in the later critique.

A similar use of space and furniture can be made with STARPOWER. Send the Squares to sit in the most comfortable chairs and put the Triangles in the least comfortable. In THE MARRIAGE GAME, the spatial arrangements recommended to the game operator include the provision that those in the wealthiest neighborhood be given the most space to move around and sit comfortably while those in the poor area have their chairs squashed together, making it more difficult to keep their things separate from one another and more difficult to avoid mixup of papers, forms, and so on.

(10) Decide upon a policy concerning visitors and/or observers. This decision will vary from operator to operator and no rule of thumb can be given. We generally refuse to allow visitor-observers; anyone interested in the game must be a participant when we run it. This is for several reasons. First, many people really would like to play but are hesitant to do so. What they require is the additional push given by saying "No, you can't observe but you're welcome to be a player." Second, the perspective gained by playing the game is often far different from that derived from simply observing and remaining marginal in the process. The third reason for our usually refusing visitors and observers is that it makes some players feel more self-conscious than they otherwise are. We believe this is unfair to them, for they are already struggling to overcome the self-consciousness that comes from playing a role in an ambiguous situation, and the presence of observers may further hinder their smooth transition into the game. Many of those who wish to observe are those in positions of more authority than those who are playing, and such observers may further hinder the players' easy role assumption.

INTRODUCTION TO THE GAME

The way in which the game is introduced to participants by the game operator may well be critical in determining the success of the experience. There are several things that you must present to participants before they are ready to begin play. These will vary in specifics from game to game. The following are a few general suggestions for ways of introducing games to maximize the probability of success.

(1) Your early comments should include references to the following: (a) gaming-simulation as an instructional medium; (b) the purpose of the specific gaming-simulation you are employing that day; (c) the rules of the game in outline form (if players have manuals, you may wish to have them read the rules and simply highlight those of importance; if you are presenting all the rules, then this part of the introduction will, of course, be longer and more complex); and *(d) the roles represented by players in the room.* Instead of your introducing roles you may wish to begin play by having

participants introduce themselves in the role. Where this is possible, it often proves a good idea because it begins their interaction.

(2) Do not take too much time for the introduction. Not only will a long explanation of the nature of the game, the rules, and the reasons you are running it not help create a successful run, but it is likely to kill it. Keep the introduction short! As questions arise later, you will be able to deal with them. Covering all points at the beginning is a poor idea, for players will forget those not seen as relevant because the questions have not yet arisen.

(3) Sound decisive; if you convey the idea that you are sure it will be a good learning experience, you will be more convincing to players. This does not mean that you must sound as though you are an expert on the game and know exactly what will happen. You must, however, explain the rules clearly and decisively so players gain confidence that although they may be confused, you know what is going to happen in general terms!

(4) Explain the expectability of initial confusion. You know from having seen many games that as play begins players are confused. But novice players may not realize that the confusion they are experiencing and the concern they feel about whether they will be successful in developing a strategy is common to all. Whereas you should not announce that everyone in the room is hopelessly confused and ready to walk out, it will be helpful to them if you say something such as the following: "I know that by now you probably are feeling confused. Don't worry about this. As play begins and you start to use the information you will surely find that it makes more sense than it does now. The rules are complex, so that play of the game can be a rich experience. If they were simple enough for you not to feel confused now, then the game would become quickly boring. So try to relax; take my word that you will feel better as soon as we get into play; and let's get started!'

(5) Acknowledge that you, the game operator, recognize the nervousness and feelings of self-consciousness that some of the players feel. In that way, they will feel that you are less critical of their early attempts to cope with a situation fraught with ambiguity. Likewise, as was suggested in 4 above, you will confirm that the feelings they have are not unique to them and thus will dispel many of the doubts they have that they will be able to play successfully.

(6) Sound enthusiastic. This, of course, is related to 3-5 above, but is sufficiently important to warrant separate mention. If you sound enthusiastic you may be able to make the feeling contagious. If you sound hesitant, bored, and as if this is a mechanical exercise and you do not know whether it will work or not, players will pick up that feeling from you. A critical ingredient in the successful run of the game often is the game operator who is able to get players into the right frame of mind as they start.

With your good preparation and a short, enthusiastic introduction, most games will run very well.

OPERATION OF THE GAME

The particulars of administration are highly variable. In one game, the operator may be constantly involved in a variety of management enterprises. In another, the operator may be largely free from such tasks and able to circulate, seeing what is going on and collecting vignettes for use in the postgame discussion-critique. There are a few kinds of activities, however, which are typically engaged in by the game operator. These will be only briefly sketched out here, since they are the elements of game operation most likely to be adequately described in the operator's manual. We conclude the section with some guides to observation during cycles.

(1) Remind players of the rules as situations arise.

(2) Give out necessary resources. In SIMSOC, for example, resources must be distributed at the beginning of each round to all travel agents, subsistence agents, and heads of groups. In METRO-APEX, computer printout reporting changes based on last-cycle decisions must be distributed as each cycle begins. This will be a major element of some games and insignificant in others.

(3) Collect forms which must be submitted to the game operator. Be sure when you get these that you establish a system for keeping track of them, or keeping them in order so that you can later locate them. It is also a good idea to put some kind of mark on forms collected, indicating either the round number or the time at which it was submitted. This is useful for later chronological analysis of what transpired.

(4) Check forms and other materials that are submitted for accuracy. If you can do this while the player is still there, it will save your running around trying to locate that person or, worse yet, attempting to remember who gave you that incorrect form.

(5) Perform the necessary calculations by hand, with a desk calculator, or on the computer, depending upon the nature of the game you are running and what is available to you. The variations in what is involved in this aspect of game operation are far too great to deal with here. If the calculations are complex, it is usually advisable to have an assistant and to find the time to cross-check one another for accuracy.

(6) Announce the time limits if there are any, and indicate whether there will be any releases from these. That is, they are not finished, will you add another five minutes or will you collect incomplete forms?

(7) Announce the amount of time left in the round at several intervals. For example, announce there are fifteen more minutes before Form C must

be turned in, then give a five-minute warning and a two-minute warning. The level of activity and enthusiasm characteristic of play of many games means the students or players will not be looking at their watches or at a room clock. Your announcement of the time remaining will be the only guide they have and should be done, therefore, with some consistency.

(8) Regulate the rhythm of the game and non-game enterprises. As mentioned earlier some games must be played straight through, in one period (such as STARPOWER) or in several consecutive sessions (such as SIMSOC). Others (such as METROPOLIS or THE MARRIAGE GAME) can be divided into consecutive rounds, or the rounds can be separated by other course activities. Whichever of these formats has been selected, the game operator's task is to move players back and forth smoothly from one activity to the other or from one round to the other, reminding them of where they were when they left off and "reintroducing" the game as necessary.

(9) Deal with unanticipated consequences. No matter how adequate the preparation, no matter how thorough the instructor's manual provided, there will be unanticipated consequences. It is important to remember that the game operator need not know all the answers or even seem to. Players are always far more tolerant of instructor's hesitation than operators usually believe! A good guide for making decisions about such things is to ask two questions: (a) Will doing what is suggested interfere with game mechanics? (b) Is there a real-world parallel for what is suggested? If the answer to the first is "no" and the second "yes," we usually allow (encourage, in fact) the proposed innovation. To answer these questions, of course, you must have an understanding of the game mechanics and of the system being simulated.

(10) The major activity of the operator during this phase is careful observation and assistance to those who require it. The central point to remember in terms of observation during the game run is that most of the participants are in a situation that is foreign to them both in terms of the subject matter that they are encountering and in terms of the context of game-play. Watch for the "hubbub factor," which indicates that a certain level of involvement has been achieved at the outset and that the players are pretty much involved on their own hooks. At that point you must watch pretty carefully to see which players *haven't* been caught up.

There are a variety of reasons why players will drop out at early stages of the game. These include a general sense of personal unease at being in the person-to-person or role-playing situation and confusion about the forms or mechanics with which they have to deal. The latter may result from a poor presentation of the game, inadequacies of the forms themselves, or just some obtuseness on the part of that particular individual. The problem is best handled by working with that person directly until mechanics have been mastered.

If the problem is the interpersonal kind, it is probably best to assign the person to a different role or location which the operator selects thoughtfully and privately. In doing this, you would look for other places in the game room where the individual might fit in better. For example, if the individual is a very passive sort, there may be a table where more passive and thoughtful types of things are going on and the operator can sometimes invent an excuse to tactfully move the person into participating in that role. In some cases, if the individual has a particular perspective that is not represented by the game, a role can be invented and assigned to the player, who will be required to generate the momentum to keep the thing going.

Probably the most significant reason people drop out during the course of the game is that their perception of reality differs significantly from that being presented in the game; their dropping out represents an objection to the material being presented. This is the most serious situation of all. It can be dealt with by stopping the game and giving the individual a chance to express personal views, but this is usually the worst alternative of all because it disrupts the whole game. A better approach is to take the individual aside until the nature of the world as the individual sees it is clarified, and why the game is seen as being wrong. If the operator is familiar with the subject matter (and the operator should be or should have some expert on hand), then a private dialogue should go on between the player and the operator until some kind of accord is reached. At this point, the player should be encouraged to set aside or hold in abeyance personal views and to continue play from the perspective represented by the game design but with the knowledge that an opportunity will be given during the critique period to express personal perceptions and to take issue with that presented in the game. If this is done, it is very important to be sure that the player is given the opportunity during the critique period.

(11) It is particularly important to watch the players when they get the results of a particular cycle. If there have been errors in the output or if there is some new material that is confusing them, simple observation of their faces will often reveal that a problem exists. Game operators are often inclined to disappear at the time that the output is presented because if they stay they have to confront the problems which might be involved with mistakes in the game mechanics. Worse yet, they fear they may not be competent to deal with the basic model that is in the game, and the best way to avoid that is not be around when people are trying to ask questions pertaining to it. A cardinal rule from our standpoint is that the operator should be present and very much alert at the time that the players receive the feedback from their decisions and should confront problems in an organized and helpful way.

(12) Another thing to watch for in player behavior is a general lassitude.

This is reflected by people thumbing through newspapers or chatting with one another about topics that don't pertain to the game, or being distracted by such things as radio, television, visitors, or events outside such as the construction of a building next door. This can be the result of poor mechanics—that is, the inability of the operator to process things quickly enough to keep people involved—or it can be the result of the distraction itself. For example, if the building next door is being put up with pile drivers and workmen banging things around, the problem was having selected the site in the first place. The introduction of competitive activity, whether it is reading material, a visitor who is not really there to think about or work with the game, or peripheral discussions going on among players can sometimes best be dealt with by either removing the distraction or rearranging the players and putting them with people that they do not know personally.

POST-PLAY DISCUSSION-CRITIQUE

If you think of a "game event" as the whole business from the time you get started until the time it is all over, you should devote between one-fourth and one-third of this to critique. Start-up time should take not more than about 10 percent, the initial cycle perhaps another 20 percent, perhaps about 40 percent of the time to actually run the game and then about the last third to go through the critique process to be described. There are three distinct phases of the postplay critique.

(1) The first phase involves letting the players vent their spleens aboout the things that happened in the game itself. That would be the arguments that have ensued, the oneupsmanship that has gone on, the hurt feelings because of a mix-up in the computer output, or anything that they just want to get off their chests—where the game "did them wrong" or where they can lord it over somebody else whom they happened to better. At the beginning of the postgame discussion, then, allow an opportunity for catharsis. Many players in the game will have become very emotional and highly involved in what transpired. Before asking them to *analyze* the experience, you must give them an opportunity to vent some of the emotions they have pent up. Some of these feelings will have been obvious to other players at time they arose; others, however, will not have been manifest. For players to fully understand the experience, they must learn how things felt to others in other parts of the game. Unless you are a trained psychologist, however, you should quickly turn them from the venting of anger and accusations ("you did this," "he did that to me," and so on) to an analysis of why those things were done and what it was about the situation or the role that led to some of the actions taken and interpretations that arose.

(2) The second stage is a systematic examination of the model presented

by the game from the perspective of the various roles. This gives everybody a chance to see what happened from the eyes of the other role players.

A good technique is to take some event such as an issue that was presented to them and have the different players speak in turn to that issue from their perspectives.

The world looks different to those in different social situations; likewise, the game looks different to those in different social roles within it. Analysis cannot take place until perceptions of what transpired have been shared between participants. Be prepared for conflicts in views and arguments about "what really happened."

(3) Finally, in the last stage of the critique, urge that the players and the operator should focus on the reality which was represented by the game rather than the game itself. This means "bringing them down" and it involves getting out of the game situation altogether and thoughtfully and at some length addressing the actual reality that the game simulated.

During this last phase, it is fruitful to have some kind of a conceptual model portrayed visually, with charts prepared in advance, worked up on the blackboard, or transmitted verbally.

It is often helpful to select some issue, event, circumstance, or problem that players *do* understand, either in a real-world context or preferably in both the context of the game and the real world, to use as a theme around which to examine the overall basic model of reality. This involves "reality-testing" the game against their prior knowledge, refining their previous perceptions, and leaving the game event with sharpened questions and answers about the world in which they live.

CHAPTER THIRTEEN

TEACHING WITH SIMULATION GAMES:
A Review of Claims and Evidence

CATHY STEIN GREENBLAT

Teachers of social science are constantly seeking better ways of conveying an understanding of systems concepts and of presenting existing theory and empirical data to students. In recent years, simulation games have gained considerable popularity as potential vehicles for such improvement in pedagogy (compare Greenblat, 1971b). These games are currently utilized in schools and colleges for a variety of purposes: heightening interest and motivation; presenting information and principles; putting students into situations in which they must articulate positions, ideas, arguments, or facts they have previously learned; or training students in skills they will later need.

This chapter stems from two interrelated problems concerning the claims and evidence for teaching with simulation games. The first is a problem in the *teaching of sociology* and can be summarized by the statement, "Those who have used games tend to be highly enthusiastic and to report very favorable outcomes, but the empirical evidence to systematically test their claims is still limited." The field is new, and much remains to be done. Many claims are as yet untested; others are only partially tested; and methodological difficulties are just beginning to be successfully overcome. Educators, game designers, and researchers have not yet fully explored the nature and range of appropriate applications of simulations to education, nor have they identified the sorts of simulations most effective for various types of learning and learners.

AUTHOR'S NOTE: I am very grateful to Marvin Bressler of Princeton University for his criticisms and suggestions on an earlier version of this paper, and to Richard Stephenson of Douglass College for his suggestions regarding this version.

The second is a problem of the *sociology of teaching,* and can be phrased in terms that are somewhat similar to the above, yet critically different: "The empirical evidence to systematically test the claims concerning the consequences of teaching with simulations is still limited, yet utilization is spreading rapidly." Perhaps it is presumptive to think that teachers—even teachers of social science who seek "hard data" to support their research hypotheses and the statements they make in classes—are often concerned about *evidence* of the effectiveness of their teaching techniques. Perhaps most of us teach more by "faith" in our methods than we would like to admit, for how easy it is to make cavalier assumptions of cause and effect relationships between our teaching and students' good examination or term paper performance. Perhaps when we purport to "see" that traditional methods do not work, we accept our innovations on similar faith. In the absence of evidence for older or newer methods, perhaps personal preference would seem the best criterion for decision-making, and the papers reviewed in this chapter would be of interest to researchers, but not to teachers. Departmental and institutional politics, however, often seem to operate to allow the traditionalists to be considered innocent until proven guilty, while the innovators are more frequently pressured to prove their contentions of superior (or at least equal) results with their new methods. Hence, perhaps, we can account for why the latter (and this author) occasionally go through the scientific process of looking for evidence in support of our personal observations. Although they may not constitute the *basis* of the decision to use a new teaching technique, positive findings help satisfy the skeptics and critics. And the process of inquiry and investigation leads to improvement of our understanding of the learning process.

These two problems, then, provide the raison d'être of this chapter: it seems fruitful, even at this early stage, to summarize the existing claims and the available evidence, so those concerned can see where we are and where we have to go.

THE POPULARITY AND PROMISE OF SIMULATION GAMES

Beliefs in the potency of games as pedagogical devices stem from several sources, including: (a) the view that the mind is an instrument to be developed rather than a receptacle to be filled; (b) the consequent position that modes of teaching are needed which will help to develop people who are excited about learning and know *how* to learn, rather than people with vast funds of information, much of which will soon be obsolete (Sprague and Shirts, 1966: 15-16); (c) the desire to develop modes of promoting engagement and curiosity, ways of looking at events and processes, and awareness of resources for finding answers; (d) the idea that students learn not because learning is a goal in and of itself, but because learning leads to goal achievement, and consequently information transmission must be seen as facilitating if it is to be effective (Coleman, 1967b: 69-70); (e) the belief that learners learn to act by acting and, hence, should be made to interact with material in an active rather than a passive way (Coleman, 1967b, 1967c; Abt, 1970; Bruner, 1961: 81); and (f) the view that, particularly in the social sciences, students must learn to examine the social world, picking out relevant variables and examining their nature and consequences; hence, modes of teaching about social systems are essential.

Simulation games relate directly to many of these notions. They represent modes of getting students to learn by provoking inquiry rather than by "feeding" information. When students cannot participate in "real" situations because direct experience is too expensive, too time-consuming, or otherwise infeasible, simulation provides an opportunity for vicariously experiencing at least some of the elements of that situation. Students experience the results of their decisions as they encounter basic processes such as decision-making, resource allocation, communication, and negotiation:

> The participants quite literally cannot avoid making decisions. They face the reality that "no decision" has as much consequence as any other decision. They must usually decide, moreover, on the basis of incomplete information, constricted by time limits, and with only partial understanding of why their previous decisions produced the consequences they did. This seems to fit much of what we know about real-life decision-making [Sprague, n.d.: 12].

In these ways students may be surrounded with environments similar to those they might not face until much later in life or might never directly experience. Finally, the classroom environment and atmosphere during the operation of a simulation differs notably from that which usually prevails. The instructor running a simulation and postgame discussion plays a role very different from the instructor teaching in a more traditional manner. There seems to be spillover to later classes, allowing more learning to take place as structural impediments are mitigated or removed.

CLAIMS ABOUT GAMES

In order to review the claims and evidence concerning the use of simulation for teaching, books, published and unpublished articles and monographs, newsletters, and advertisements from games' publishers were reviewed.[1] The numerous propositions (phrased explicitly or implicitly) found in these materials were organized into six general categories, and are listed here in detail in order to present a relatively complete inventory prior to reviewing the available research and offering suggestions for further investigations. In general, the sources are not identified in the list that follows, as the same claims are made repeatedly, and thus multiple sources would have to be cited for each. The claims presented below are phrased in simple descriptive form (for example, "participation in simulation games generates greater interest in the topics simulated"); almost all, however, have explicit or implicit counterparts which are *comparative* (for example, "participation in simulation games generates greater interest in the topics simulated; this increment in interest is larger than the increment with other modes of teaching"). In the interest of economy of space, only the descriptive form is given here; the reader should add the comparative form to each entry.

(1) Motivation and interest
    (a) Participation in simulation games is itself interesting and involving.
    (b) Participation in simulation games increases interest in the *topics* simulated.
    (c) Participation in simulation games increases interest in the *course* in which the simulation is employed.
    (d) Participation in simulation games increases interest, enthusiasm, and commitment to *learning in general*.
(2) Cognitive learning
    (a) Participants in simulation games gain *factual information*.
    (b) Participants in simulation games acquire *explicit referents for concepts* used to describe human behavior; abstract concepts such as "organization," "power," "stratification," and "negotiation" take on concrete meaning.
    (c) Participants in simulation games learn *procedural sequences*. "The actors must, of course, learn the rules, comprehend the essential features of the environment, understand the implications of the alternatives open to them, and develop increasingly elaborate strategies. They must be taught to operate the simulated system, in this instance in the hope that they will acquire a better concept of the larger system through a highly concentrated experience" (Meier, 1967: 157).
    (d) Participants in simulation games learn *general principles* of the subject matter simulated (such as, the need for social control, good communications, and long-range planning).
    (e) Simulation games provide simplified worlds from which students can stand back and understand the *structure* of the everyday, "real" world. "Games seem to display in a simple way the structure of real-life situations. They cut us off from serious life by immersing us in a demonstration of its possibilities. We return to the world as gamesmen, preparing to see what is structural about reality and ready to reduce life to its liveliest elements" (Goffman, 1961: 34).
    (f) Participants in simulation games gain in *explicitness:* "The capacity to identify consciously elements of a problem in an analytic or technical sense."
    (g) Participants in simulation games learn a *systematic analytical approach*.
    (h) Participants in simulation games learn better *decision-making skills*.

      (i) Participants in simulation games learn *winning strategies* in those situations simulated.

(3) Changes in the character of later course work.

      (a) Participation in simulation games makes *later work* (such as, lectures, reading) *more meaningful*.

      (b) Participation in simulation games leads students to *more sophisticated and relevant inquiry,* for discussion of the simulation leads to questions about real-world analogies.

      (c) Class discussions following a simulation will involve *greater participation* by class members, as they will have had a shared experience.

(4) Affective learning re: subject matter

      (a) Participation in simulation games leads to *changed perspectives and orientations* (for example, attitudes toward various public and world issues, attitudes toward the importance of collective versus individual action, attitudes toward deviant life styles).

      (b) Participation in simulation games leads to *increased empathy* for others (such as national decision makers, ghetto residents) and increased insight into the way the world is seen by them.

      (c) Participation in simulation games leads to *increased insight into the predicaments, pressures, uncertainties, and moral and intellectual difficulties of others* (such as, decision makers, ghetto residents).

(5) General affective learning

      (a) Participants in simulation games gain increased *self-awareness*.

      (b) Participants in simulation games gain a greater *sense of personal efficacy and potency*.

(6) Changes in classroom structure and relations

      (a) Use of simulation games promotes better *student-teacher relations*.

      (b) Use of simulation games leads students to *perceive greater freedom to explore ideas*.

      (c) Use of simulation games leads to *students becoming more autonomous,* thus changing teacher-student relationships.

      (d) Use of simulation games leads to *students perceiving teachers more positively*.

      (e) Use of simulation games produces *more relaxed, natural exchange between students and teachers*.

      (f) Use of simulation games leads to increased *knowledge of other students* (by students) and greater *peer acceptance* (Abt, 1970: 121).

      (g) Use of simulation games involves a *diminishing of the teacher's role of judge and jury*.

      (h) Use of simulation games leads to *teachers perceiving students more positively*.

EMPIRICAL STATUS OF THE PROPOSITIONS

Research dealing with various aspects of teaching with simulations varies in both volume and quality. Hence, the level of verification of the specific propositions is very uneven. Many are generally supported by anecdotal reports, but few have received careful attention through systematic testing.

No evidence, for example, was found for any of the propositions relating to changes in the character of later course work (section 3 of the list), though Feldt (1966a: 20) reports as follows concerning the Community Land Use Game (CLUG):

No systematic attempt has been made as yet to determine the overall effective-ness of the game. The volunteered opinions of persons who have played it, however, are generally highly favorable. Many students have reported that course work in municipal finance, decision theory, zoning law, urban design, and economics, as well as courses in urban ecology and geography, have been much more meaningful and important to them as a result of having played it. Others have reported that they could better understand changes in urban growth patterns they had observed after having seen similar patterns of devel-opment in the course of the game. On the whole, it seems reasonable to argue that the game provides a certain amount of field experience to the participants which makes further course work in planning and related areas more signifi-cant to them.

There is a similar paucity of data concerning the propositions about changes in classroom climate and relations (section 6 of the list). Discus-sions of the reasoning behind these claims were found; Abt (1970: 31), for example, notes that the teacher role is to decide what concepts can be taught most effectively, by what method they can be communicated most memora-bly, and at what point review and evaluation are needed for "closure." The teacher also runs the "debriefing" or postgame analysis; "this should be a structured, directed discussion of the limitations and insights offered by the game and of the performance of the players in both representing and solving their problems effectively. Here the players will consider the teacher as a vital part of the game's operation and resolver of meaning, rather than as a person who interferes with classroom activities." Boocock and Coleman (1966: 219) speak similarly in suggesting that games are self-disciplining and self-judging, thereby changing the teacher's role. No evidence, how-ever, was located concerning this set of propositions. Some could easily be tested using student or teacher questionnaires or sociometric techniques, but if this has been done, it has not been reported in the literature surveyed.

Other propositions have received more scrutiny by researchers. Some work has been done concerning affective learning re: subject matter (section 4 of the list) resulting from simulation participation. Studies with the LIFE CAREER game suggest that participants gain an appreciation of the com-plexity of "real-life" planning. This is illustrated by students' statements and by increases in the number who after playing believe that "it is hard to plan your life in advance" (Boocock and Coleman, 1966: 229-231). Players were also found to gain a deeper understanding or empathy for the roles they played in the game.

For example . . . boys who worked on teams assigned to a profile of a girl
student tended, by comparison with boys who planned for a boy in the game,
to move toward a more "liberal" attitude toward the appropriate role for
women. This was indicated by their greater willingness after the game to agree
that women who wished to do so should have jobs and other interests outside
of the home and family [Boocock, 1967b: 332].

Responses to a checklist of twelve personal characteristics that subjects
thought described what a typical dropout was like were utilized to measure
changes in empathy for dropouts. Boys who played the potential dropout
role developed more positive images if they already had some feeling of
identification; girls playing this role became more negative toward dropouts. Thus, the researcher points to the need for caution in using this kind of
teaching device: "If simulation games do indeed change attitudes as effectively as they appear to do, one must be clear as to the direction and desirability of changes" (Boocock, 1967b: 332).

Other evidence concerning the development of empathy is largely anecdotal. The following are examples that convey the nature of such reports:

Finally, one student said: "Another important thing I now understand better is
communism. I realized to my amazement when we made out the decision
sheet for Ingo that even those of us who claimed to be staunch conservatives
were advocating pushing economic development as hard as we could, disre-
garding as far as we dared the validators. Our 'motto' was to bring the people
as close as possible to starvation without there being a revolution. Now I can
see why communism has such appeal among the underprivileged nations of
the world. The temptation to move swiftly ahead at all costs is a strong one
indeed, and this is especially true if you have nothing to conserve (thus why be
a conservative?) [Carlson, 1969: 70].

Goldhamer and Speier (1959: 79) report that RAND gamers claim
players acquire "new insights into the pressures, the uncertainties, and the
moral and intellectual difficulties under which foreign policy decisions are
made." The instrument used is not described in their report.

Robinson (1966: 118) found some attitudinal change in Inter-Nation Simulation participants, and discussed the possible significance of evidence of
even minimal attitude change:

The challenge to educators is to find ways to penetrate the firm 'set' that
college students bring to courses on politics and international relations. Students' perspectives and orientations toward public and world affairs are ordinarily developed by the time they reach college and are largely beyond amend-
ment, except for some unlikely confrontation with an irreversible learning
experience. It would be too much to claim, at this point, that simulation
constitutes such an experience, but our data indicate small and important
differences whereas other methods yield virtually no differences. We cannot

yet boldly recommend revision of instructional policies, but we have grounds for confidently recommending further research and replication to help decide whether our vision of an effective technique is a reality or a mirage.

Less evidence is available concerning general affective learning (section 5 of the list). Earlier it was reported that male participants in LIFE CAREER changed their attitudes toward women pursuing careers. The researchers also report a before-after change in the percentage of female participants who agreed that "an intelligent girl with a good education really should do more with it than just get married and raise a family." This, Boocock and Coleman (1966: 232-233) suggest, is evidence not only of attitude change, but also of learning to feel greater control of one's environment. In another report of LIFE CAREER participants, Boocock (1967: 333) reports that "at the same time that they become aware of the amount of information they must assimilate and the amount of planning necessary to make intelligent career choices, many students also gain confidence in their ability to do so." The evidence is not given, however, and there is no discussion of persistence of the increase in confidence.

Researchers investigating the outcomes of play in a legislative game report more change in the experimental group than in the control group away from the belief that "people like me don't have any say about what the government does." Impressionistic data were also gathered concerning an increased sense of interconnections between various aspects of a situation and interdependence in the environment (Boocock and Coleman, 1966: 234). Boocock and Coleman (1966: 233) and Inbar (1970: 241) report gains in feelings of personal potency by participants in COMMUNITY DISAS-TER. Some players in trial runs of THE MARRIAGE GAME have reported to the designers about considerable growth in self-awareness and insight into others as a result of the simulation experience. One girl who participated with her real-life partner reported in a personal note to this author, "It's sad and hard to admit, but I think I learned more about someone and our relationship through 8 hours of participation in the game than through 3 years of living together." Again, however, the evidence is anecdotal.

More evidence is available concerning the propositions relating to cognitive learning (section 2 of the list), but the empirical status of these claims is still weak. Specific learning from playing LIFE CAREER and a legislative game was measured by means of "test-like" items (Boocock, 1967b, 1966a). Participants in both games scored higher in before-after score differences than did those in the control groups. Since players in each game served as the control group for those in the other game—and, therefore, the control groups were not taught the same material by an alternative method—evidence is available for the descriptive claim about learning but not for the comparative one. Participants in the legislative game were also found to change in their perception of the best strategy in the game. There is, however, no evidence that the learning of game strategy was paralleled by learning of "real-life" strategy.

Anderson (1970: 49-51) attempted to test learning with a consumer game by a paper-and-pencil test and also by an exercise in which students had to *apply* what they had learned by reading contracts and selecting the best. The control group in this case was taught the same material by conventional methods. He reports that there were no differences in factual learning for those taught by simulation and those taught by conventional methods; behavioral learning was better with simulation for some subpopulations.

Other researchers used student questionnaires to examine the extent of learning (Attig, 1967). Alger's (1963: 179) students reported six kinds of learning with the INTER-NATION SIMULATION: (1) vividness and understanding beyond what one got from textbooks; (2) realization of the complexities of conflicts between rival nations; (3) importance of having reliable knowledge and the importance of communication in international relations; (4) better understanding of the problems and goals of nations not like the United States; (5) better understanding of the problems of decision-making; and (6) difficulties of balancing the requirements of internal and external affairs.

Many researchers (Boocock and Coleman, 1966; Boocock, 1966a; Feldt, 1966a; Inbar, 1970) report that learning is in general terms. They suggest that students gain in awareness or that they are sure that they learn but find it difficult to specify just what the content of the learning is. Participants often are able to articulate general dimensions of their learning, but not specific facts.

In summary, researchers express a conviction that cognitive learning takes place, but measurements provide limited data. Self-reports of participants suggest learning, but information about how many or what proportion of participants report this is generally lacking. Learning that takes place seems to be difficult to specify or articulate, but it appears that it is learning of principles and procedural sequences and the acquisition of referents for concepts, rather than learning of factual information.

Finally, the greatest amount of discussion in the literature centers on claims about the heightening of motivation and interest (section 1 of the list). There is a great deal of anecdotal information concerning student involvement by simulations. Researchers report written and oral statements by participants testifying to the "motivating and self-sustaining quality of the activity" (Boocock and Coleman, 1966: 224). Some describe the degree to which students have evidenced emotional involvement (anger, disappointment, frustration) as evidence of interest (Feldt, 1966a: 20; Sprague, n.d.: 16). Other behavioral indicators of interest are implied in the following statements: "After the first day students agreed to bring their lunches for the rest of the week so they could have an extra 40 minutes play each day" (Boocock, 1967b: 330); "An indication of student enthusiasm for the game was the number of students who desired to attend class for purposes of conferences and negotiations on days when the other section was meeting" (Attig, 1967: 26); "It is not at all uncommon for players scheduled to play for four hours to insist that they be allowed to continue to play for an additional four hours, often without stopping to eat" (Feldt, 1966a: 20).

A study by Robinson et al. (1966: 57) is the only one found which utilized several indicators and investigated the extent to which interest generated by the simulations was greater than interest generated by other modes of teaching. One course was taught entirely by simulation and another by case study. The measures of interest employed were:

(1) comparisons of students' interest in the course with interest in other courses taken simultaneously;
(2) perceptions of interest in this course;
(3) perceptions of interest in political science;
(4) preference for case or simulation;
(5) descriptive evaluation of the course at the end of the term;
(6) reports of the amount of students' reading on the subject of the course;
(7) use of special reading materials placed on reserve in the college library;
(8) visits to the professor's office;
(9) attendance in class; and
(10) rate of participation in "lab" section.

As the reader will note, differences in many of these measures—particularly the behavioral indicators (6-10)—may reflect differences in variables other than interest: clarity of presentations, understanding of materials, and so on. In addition, due to the unusually extensive use of simulation and case study, the measures are measures of interest in the course as well as interest in the method of teaching (simulation). Robinson's findings indicated that "case method succeeds more than simulation in eliciting student interest as measured by students' perceptions, but measures of student behavior indicate that simulation succeeds more than case in affecting student interest and involvement."

Little attention has been focused on the question of whether the interest manifested by students participating in a simulation games is due to the *novelty* of the approach and represents a Hawthorne effect. If such were found to be the case, it would suggest use of simulations only until these "novelty effects" wore off or diminished beyond some point. Furthermore, as Cohen (1962: 371) suggests in his critique of simulations, "no one has ever systematically investigated the possibility, for example, that those whose interest and enthusiasm are visibly enlisted by games are those who are most interested and enthusiastic about the subject in the regular class, and hence that there is little net increase in interest in the subject." This is a problem of study design, and will be discussed in the next section.

In summary, then, it appears that there is a considerable amount of anecdotal material about affective involvement of students at the time of participation, and some evidence that student interest in simulations is very high. There is, at the moment, little hard data to show that such participation leads to greater interest in the subject matter, the course, or learning in general.

METHODOLOGICAL PROBLEMS IN GAMES RESEARCH

The foregoing discussion has pointed to the fact that many of the claims made about consequences of teaching with simulation games are supported by anecdotal data rather than empirical evidence. An additional problem arises in discussing even the little evidence that has been compiled; this problem stems from the methodological shortcomings of many of the research studies. A great many do not meet the canons of scientific inquiry; the deficiencies include both conventional ones and specific problems with this type of research.

The first category includes problems of research design, sampling, operationalizing of concepts, and lack of control for relevant sample characteristics in the analysis.

Many of the studies suffer from poor research design: "after-only" tests which preclude measurement of change; lack of control groups even where the intention is to draw conclusions about the value of simulations compared to other techniques; failure to consider Hawthorne effects; and poor criteria for accepting or rejecting hypotheses.

A related set of problems stems from the sampling techniques. In many instances, the subjects were students available to the researcher, and were known to be unrepresentative of students at that academic level. In other cases, the participants were of the age and ability level one would ordinarily teach with the game being investigated, but were sampled while out of their student roles—such as high school students at an organizational conference for a weekend. Their definitions of the situations and thus of the activity might well be different from the definitions by the same students if they were playing the game in a class. Surely teaching and learning take place outside classrooms, but, if generalizations are to be drawn about the use of simulations in schools, the relevant sample would seem to be students in classes.

An additional sampling problem is the very heterogeneous nature of some of the samples. Several games were run with multiple groups of people of differing ages and academic backgrounds. These subsamples were then merged to create a large enough n for subsequent analysis. It is difficult to define the relevant population for generalization from such findings, and subsample differences are not reported.

Another problem in many studies relates to poor operationalizing of concepts. Frequently the multidimensionality of such concepts as "interest" is not recognized; "learning" is often treated as a "yes" or "no" thing; and little attention is paid to the tenacity of the learning. The measures employed often bear little relationship to the learning objectives specified by the game director or by the administrator. Thus Shirts (1970: 82) remarks,

> It seems to me that there are several possible reasons for the discrepancy between the research results and the expectations of knowledgeable persons. For one thing, it appears that the design of most of the research has been guided more by what is convenient, tidy, and available than by an honest attempt to determine the impact of the use of simulations. For what other reason would a person compare simulations with traditional didactic methods on their effectiveness in teaching students numerous facts and ideas as measured by an objective test? Books and lectures present carefully processed ideas and facts to the students in grade-A, enriched, homogenized form. The students, in turn, have been trained by many years of conditioning to accept this rich diet and to return it to the lecturer on demand. In simulations on the other hand, facts are frequently hidden in scenarios, messages from other participants, decision-making forms, statements by people in hot debate, and announcements from the directors or the simulated mass media. Other facts are specific to the game being played and have to be translated before they have any meaning in the real world.

Raser (1969: 133), too, attributes the problem of poor evidence to inadequate measuring devices; "emphasis has been on developing measures to tap the acquisition of punctiform data—the retention of factual material. Only a few isolated efforts have been made to measure learning of concepts and relationships, or even to discover how much learning is facilitated, and none have [sic] been directly applied to gaming."

Finally, a general methodological shortcoming in the studies reviewed is the frequent lack of control for relevant student characteristics. In most instances, only scores for the total sample are reported. In many studies, such factors as sex of players and sex balance of groups, social class background of participants, intelligence, school records, and pregame motivations of participants are not employed as independent variables to examine the differential effects of participation on students varying in these characteristics, although some researchers (compare Stoll, 1969) have found them to be important. Robinson (1966) controlled for cognitive style, need for achievement, need for affiliation, and need for dominance in analyzing his data; such factors are suggestive of the nature of further differentiations that might be made in attempts to ascertain who learns what from simulations.

In addition to these general problems, there are also problems specific to "games" research. Many are difficult to overcome, but the researcher contemplating investigations or the teacher viewing studies should be aware of these dilemmas.

There are a number of game variables that may be important in explaining differential outcomes, including length of play, size of playing group, and amount and quality of pregame preparation (compare Inbar, 1966). A special instance is the conditions of administration: how the simulation is employed. In some instances, research has been done where simulations were used in courses with correlate readings, lectures, and discussions. Testing for the consequences of use under these (recommended) conditions of administration is quite different from testing the teaching potential of the same simulation when it is run in an afternoon as part of a conference. In addition, characteristics of the game administrator have been found to be of considerable importance in explaining the outcomes of participation (Inbar, 1966); yet discussion of such factors as administrator competence, preparation, and familiarity to students is often lacking. A final set of game variables infrequently controlled is the roles played by the participants. Those playing different parts often have different experiences, but this has not generally been examined.

A large problem arises because, in many studies, "games" and "simulations" are at least implicitly treated as homogeneous. Despite great variations in games, conclusions from studies with one game are generalized to games in general. In point of fact, even the best-designed study could not provide a full test of any of the propositions outlined above; it could reasonably yield only generalizations about the particular game investigated or possibly that type of game. This idea of the heterogeneity of games also presents difficulties of interpretation of reports in which the findings from several studies are put together to test hypotheses about games (Cherryholmes, 1966).

Finally, there is the problem of definition of the proper "end" of a simulation experience. An integral part of all instructional simulations is the postplay discussion and analysis. Students are often unable to observe or to know of the overall course of events and thus to draw relevant conclusions without a discussion of what happened. Debriefings also focus upon the "fit" between the simulation model and the real world and thus allow students to learn from their play activities. The studies reported, however, generally fail to note whether postplay questionnaires and other measuring instruments were administered before or after such debriefings. In this author's opinion, the appropriate measurement time is *after* discussion, as the discussion is *part* of the simulation, not an appendage to it. This, of course, contributes to greater problems of administrator effects, but differential administrator competence *is* an important factor in accounting for the learning outcomes of the use of simulation games.

CONCLUSION: FUTURE DIRECTIONS

The foregoing review points to the lack of sufficient data to prove that games meet their pedagogical promise. For a number of reasons, this should not be taken as an argument for abandonment of their use in teaching.

First of all, it is difficult to tell at this point whether the lack of evidence in support of the propositions stems from poor outcomes or poor measurements. Some of the difficulties plaguing the games researcher have been outlined above, and better ways of dealing with them may be devised.

Second, although there is little evidence that students learn more when taught by games than by conventional methods, there is no evidence that they learn *less*. In fact, studies of cognitive learning point to "no difference" or "differences in favor of games that are not statistically significant." Hence, games seem to be at least as effective as other modes of teaching, and further studies may show yet more significant results.

Third, one must keep in mind the *general* scarcity of demonstrable evidence in social science and in education. Where, for example, is there good evidence that students learn when teachers lecture and class members take notes?

Fourth, a "data-based decision" to use games for teaching obviously should not be dependent upon evidence in support of *all* the claims outlined. If, for example, it were found that games stimulated interest and motivation and did nothing else, their use to get students involved and questioning might well be warranted.

Despite the general paucity of evidence, then, it is to be hoped that games will continue to be employed, and that they will receive closer scrutiny by researchers and educators. I am hopeful that, in addition to trying to test the propositions offered above, those who design, utilize, and evaluate games will turn their attention to the following types of questions.

(1) How and when and how much should games be used, and what is the best way of integrating them with other modes of teaching? Rather than introducing simulations in an ad hoc manner into a class, we should seek ways to make them parts of units of study, tied with correlate readings and other experiences.

(2) As noted earlier, questions of use cannot be answered for games in general. Rather, we must ask which games (or which types of games) best meet specific instructional goals, and thus how and when they should be employed. For some games, Bloomfield and Padelford's (1959: 1115) comment on political games seems highly appropriate:

The political exercise is by no means a substitute for systematic rigorous analysis by teacher and student in either international or domestic politics. Indeed, the gaming technique should be used only after the student has had extensive reading and thorough instruction on the political process, the nature and operation of institutions and laws, group dynamics, and the substance of political problems themselves. Otherwise the gaming is likely to become artificial, pursued largely on the basis of hunches or intuitions rather than of knowledge and understanding.

Other games, however, require little advance information or knowledge, and their primary value is their motivating power. Their contribution seems to lie in heightening students' interest in the topic and in sensitizing them to the complexities and variables involved in the social structure or social process simulated. We must, then, attempt to develop a taxonomy of games to guide the user or potential user.

(3) If, as has been suggested, participation in simulation games leads to attitudinal change, serious thought must be given to the dangers as well as to the promises of the technique. What are the underlying assumptions and values of the models developed and used? What are we *deciding* to teach, and what are we teaching *inadvertently?* When does "attitude change" become "brainwashing?"

(4) What are some of the less obvious personal consequences of participation in simulations? For example, where involvement is high and is manifested by severe frustration, anger, depression, and so on, are there "costs" to students that must be weighed against the gains? And how do these costs compare to those stemming from the frustration, anger, and depression created when students are "talked at," kept still and obedient, and the like in the regular classrooms?

(5) Finally, if further testing lends greater support to the propositions listed earlier, we then must continue our investigations to attain a greater understanding of *how and why* games have these effects. Through this type of query, researchers can make a contribution not only to those interested in this educational technique, but to those in all fields concerned with the nature and process of learning.

NOTE

1. Happily, the number of studies is steadily increasing; hence any review such as this is quickly dated. The reader is urged to consult recent issues of *Simulation and Games* (quarterly journal published by Sage Publications, Inc.) for reports published since September 1971, when this paper was completed.

CHAPTER FOURTEEN

THE EDUCATIONAL EFFECTIVENESS OF SIMULATION GAMES:

A Synthesis of Findings

MARY E. BREDEMEIER
CATHY STEIN GREENBLAT

In considering what we know about evaluating the effectiveness of simulation games, we need to supplement the old joke:

"So how's your wife, Sam?"

"Compared to what?"

We need to add, "For what purpose, under what conditions, and how can we be sure?"

CONDITIONS

The most important recent clarification of assessment efforts has been recognition of the many complex ways in which a given game is not the same experience for everyone and may not be the same experience for anyone (for a discussion of the "multiple realities" possible in games, see Greenblat and Gagnon, 1979). The tendency to think and write about *the* learning from *the* experience of *a* game must give way, in the first place, to recognition that what anyone learns from any experience depends on a host of circumstances: what the person is looking for; the detailed "shape" of the experience (a term explicated below); the nature of the person; opportunities to practice; similarities of that experience to other experiences; the intrinsic pleasantness/ unpleasantness of the experience. Such variables obviously affect what we all learn from *any* experience, whether it be a lecture, a cocktail party, or a movie; and it should be clear that they affect what people learn from *a* simulation game, not to mention "simulation-gaming."

What Is Being Looked For

In most formal or purposive instruction-learning situations, the standard formula is to say, in effect, "Here is what you are supposed to learn; now learn it; now display that you have learned it." Chartier (1973) feels that the simulation-gaming experience has more satisfactory outcomes when a learning "set" is established through specification for students of why they are playing, what is expected of them, and what they can expect to learn. However, it is just at this point that some philosophies of simulation-gaming complicate assessment efforts, insisting that part of the special nature of simulation-gaming instruction is *not* to make clear in advance what is to be looked for. Indeed, from this view, much if not all of the point of the simulation-gaming experience would be lost if participants knew the point in advance.

Simulation-gamers are by no means of one mind on this issue, as our discussion of "the shape of the experience" makes clear. However, the existence of this point of view distinguishes simulation-gaming learning from much other learning at the outset, and leaves (purposely, perhaps) the question of *what* will be learned up to variables outside the instructor's control, except to the extent that they can be controlled during the debriefing session. In comparing simulation-gaming learning with learning from more conventional pedagogies, this perspective complicates the problem of defining the dependent variables.

Even if the "point" of a simulation-gaming experience might be lost if it were to be discussed in advance, there remains the question of what that point is. There seem to be two major categories of answers. One is that the instructor has the point clearly in mind and considers that the experience will certainly produce it in the minds of the participants. The other seems more radically to distinguish simulation-gaming from other techniques and to make conventional comparison with those techniques irrelevant—beside the point—by saying that the point is not to have a specific point. Rather, it is to show that different people will learn different things, or it is to stimulate creativity, heighten awareness, provide for surprise, or reinforce sentiments.

In that case, however, comparisons can still be made; it simply becomes necessary to identify clearly the dependent variables *as* creativity, surprise, reinforcement, and so on. Simulation-gaming becomes more like an artistic experience than a conventionally defined learning experience, or even, perhaps, more like a religious or initiation ceremony experience. (What are people supposed to learn from puberty rites?)

The point of all this is to emphasize the pointlessness of comparative assessments of effectiveness without clearer specification of any rationale for the outcome to be measured than is often found in the assessment literature.

The Shape of the Experience

Participation in a given simulation/game with administrator A, in form B, at time C, with other participants of type D, and with incentive E is not the same experience as participation in the "same" game under different instances of those variables. With respect only to those five variables, and assuming that any of them can take on only four values, we already have 1024 different experiences. We do not know how much difference each of them makes, but if any makes any difference, often any comparison between the simulation/game outcome and other techniques will be confounded unless the variables are controlled.

There is evidence that some of them do make a difference.

ADMINISTRATIVE VARIABLES

How a game is run and who runs it appear to make a difference. Shirts (1976a) points out that instructors' attitudes toward simulation-gaming and toward students, as well as their knowledge and skill in administering games, can affect the experiences students have with simulation-gaming. Livingston (1970) found significant differences in attitude change between groups of students who played the same simulation game under different instructors.

Other procedural variables, such as the introduction, variations in game play, and the debriefing, affect the simulation-gaming experiences of players. Chartier (1973) delineates aspects of the introduction which are presumed to affect game experiences and learning outcomes. The popular games STARPOWER and BAFÁ BAFÁ are quite versatile; game play and debriefing can be varied to highlight quite different real-world settings and problems. (For further discussion of uses of these two games, see Carranza, 1974; Bredemeier, 1978; and Jackson, 1979.) Allen et al. (1978, 1979) have demonstrated ways to vary game play and scoring with EQUATIONS to enhance learning outcomes. For instance, the "snuffing" version of EQUATIONS provides more incentive than the standard form of this game for players to engage in idea-swapping, and has been found to result in achievement gains in mathematics.

The postgame discussion, or debriefing, is widely regarded as essential for maximum (or even correct) learning to occur (see Livingston and Kidder, 1973; Coleman et al., 1973; Stadsklev, 1974). This is the point at which generalizations and symbolic meaning are generated out of players' concrete experiences. Spelvin (1979) stresses the leader's role in eliciting "learner-discovered" principles, in assisting students' attempts to organize their ideas and experiences into increasingly higher-order generalizations, and in providing the discussion and assignments which will relate the experiences of the game and the generalizations to students' real-life experiences.

The research does not always show enhanced learning from debriefing, however. Livingston (1970) found no effect on understanding the game, and only a slight effect on attitudes, of postgame discussions of GHETTO. Chartier (1972) reports an experiment with GENERATION GAP to compare learning from (1) simulations with discussions, (2) simulations without discussions, (3) discussions without simulations, and (4) independent learning involving neither simulations nor discussions; the only significant difference in outcome was greater expressed satisfaction with perceived learning outcomes from participants in the debriefed simulations. It may be that the *quality* of the discussion is the crucial determinant of its effects; it may be also that games differ in their need for debriefing. The purposes of GHETTO are fairly obvious; the purposes of STARPOWER are not so obvious.

INTERNAL GAME VARIABLES

The internal structure of games may be a major source of variation or consistency in experience and variability of outcomes. If the content of a game does not truly represent the reality it is supposed to represent, participants may enjoy the game experience but cannot be expected to learn the "right things" from it. (For more on game content as a source of error variance, see Boocock, 1972b; Smith, 1972; Chapman et al., 1974; Shirts, 1976b; and Greenblat, 1980.)

Orbach (1977) contends that more positive research findings will be obtained through designing theory-based game models specifically to attain previously specified outcomes. If the goal is attitudinal change, for instance, Orbach proposes that the design model would need, built into the *roles,* the kinds of behavioral expectations likely to produce the desired identifications. Greenblat (1975e, 1980) also calls for more attention to the design process, and suggests that some general taxonomy of games is needed to enable designers to relate game components to specific goals. Lester and Stoil (1979) reasoned that such a taxonomy might be provided by classifying simulations as "role-specific" (those in which roles directly correspond to real-world roles) or "role-general" (noncorrespondence of game and real-world roles), each of which is thought to have quite different instructional purposes. Factual learning, they speculated, should require that the simulation be role-specific, while comprehension of general principles and relationships might be more effectively induced through the role-general simulation. They designed a role-specific simulation on international ocean resource issues for an introductory course in international political economy, and compared its effects on student knowledge, motivation, and course evaluation with a nonsimulation control group. (They did not, however, compare outcomes from the role-specific simulation with any role-general simulation experience.) The "knowledge" measure was a pretest, posttest, 18-item, multiple-choice instrument dealing with diplomatic process issues and factual knowledge of ocean politics. Course evaluations were (as usual!) higher in the simulation experience; however, gains in scores on *process* learning were greater for the simulation group, while the control group showed more gain in substantive information—outcomes directly opposite those expected. The authors see a need for further study of the proposed typology and suggest another: the classification of simulations as predominantly active participation/predominantly passive participation.

Williams's (1980) efforts to demonstrate that improvements in the design process, including more satisfactory synthesis of game theory and learning theory, will result in demonstrably better outcome assessment are discussed below.

GROUP VARIABLES

It is probably the case with all pedagogical techniques, including simulation-gaming and other experiential exercises, that decisions about group size are more often made on the basis of expediency than on any consideration of how best to facilitate learning. To ascertain the extent to which the considerable body of research on group size and learning might apply to the simulation experience, Gentry (1980) investigated the relationship between group size and various attitudinal and performance variables in three undergraduate business logistics classes. There was a positive relationship between group size and amount of dissension in the group, but no relationship between group size and game performance. Group performance was more satisfactorily explained by the quality of the group's leadership than by its size. Since the larger the group, the higher its probability of getting a talented leader, Gentry speculates that more effective leadership in large groups may have overshadowed any disadvantages to performance from high dissension, as well as any advantage inherent in small group size.

Greenblat (1980) calls for researchers to give more attention to the dynamics of groups, including their negative as well as positive effects on members, and the effects of members' triadic role set as simultaneously being players of simulation roles, players in a game, and students in a class.

There is some evidence (for example, Remus, 1977) that winners and losers have different attitudes toward a game, both in terms of enjoyment and of perceived learning. What students learn from STARPOWER is likely to be much influenced by their luck of the draw in becoming members of the Square, Circle, or Triangle groups, each of which has very different experiences of success and failure in the game. One observes Squares becoming progressively more animated and involved, while the Triangles tend to display increasing alienation and sometimes outright hostility. (Variations occur; one of us recalls a Triangle group which developed strong group cohesiveness and a song, "We have more fun in the Ghetto.") Whether success in a game is determined individually or according to some criterion of grouping, Remus (1977) may be correct in regarding outcomes of "rank" in competitive success as a major source of uncontrolled error in simulation-gaming research and a possible explanation for inconclusive or negative results in many studies.

No significant effects of sociometric grouping have yet been discerned in the few studies so far undertaken. Brand (1980) investigated the effects of two sociometric variables on fifth-grade learning from simulation-gaming: mutual selection of partners and membership in a cohesive group. The results corresponded to those of Fletcher (1971b); pretest and posttest measures confirmed that learning had occurred from the activity but it was not related to the sociometric variables. Norris and Niebuhr (1980) found a correlation between group cohesiveness and gaming performance, but cautioned that cohesiveness might have been an effect rather than a cause, possibly increasing for winners and decreasing for losers as the game progressed. No effects were found on either cohesiveness or performance of voluntary, as compared to assigned, group membership.

The Nature of the Persons

In addition to the effects of the variety of "shapes" a simulation-gaming experience may provide, experiences in a given game are also likely to be affected by various characteristics of the learners themselves. As already noted, the less the instructor structures what is to be learned, the greater the scope left for personal characteristics of the players to determine what is learned. Indeed, researchers tend to agree that the inconsistent findings of past research on simulation-gaming outcomes may result in part from the varying effects of a game on different players (see Fletcher, 1971, 1971b; Edwards, 1971, 1971b; Greenblat, 1980). Characteristics such as attitudes toward the game (Remus, 1977), attitudes of players prior to the game (Lee and O'Leary, 1971), personal relationships among players (Babb et al., 1966), prior acquaintance with other players (Livingston et al., 1973), and sex of the players (Fletcher, 1971b) have been found to affect game performance and/or outcomes. Most recent research has focused on one or more of three sets of learner characteristics: (1) personality variables, (2) cognitive style variables, and (3) the relationship between game ability and academic ability.

PERSONALITY VARIABLES

A major difficulty in simulation-gaming outcome assessment has been the failure of most researchers to take account of the fact that some students learn from games while others do not, and therefore to treat individual differences in outcomes as error variance. Pratt et al. (1980), using the Myers-Briggs "Thinking/Feeling" scale as the measure of individual differences, explored the effects of this variable on perceptions of personal participation, group functioning, and effectiveness of seven simulations/games or simulations. Persons scoring high on the "Feeling" dimension perceived themselves as participating more, and expressed more positive attitudes toward group functioning and the game as a learning experience than did those scoring high on the "Thinking" dimension. No other outcome measures were used. Schneier (1976) reports finding relationships between personal characteristics of players and attitudes toward the simulation-gaming experience. The relationship between these attitudes and the cognitive/affective learnings that occur remains to be explored.

COGNITIVE STYLE VARIABLES

Among those investigating the relationship between cognitive style and a variety of possible learning outcomes from simulation-gaming are DeNike (1973), Fletcher (1971b), Edwards (1971b), and Johnson and Stratton (1978). Lee and O'Leary (1973) found with the simulation game INTER-NATION that those who seemed to gain least from the experience differed from those who gained most in displaying less empathy, preferring symbolic methods of learning (reading and writing) to listening and experiencing, and liking independent work more than group interaction.

The underexplored variables of personal and cognitive style would seem to merit considerable research focus, as they may provide the key to matching learners with the appropriate educational treatment or to altering simulation-gaming circumstances to increase learning for resistant participants. In an extensive review of the research on the general effectiveness of schools, Averch et al. (1972) concluded that a major reason for the failure of educational research to show a positive relationship between treatment and outcomes is the failure to match student characteristics with specific modes of instruction.

GAME ABILITY AND ACADEMIC ABILITY

There is a growing body of evidence that game ability may differ in significant ways from other academic abilities which rely heavily on the capacity to think abstractly or on verbal ability. Researchers have found varying degrees of relationship between the two variables, very likely due to the varying criteria used to assess "performance," as well as the differences in the *nature* of the performance required by different games. Livingston et al. (1973), for instance, found that high-ability students were more successful in drawing analogies from GHETTO to the real world, and Vance and Gray (1967) found students' grade point averages strongly correlated with their performance on a business game, while Braskamp and Hodgetts (1971) found a negative correlation of $-.37$ between students' grade point averages and their performance on a business simulation game. Estes (1980), using a computerized simulation in a basic management course, found considerable difference between students earning "A" on the simulation and those earning "A" in the course, even though the simulation grade counted as one-fourth of the course grade. There were more "Fs" on the simulation than on the course itself; one student earned "A" in the course with a simulation grade below 20 (100 being the highest possible score). The performance measure in this case was effectiveness of decision-making in earning points for one's team.

Other evidence that different abilities may be required for game performance is provided by Seginer's (1980) study of preadolescent boys in Israel using the simulation game GENERATION GAP. The game was selected for its procedural ease and its differentness from traditional instruction. The study assessed the effects of SES, verbal/logical cognitive abilities, and self-esteem on game ability (competence and comprehension) and academic ability (verbal and mathematical). Correlations between the measures of game ability and academic ability were low, although significant at the .05 level. An important finding of this study is that game performance was less dependent on social background than was academic performance. Seginer (1980: 419) specifies the respects in which game ability may differ from academic ability: (1) the cognitive processes involved may be ability to perceive relationships rather than language command; (2) it is more independent from self-perceptions of competence and control; and (3) it is not directly affected by social background. Although noting the need for further research in other settings, Seginer suggests that simulation-gaming may be a promising avenue to reduce some of the conventional classroom advantages of high SES students.

Seginer's findings lend support to Coleman's (1970) view that simulation-gaming may be particularly effective in teaching disadvantaged students whose language skills are not well developed. Seginer sheds light on the commonly observed phenomenon that students in simulation situations often develop and use successful strategies that they cannot verbalize. For these strategies to "pay off" in the long-run academic competition, however, would obviously require that instructors be aware of, and utilize in a variety of ways, the different cognitive and affective abilities identified by researchers, and that they use assessment tools and techniques which in fact tap these resources.

HOW CAN WE BE SURE?

These issues are intimately related to the methodological problems of assessment and to the continuing discrepancy between directors' and participants' impressionistic evidence and subjective reports on one hand, and "objective," "hard," or "psychometric" evidence on the other. A case that illustrates nearly all the issues in the methodological debate is Megarry's (1979) criticism of Jackson's (1979) research.

Jackson had 272 Australian students play BAFÁ BAFÁ and STARPOW-

ER. Megarry's description (1979: 170) gives the flavor of the debate: the participants were "subjected to a test of eleven demographic items in addition to Preliminary Tests, Post Tests, and Retention Tests (50-item, two-choice questionnaires). The article is 'supported' by sixty references (including one to document the state of the weather at the time of the Preliminary Test!)."

The results were drearily familiar; 4 out of 26 hypotheses were statistically supported. Jackson considered the conclusion "inescapable" that the games had little effect on attitudes, cognitions, and affect; and then tried, as Megarry enjoys pointing out, to escape it anyway by pointing to the "sharp contrast" between those findings and "the impressionistic evidence reported by all concerned" of students' "favorable reactions" and "degree of awareness manifested in the debriefings." Jackson (1979: 134) considers two possible explanations: (1) the problem may lie in faulty conceptual linkage between the experiences of the games and the measures used, and (2) students' *liking* the experience may not necessarily mean they *learned* anything from it.

Megarry's (1979: 171) inference from this typical study is that "the black-box input/output style of evaluation" needs to give way to "a wide-ranging, responsive, qualitative evaluation which studies process as well as product." (For related discussions of this issue, see Boocock and Schild, 1968; Foster et al., 1980; Greenblat, 1975e, 1980; Pierfy, 1977; Remus, 1981; McGinley, 1980.)

We think the matter should be put a little differently. There are two separate questions. One is what to study—for example, "process" or "product" (and, of course, *what* process and *what* product). The other is how to study it. The first is a theoretical-conceptual problem to which we return below. The second is a methodological problem. The two are too often confused by vocabularies of "psychometric" versus "qualitative," or "objective" versus "subjective."

If there is a theory (the first problem) about the impact of some simulation-gaming experience as compared to some other experience, the theory may refer either to a process or a product, which is to say, to something within the "black box" or to some "output." Whatever it refers to must dictate the kind of evidence needed to determine whether the impact occurred differentially or not. If, for example, one supposes that BAFÁ BAFÁ provides a more vivid experience of culture shock than does reading an ethnographic account, one obviously must devise some measure of culture shock and of "vividness." Whether that measure should be an intensive interview, a semantic differential, a galvanic skin response, or the like, may be debatable (and will be settled only by research), but the issue is certainly not simply one of "qualitative" versus "psychometric." Then, of course, whether those who do experience culture shock subsequently become more or less curious about foreign cultures or more or less accepting of others' differentness from themselves are still other matters requiring still other measures.

The general point is a familiar but frequently ignored one: that what should be measured is what the theory (originating from whatever impressions) precisely says will be an effect; and how it should be measured depends on what it is.

WHAT SHOULD BE MEASURED?

Modifying Greenblat's (1975e) classification of "claims" for the effects of simulations/games, we have identified three major categories of dependent variables that are often said to be affected. One is substantive learning, which may be either cognitive or affective/evaluative learning, and may entail learning about the self or about some external subject or phenomenon. A second concerns motivation to learn something, and a third concerns the nature of student-teacher relations—what might be called the "atmosphere" of learning. The last two claims usually, at least implicitly, are linked to the further hypothesis that motivation and atmosphere affect substantive learning. However, this latter hypothesis is rarely, if ever, investigated.

Substantive Learning

COGNITIVE SUBJECT MATTER LEARNING

One claim of simulation-gaming advocates is that the method experientially teaches facts, concepts, and procedures more effectively than conventional techniques. Greenblat (1975e), in reviewing the claims and evidence, suggests that games may be more effective in teaching principles, procedures, and concepts than in teaching facts. Hearn (1980) speculates about their possible efficacy in removing learning blocks, facilitating preparation for examinations, and providing linkage for various course concepts.

As noted earlier, there is a substantial body of testimonial and impressionistic evidence in support of these claims (see Bredemeier, 1978, 1981; Rosen, 1981; Tiene, 1981); but the "hard" evidence favors simulation-gaming over conventional methods only with respect to *retention* of what is learned. Approximately as many comparative studies report superior subject matter learning from simulation-gaming over conventional classroom methods as report the reverse; the majority of studies to date have found no significant differences.

Pierfy (1977) reviewed 22 research reports on experiments with social studies simulations/games which compared their effects with those of con-

ventional instruction on a variety of learning outcomes, including two measures of cognitive achievement: acquisition of facts and retention. The
results of 3 studies showed significant differences in favor of simulation-
gaming as a technique for acquisition of facts and principles; 3 found the
differences in favor of conventional methods; and 15 found no significant
differences. Table 1 provides the relevant information (adapted from Pierfy,
1977: 258-259).

Of the studies surveyed by Pierfy, 11 assessed *retention* by administering
the posttest a second time, considerably after the first administration. Of
these, 8 found retention significantly better with simulation/gaming, while
three found no difference. The 8 studies, and games used, were: (1) Baker
(1968), AMERICAN PRE-CIVIL WAR PERIOD; (2) Curry and Brooks
(1971), LIFE CAREER; (3) Johnson and Euler (1972), LIFE CAREER; (4)
Keach and Pierfy (1972), SAILING AROUND THE WORLD; (5) Lucas et
al. (1974), FARMING, PROMOTION, THE CITIES GAME; (6) Postma
(1973), FARMING, PROMOTION, THE CITIES GAME; (7) Riegel
(1969), ECONOMIC DECISION GAMES; and (8) Wing (1968), SUMER.
The three "no difference" studies were: Garvey and Seiler (1966), INTER-
NATION; Johnson and Euler (1972), LIFE CAREER; and Wing (1968),
SIERRA LEONE.

In more recent studies, Shade and Paine (1975) found more effective
transfer of information through simulation than through conventional
methods, and Allen et al. (1978, 1979) have shown in several experiments
that playing EQUATIONS as part of the regular classroom curriculum improves both math achievement and attitudes toward school. Szafran and
Mandolini (1980) assessed the effects of SIMSOC on two types of cognitive
knowledge: objective test performance and concept recognition. As compared with the control group, SIMSOC participants showed a slight but not
significant negative difference in test performance and a slight, positive,
nonsignificant difference in concept recognition.

In sum, the available evidence suggests that simulations/games are at
least as effective as other methods in facilitating subject matter learning and
are more effective aids to retention.

AFFECTIVE SUBJECT MATTER LEARNING

Simulation games are widely believed to have great potential in the area
of affective learning; it seems plausible that experiencing the worlds of
others would be more effective than traditional teaching methods for increasing empathy and might lead to changed perspectives and orientations.

Assessments of the effects of simulation-gaming on attitudes show, as
Jackson (1979: 102) puts it, a "checkered" pattern. Cherryholmes (1966)
found, in a review of six studies, no evidence for greater simulation-gaming

effectiveness in changing attitudes. Pierfy (1977) found, however, that in eight of eleven studies which investigated attitude change, simulation-gaming was more effective than conventional instruction. Pierfy identifies the nature of the change as being in the direction of greater empathy and "realism." The studies and games used were: Baker (1968), AMERICAN PRE-CIVIL WAR PERIOD; Boocock (1963), ELECTION CAMPAIGN GAME; Curry and Brooks (1971), LIFE CAREER; Lee and O'Leary (1971), INTER-NATION; Newman (1974), SUNSHINE; Stadsklev (1969), CONSTITUTION TODAY; Targ (1967), INTER-NATION; and Vogel (1973), CITY COUNCIL. The three "no difference" studies and games used were: Alley and Gladhart (1975), MAYORAL ELECTION GAME; Boocock et al. (1967), LIFE CAREER, DEMOCRACY; and Garvey and Seiler (1966), INTER-NATION.

Reid (1979) reports the effective use of simulation-gaming in developing attitudes of awareness and appreciation regarding science education in a study involving 1100 14-16-year-old British students. Shade and Paine (1975) found that declines in political cynicism were produced more effectively through simulation than through conventional teaching methods. Livingston and Kidder (1973) also report changing political attitudes of high school students with DEMOCRACY. GHETTO (Livingston et al., 1973) and STARPOWER (Chapman, 1974) are reported to have been more successful than traditional instruction in changing racist or sexist attitudes.

The "checkered pattern" persists, however. Jackson's (1979) research with BAFÁ BAFÁ and STARPOWER revealed no significant difference in attitude change between treatment and comparison groups. Some studies have shown evidence of negative attitude change, such as increased pessimism and cynicism toward the urban poor from playing GHETTO (Kidder and Aubertine, 1972). Williams (1980), hypothesizing that more effective synthesis of game and learning theories would result in more effective attitude change and better research results, tried to achieve the "union with theory" called for by Smith (1972). Williams's two experimental groups were an "incentive" group (motivated by expected "reward" for attitude change) and a "dissonance" group (motivated by the need to change attitudes to reduce cognitive dissonance); 109 college students were randomly assigned to these groups and to a control group. Subjects represented villainous medieval nobles (about whom they had previously read in a short history of a fictitious conflict) in a 20-minute simulation game. *All three* groups showed significant positive attitude change, with no significant differences between the two experimental groups. Williams's interpretation of this puzzling result is that *identification with the role* superseded either dissonance or incentive in the two experimental groups as the controlling variable. After taking account of a variety of complicating factors, Williams

(1980: 194) concludes that (1) the major hypothesis of the study was supported, and (2) both experimental conditions were more successful than the control condition in changing attitudes.

The available evidence thus suggests that, under certain circumstances and for some students, simulation-gaming can be more effective than traditional methods of instruction in facilitating positive attitude change toward the subject and its purposes.

LEARNING ABOUT THE SELF

Game directors and researchers often find that participants in a simulation/game report a variety of self-integrating outcomes, including tension release, receipt of valuable affective feedback from others or from the experience of the game, increased self-awareness, and greater sense of personal power or self-confidence (Bligh, 1972; Bredemeier, 1978, 1981; Rosen, 1981; Tiene, 1981). Lee and O'Leary (1971) found students reporting more confidence in their decision-making abilities and tolerance for ambiguity after a simulation experience. On the other hand, players who do not do well in the game, who are overly sensitive to others' disapproval, or who have difficulty playing roles sometimes report negative affect (Taylor and Walford, 1972).

Johnson and Nelson (1978) report on some promising outcomes of simulation/game playing with juvenile delinquents. Their research subjects were 14 male first offenders between 12 and 15 years of age, randomly assigned to control and experimental groups. Three games of rapport—ROLES, JUSTIFICATION, and PENALTIES—were played with the experimental group in an effort to improve communication between clients and counselor. Experimental subjects, although not perceiving themselves as having increased self-awareness from playing the games, showed significantly greater positive change than the control group in willingness to communicate, according to observations of counselors and scores on the "Unwillingness to Communicate" scale which correlates with apprehension, anomia, and alienation.

Motivation to Learn

In course evaluations, students frequently mention the simulation-gaming experience as outstanding, report high satisfaction with the course, express appreciation of knowledge gained about simulation-gaming as an instructional technique, and perceive the experience as having stimulated their motivation and interest. Numerous studies support the impressionistic and testimonial evidence. Reviews of the literature and/or research by Cherryholmes (1966), Chartier (1972), Taylor and Walford (1972), Brenenstuhl (1975a), Orbach (1977), and Jackson (1979) provide documentation for the alleged motivational outcomes of simulation-gaming. In seven of eight studies reviewed by Pierfy (1977), which compared student interest in the simulation-gaming treatment with interest in the standard "control" treatment, significantly greater interest is reported to have been stimulated by the simulation-gaming approach. The studies and games used are: Boocock (1963), ELECTION CAMPAIGN GAME; Clements (1970), MONEY AND CREDIT MANAGEMENT; Keach and Pierfy (1972), SAILING AROUND THE WORLD; Lee and O'Leary (1971), INTER-NATION; Newman (1974), SUNSHINE; Postma (1973), FARMING, PROMOTION, THE CITIES GAME; and Stadsklev (1969), CONSTITUTION TODAY. The remaining study, by Johnson and Euler (1972), using LIFE CAREER, found no significant difference in interest development between the simulation/game and comparative treatments.

Little is reported about the "whys" of motivation and interest stimulation by simulation games. Interest appears to depend on a variety of interactive variables, including learner style, person-role fit, rank in outcome of competition, and many other factors about which further research is needed (Orbach, 1977). Remus's (1977) answers to his own question, "Who likes business games?" is "the winners!"

Learning Atmosphere

The claim that simulation games change classroom structure and relations may be closely related both to claims regarding their success as motivational tools and to claims that they alter the character of later course work. Greenblat (1975e) identifies three claims often made for changes in the character of course work: (1) it becomes more meaningful; (2) students participate more openly and vigorously; and (3) the quality of inquiry is more incisive. Boydell (1976) speculates that the experiential learning that occurs in a simulation enables participants to generate ideas, to see, feel, and interact with meaningful problems, experiences which may provide a motivational link between past, present, and future cognitions and affect. Bredemeier (1978), Tiene (1981), and Rosen (1981) provide current anecdotal reports on changes in classroom structure and relations which include more relaxed atmosphere, reduced social distance, and more open and vigorous communications. Roberts (1975) compared experimentally the effects of conventional lecture and classroom games formats in the introductory American government course, and reported more relaxed social relationships among students and between students and instructor as a major positive outcome.

It is possible, of course, that some of the changes in classroom atmosphere and social relations attributed to the simulation-gaming experience may result from differences in teaching styles and personalities between instructors amenable to the use of simulation-gaming and those who are not. Are people who use simulation-gaming likely to be people who stimulate relaxed classrooms? The variable of *instructor* style and personality in affecting simulation-gaming outcomes merits some attention from researchers.

SUMMARY

We do not yet have (1) a theoretically based taxonomy of games with (2) clear theories about (a) what aspects of them are expected to have (b) what sorts of distinct effects (c) on what sorts of students (d) for what reasons. Until these tasks are addressed, we shall probably continue to see results of investigations about "effectiveness" that are inconsistent, ambiguous, and nondefinitive in support or revision of widespread "impressions."

It is not likely that many of the antecedent or intervening conditions and contingencies mentioned in this review as possibly contaminating relationships can be controlled. That probably makes imperative the urging by Remus (1981) and Campbell and Boruch (1975) that subjects be randomly assigned to experimental and control conditions as a way of controlling for the possible contamination. Even then, however, it would seem desirable to include "turnover" analyses of the data, rather than to rely only on comparisons of group averages, to explore the possibility of differential canceling effects on different students. No methodological or technical refinements of data analysis, however, are likely to substitute for the first request of careful specification of the theoretical reason for expecting any effects at all.

CHAPTER FIFTEEN

GROUP DYNAMICS AND GAME DESIGN:

Some Reflections

CATHY STEIN GREENBLAT

When I first saw the theme for the 1980 ISAGA conference—"How to Design a Simulation Game"—I immediately thought of attending, for game design is the primary area of my gaming interests these days. Hopes of attendance were accompanied by thoughts of making a presentation. Shortly thereafter I received an invitation from Dr. Bruin in behalf of the organizing committee, with a specific request that seemed to make the task of preparing a paper even easier. They suggested that I first summarize what I had written a number of years ago about the claims made for learning with simulations and the evidence (or lack of it) to support these claims. They then proposed that I indicate the implications of this for game design. It did not seem a difficult undertaking; after all, I was to review my own earlier writing, and take the material one step further.

But my initial optimism about the ease of the task was diminished when I reread the paper. I started to see holes in the formulation I had presented and more problems in the way those concerned with the design, use, and evaluation of gaming had examined the enterprise.

The first part of the original paper (Chapter 13) was based on a review of books, published and unpublished articles and monographs, newsletters, and advertisements from games publishers. Implicit and explicit propositions found in these materials were extracted and organized into six general categories: motivation and interest in the subject matter, cognitive learning, changes in the character of later course work, affective learning about the

AUTHOR'S NOTE: The author wishes to express her thanks to Dr. Mary Bredemeier for her helpful comments and criticisms while this paper was being written, and to the Rutgers University Research Council for providing funds toward attendance at the ISAGA meetings.

subject matter, general affective learning, and changes in classroom structure and relations. The claims were phrased in simple descriptive form—for
example, "participation in simulation games generates greater interest in the
topics simulated"—but I noted that almost all had explicit or implicit counterparts which were comparative: for example, "participation in simulation
games generated greater interest in the topics simulated; this increment in
interest is larger than the increment with other modes of teaching." Due to
space limitations, only the descriptive form was offered; the reader was
urged to add the comparative form to each entry.

Since some of you are newly entering the game field, let me present that
list here. It suggests all those things people thought might happen to students
or other participants in games. Probably nobody thought all these would
happen, but the list was surely suggestive of the degree of optimism among
gamers. If anything, it seemed too long, rather than incomplete, at the time I
wrote it (Greenblat, 1975e).

(1) Motivation and interest
  (a) Participation in simulation games is itself interesting and involving.
  (b) Participation in simulation games increases interest in the topics simu-
      lated.
  (c) Participation in simulation games increases interest in the course in which
      the simulation is employed.
  (d) Participation in simulation games increases interest, enthusiasm, and
      commitment to learning in general.
(2) Cognitive learning
  (a) Participants in simulation games gain factual information.
  (b) Participants in simulation games acquire explicit referents for concepts
      used to describe human behavior; abstract concepts such as "organi-
      zation," "power," "stratification," and "negotiation" take on concrete
      meaning.
  (c) Participants in simulation games learn procedural sequences. "The actors
      must, of course, learn the rules, comprehend the essential features of the
      environment, understand the implications of the alternatives open to
      them, and develop increasingly elaborate strategies. They must be taught
      to operate the simulated system, in this instance in the hope that they will
      acquire a better concept of the larger system through a highly concentrated
      experience" (Meier, 1967: 157).
  (d) Participants in simulation games learn general principles of the subject
      matter simulated (such as the need for social control, good communica-
      tions, and long-range planning).
  (e) Simulation games provide simplified worlds from which students can
      stand back and understand the structure of the everyday, "real" world.
      "Games seem to display in a simple way the structure of real-life situa-
      tions. They cut us off from serious life by immersing us in a demonstration
      of its possibilities. We return to the world as gamesmen, preparing to see
      what is structural about reality and ready to reduce life to its liveliest
      elements" (Goffman, 1961: 34).

(f) Participants in simulation games gain in explicitness: "The capacity to identify consciously elements of a problem in an analytic or technical sense."

(g) Participants in simulation games learn a systematic analytical approach.

(h) Participants in simulation games learn better decision-making skills.

(i) Participants in simulation games learn "winning strategies" in those situations simulated.

(3) Changes in the character of later course work

(a) Participation in simulation games makes later work (such as lectures, reading) more meaningful.

(b) Participation in simulation games leads students to more sophisticated and relevant inquiry, for discussion of the simulation leads to questions about real-world analogies.

(c) Class discussions following a simulation will involve greater participation by class members, as they will have had shared experience.

(4) Affective learning re: subject matter

(a) Participation in simulation games leads to changed perspectives and orientations (for example, attitudes toward various public and world issues, attitudes toward the importance of collective versus individual action, attitudes toward deviant lifestyles).

(b) Participation in simulation games leads to increased empathy for others (such as national decision makers, ghetto residents) and increased insight into the way the world is seen by them.

(c) Participation in simulation games leads to increased insight into the predicaments, pressures, uncertainties, and moral and intellectual difficulties of others (such as decision makers, ghetto residents).

(5) General affective learning

(a) Participants in simulation games gain increased self-awareness.

(b) Participants in simulation games gain a greater sense of personal efficacy and potency.

(6) Changes in classroom structure·and relations

(a) Use of simulation games promotes better student-teacher relations.

(b) Use of simulation games leads students to perceive greater freedom to explore ideas.

(c) Use of simulation games leads to students' becoming more autonomous, thus changing teacher-student relationships.

(d) Use of simulation games leads to students perceiving teachers more positively.

(e) Use of simulation games produces more relaxed natural exchange between students and teachers.

(f) Use of simulation games leads to increased knowledge of other students (by students) and greater peer acceptance (Abt, 1970: 121).

(g) Use of simulation games involves a diminishing of the teacher's role of judge and jury.

(h) Use of simulation games leads to teachers perceiving students more positively.

At the time, the list itself constituted a major contribution to the field, for previously claims were scattered in various locations and no one had offered a compendium of them, no less a full classification scheme. The paper continued with two further sections: a review of the evidence and a lengthy discussion of the methodological problems of games research. The major conclusion offered in the first of these sections was that there was very scanty data to support the claims that were offered. We knew more about some of the propositions than about others. For example, there were no data regarding the third category—changes in the character of later course work—and none for the last—changes in classroom structure and relations. The best evidence was for increased motivation and interest, which seemed to improve due to participation. And there was some evidence on cognitive learning and on affective learning about the subject matter, such as the development of greater empathy. Anecdotal reports were abundant; "hard data" were clearly lacking. A number of methodological problems in evaluation were then noted in a general section on problems plaguing the researcher, and urgings for future study.

One of the critical problems I pointed out at that time concerned the failure to view students as individuals or different learners. Student-players were considered a homogeneous collection:

> Finally, a general methodological shortcoming in the studies reviewed is the frequent lack of control for relevant student characteristics. In most instances, only scores for the total sample are reported. In many studies, such factors as sex of players and sex balance of groups, social class background of participants, intelligence, school records, and pregame motivations of participants are not employed as independent variables to examine the differential effects of participation on students varying in these characteristics, although some researchers have found them to be important. Robinson (1966) controlled for cognitive style, need for achievement, need for affiliation, and need for dominance in analyzing his data; such factors are suggestive of the nature of further differentiations that might be made in attempts to ascertain who learns what from simulation [Greenblat, 1975e: 280-281].

A few years later, when Dick Duke and I collaborated on the writing of *Gaming-Simulation: Rationale, Design, and Applications,* we reprinted that paper with an update by Frank Rosenfeld (1975). The conceptual scheme still held up, and a bit of progress had been made in establishing that games were effective for some pedagogical goals.

But in a paper written for that volume, I expressed some new concerns (Greenblat, 1975b). In a section on "Unanswered Questions," I suggested we needed to pay attention to such issues as the potential *harm* of bad simulations, the potential *harm* of bad games, to students who don't like and don't learn from games, to the effects of teacher or administrator inputs, to the timing of gaming experiences, and to the number of games used within a course. Some of these questions had not been raised in print before and, unfortunately, none had been adequately answered.

Again, I echoed concern about individual differences in learning, albeit in a slightly different form. In a section headed "How can we understand the asymmetrical learning experiences of students who participate in the same game?" the following statement appeared:

> Discussions of the experience of being a player seem to treat participation as a constant factor. Yet in most gaming-simulations, students are cast in very different simulated roles (e.g., poor person, city administrator, clergyman, etc.) with different goals, constraints, resources, etc., attached to them. By internal definition, then, the experiences are different, and it could be anticipated that the nature and extent of learning by those in different roles would differ. In good post-game discussions there is of course a sharing of experiences and perceptions, but it is unlikely that this vicarious experiencing can fully equalize the differential learning. Attention thus must be directed to understanding and dealing with asymmetrical learning from the same gaming-simulation [Greenblat, 1975b: 191].

And then I made what I think was an important point, which I immediately dropped, not knowing where to take it at that time:

> The problem of differential learning is compounded when we consider that the participant is really in three simultaneous roles: in addition to playing the simulated role, students are players in a game and students in a class. Those writing about games often ignore the latter two or assume that they are of no importance. Yet either of these may be dominant at any particular time and may seriously affect the learning that transpires. Add to this the effects of peer pressure, and the complications in understanding what is happening are magnified further. Teachers and researchers can ill afford to ignore the "treble role" of players and must try to understand the factors contributing to dominance of one or the other at any given time [Greenblat, 1975b: 191-192].

Some of you are probably hoping (and I wish it were true) that today I am going to go back to these points—the evidence in general support of the claims and the problem of failure to look at individual learner differences—and indicate how much has been learned since that time, and what implications it has for game designers. Unfortunately, I do not believe that much additional evidence has been accumulated, and those studies that have been done have suffered many of the problems of the early studies (problems which I now realize are much more generic to the type of research and derive to a large degree from educational politics and problems of support rather than from the limited insight or sophistication of the researchers).

But I have also found some problems in my own formulation. Think for a moment of the last point I made: that students are in a treble role—the simulated role, a player in a game, and a student in the class. The focus and concern of game designers has been generally only on the first or on the first and second. That is, we concern ourselves with the quality and qualities of the simulated role: Is it realistic? Are players given the correct resources? Are the constraints on action similar to the real-world role player's constraints? When we look at the student as a player in a game, we concern ourselves with such questions as: Are the instructions clear? Is the game interesting for people in different roles? Is the tempo fast enough? Is there enough feedback?

But we neglect the third dimension: The student/player is also a student in a class. Thus, not only must the pregame factors suggested above be taken into consideration in evaluative studies, but we must think about them when we design and employ the games. And more critically, we must think about how game performance and learning might affect postgame relationships.

In the early formulation, speculations were offered about the effect on classroom structure and relations, but the list now seems to me to be incomplete. Furthermore, like the earlier propositions, these were all phrased positively. While the phrasing of the claims on attitude change allowed the possibility of negative change (it only said participants would change their attitudes), the claims about cognitive learning posited increased learning (nobody suggested that participation might lead to greater confusion than had existed before), and the items about general affective learning talked of increased self-awareness and increased potency, but did not mention the possibility of negative self-esteem, lowered morale, or a decrease in one's sense of efficacy as possible results of participation in games. In the last proposition (on class structure and relations), it was assumed that participation would make no difference (the null hypothesis), or that it would improve relations within the class.

If my earlier concerns were that we thought of students as homogeneous, I realize now that we nonetheless thought of them as individual learners in the classroom. But each player also has that role as a student in a class, and a class is not just a collection of independent individuals. Prior to introduction of the game, there are patterns of like and dislike, trust and distrust among students and between students and the teacher. Some of these are based on "personality" factors; some are based on race, religion, ethnicity, or gender; some are based on demonstrated competence and achievement. There are also elaborate ways students develop and maintain "reputations" with each other and with the teacher. And a game, it seems to me, may challenge and affect these relationships and reputations, for better or for worse.

Yet, nowhere in the list of claims is there attention to such factors as the student's self-concept as a learner, as competent or incompetent in a number of areas (only general feelings of potency are mentioned); no attention is paid to relationships between students, to liking or disliking, trusting or distrusting them, to better understanding of other players as people—for example, more knowledge of who they are and what they think and believe. Neither is attention paid to responses to particular social categories players/ students represent (not in their simulated roles, but in real life). For example, what if members of a minority group perform poorly and are seen as the cause of failure of one's group. Do players make generalizations from that? What if there is high competition between players? What does this mean in terms of postgame interpersonal relationships?

The initial claims now strike me as incomplete—as naive in their assumption that if interpersonal relations were affected, they would be affected in a positive way. It is like the early hypotheses about the effects of interethnic or interracial contact: if only people would get to know one another better, there would be more harmony. We now know that is not the necessary outcome. Similarly, we should think about the hypothesis that gaming will improve interpersonal relations in the classroom and ask "under what conditions?"

Those interested in gaming have perhaps gone further than many other educators in recognizing the potential of group effects. They have taken to heart theories and data about the social nature of learning, and have attempted to structure classroom experiences in which students learn from one another. Seymour Sarason (1971: 190) urged:

> By and large, however, teachers do not think in terms of how a group can be organized and utilized so that as a group it plays a role in relation to the issues and problems that confront the group. . . . In their training teachers have been exposed, almost exclusively, to a psychology of learning that has one past and one present characteristic: the latter is its emphasis on how an individual organism learns, and the former is that the major learning theories were based on studies of the individual Norway rat. If instead of putting one rat in the maze they had put two or more in the maze, the history of American psychology would have been quite different. Conceivably, the social nature of learning might not need to be rediscovered.

Though we have tried to utilize group dynamics for learning, however, I think we have stopped too short in our reflections on the full implications of using the group. There are three main areas that I think we must more deeply concern ourselves with in designing games and later in using them. Let me present these briefly, and then expand upon each.

First, we know that groups are powerful agents of attitude change. Despite the paucity of evidence on attitude change from game participation, there is strong theoretical support for these claims, and research in other domains suggests that more careful study in gaming situations might well reveal this outcome. If so, we must direct careful attention to the values that are built into games, deliberately or inadvertently.

Second, there are a number of group dynamics outcomes to which we have paid insufficient attention. We have thought if we put several students together in a situation in which they must cooperate in order to successfully compete against other groups, we would foster better relationships. But researchers in other domains have noted that there may be negative results in terms of attitudes toward others and interpersonal relations from such group competition—especially in terms of members of groups that *lose*. Again, I note that this research is not research done in game situations. But it is perhaps even more important to us because some of our losers are such not by lower ability or less effort, but because we have deliberately given them unequal resources to win because their real-world counterparts have unequal resources. To simulate accurately, we have created conditions for failure in some groups and generated feelings of failure in attaining group goals or in "winning the game." But now, I suggest, we must ask what consequences this has for interpersonal relations in the classroom.

Third, we have often argued that a virtue of gaming is that students cannot be passive recipients of information from the teachers but must be active participants in the learning process. To be a more active participant, however, means the student must offer a "performance" to an audience of fellow students. In that performance, personal revelations will be made: the students may be required to reveal values or attitudes that could be kept to themselves in the traditional classroom. Or they may be forced to show their aptitude or ineptitude at various things to other students, as well as to the teacher. One's skills, knowledge, and values may thus become much more "public knowledge." I think we must ask about the personal consequences of this to the student, and ask how many protections we offer for the student who is threatened or hurt by making these revelations. I am not implying by these three concerns that they are problems in the pejorative sense. Rather, I am suggesting that group dynamics factors must be given more consideration than has been the case to the present.

One could, I suppose, argue that these concerns are for the teacher. I do not accept this. My stance has consistently been that game *designers* have a responsibility to both the operators and the participants in their games. They must be specific about what the game model is, about what outcomes are expected and which ones are possible, and must offer guidance about how to effectively employ the game and to what ends.

The remainder of this chapter is not an exhaustive review. Rather, it is an attempt to suggest the kinds of things we might think about in applying knowledge of group dynamics when designing and using games.

Let us look first at groups and attitude change and the implications for game designers. Michael Zey, a graduate student in sociology at Rutgers, has written a useful summary of some of the current literature on the potency of groups in influencing values and attitudes (Zey, 1979). Some researchers, studying adults in organizational settings, have noted that the formation of recruit peer groups increases the likelihood of successful organizational socialization (Evans, 1963). Becker (1963) claims that when a "cohort" group experiences the socialization program together, the outcomes are likely to be more uniform than if they had been processed individually, as the group serves as a mediating force and, on the primary level, acts as a direct socializing agent. Van Maanen (1976: 93) argues, "virtually all organizational members are part of a smaller group which constitutes a key source of learning."

Research in other contexts yields similar findings. In an analysis of several experiments in group behavior Kurt Lewin (1952) deduced a number of conditions necessary for the occurrence of attitude change in the individual. A main point of Lewin's argument is that a group procedure for changing social conduct is more effective than an individual method. Lewin (1952: 472) claimed that

> experience in leadership training and in many areas of re-education regarding alcoholism and delinquency indicate that it is easier to change the ideology and social practice of a small group handled together than of individuals.

He suggests that the individual is unwilling to depart too far from group standards, so that a group change will lead to an individual change—a claim reflected in later "reference group" literature.

Lewin had also observed experiments involving manipulation of food habits in laboratory settings, and had noticed that various lecture methods did not attain the desired value changes in the subject. He (1952: 463) argued:

> Lecturing is a procedure by which the audience is chiefly passive. The discussion, if conducted correctly, is likely to lead to a much higher degree of involvement. . . . . Although he may physically be part of a group listening to a lecture, for example, he finds himself psychologically speaking in an individual situation.

On the other hand, "If the group standard itself is changed, the resistance which is due to the relationship between individual and group standard is eliminated" (Lewin, 1952: 472).

E. H. Schein has expanded upon the process by which the participative group allows for value change in the individual. Basing his analysis on Lewin's process description, Schein refers to the "unfreezing" of a new member's old values which are at odds with the organization's values. In Schein's (1972) view, the organization provides a series of *upending* events which lead to the failure of the individual to receive confirmation of self. At this point, the subject is motivated to seek what Schein calls "psychological safety" by rearranging expectations and/or self-image. This theory is heavily based on the expectancy theories of Lewin, Fishbein, and Festinger, which see attitude change as primarily a social influence process relying on communication. Summing up a number of expectancy theory studies, Cohen (1964) states, "group decision may be effective, then, because it trades on the pressures in a group toward conformity to group norms . . . these pressures can help to bring about adherence to a new norm the group had adopted."

While this body of material provides continuing encouragement for investigating the claim that games are effective instruments of attitude change because they entail group dynamics, it also should support the need for caution. If simulations indeed do change attitudes, we must be clear about the direction and desirability of changes. Sarane Boocock, Garry Shirts, Nancy Glandon, and Jaquetta Megarry are only a few of the persons who have urged that we must pay careful attention to the value implications of games and to the type of attitudes they may foster.

At the ISAGA meetings in Caracas, John Gagnon and I presented a paper in which we argued that *no* games are value-neutral—all have the values of the designer built into them either explicitly or implicitly. That paper was published in a revised form in *Simulation & Games* (1979) [and as Chapter 10 in this volume] and thus I shall not take the time to reiterate the thesis. But I cannot emphasize too strongly my belief that since games seem to have the potential for attitude change, we must be very careful about the values we build into our games, we must make more sensitive and conscious decisions, and we must be much more explicit about these in the game manuals we prepare for users. There is no way to avoid the game being a form of "propaganda"; but at least we can be open about what it is advocating, so teachers and other operators can make *their* value judgments about whether to employ it. Hopefully, they will point out the game biases to participants so they, too, have greater freedom of choice.

My second area of concern is with the possible consequences of group activity in games for postgame interpersonal relations. A vast literature has arisen in the social sciences examining some of the interpersonal carry-overs of group participation under different conditions. For example, several researchers studying communication patterns in task-oriented groups have found that persons occupying central positions in communications networks, and hence participating more, had higher group morale than persons occupying more peripheral positions (Bavelas, 1950; Bavelas and Barrett, 1951; Leavitt, 1951). The same conclusion was reached in a number of industrial studies focusing on a special type of participation—namely, participation in decision-making activities (Coch and French, 1948). What are the implications of these findings for us, as we put students into roles in simulations in which, as I noted earlier, one finds both unequal participation and different degrees of decision-making?

Other important research has shown that it is not just putting people together in cooperative groups that is important, but how this group cooperation is rewarded and whether it leads to success.

James Michaels (1977) suggests that there are four "pure" types of reward allocation employed in schools:

(1) IC—Individual Competition. Here rewards are differentially allocated among individuals according to their *relative* performance (as when grades are given on a curve).
(2) GC—Group Competition. Here rewards are differentially allocated among groups according to their relative performance (and usually equally within the group).
(3) IRC—Individual Reward Contingencies. Each individual is compared with previously established standards to determine reward allocation.
(4) GRC—Group Reward Contingencies. In this case, each group is compared with previously established standards.

In the competition situations (IC and GC), there is negative reward interdependence among units, for standards are set by other competitors. With reinforcement, there is general independence among units, for standards are set by external units.

Michaels (1977) then reviews several studies that examine the relative effectiveness for academic performance—cognitive learning—and concludes that for students on the whole, Individual Competition is better than Group Competition, Individual Reward Contingencies seem to be about the same as Group Reward Contingencies, and Individual Competition is better than either Individual or Group Reward Contingencies for bringing about cognitive learning. Group Competition may be better than Group Reward Contingencies, but the evidence is incomplete. Table 15.1 summarizes these studies.

If we are concerned with cognitive learning, then we as game designers must pay attention to these findings. But Michaels also points out that while the *overall* superiority of individual competition appears clear, Individual Competition is not equally effective for many students, particularly the initially low performers. Thus, the traditional classroom reward structure, based on Individual Competition, may be largely restricted to the top third of the class, for these are the students who are apparently most responsive to it.

If we are going to claim that games are useful because they get everyone involved, then we must ask whether everyone is involved in a gaming situation based on individual competition. If so, perhaps we are putting old

TABLE 15.1 Summary of Reward Structure Comparisons

Study	Subjects	Task	Relative Effectiveness
Hamblin et al. (1971)	4th graders	Mathematics, reading, spelling	IRC – GRC[a]
Clifford (1971)	5th & 6th graders	Digit-letter substitutions	IC > IRC
Scott & Cherrington (1974)	College students	Test scoring	IC > GC = IRC
Julian & Perry (1967)	College students	Psychology lab exercises	IC > GC = GRC
Maller (1929)	5th–8th graders	Mathematics	IC > GC
Sims (1929) (Study 1)	College students	Digit-letter substitutions	IC > GC
Sims (1929) (Study 2)	College students	Reading	IC > GC
de Charms (1957)	College students	Mathematics, scrambled words	IC > GC
Michaels (1975)	College students	Mathematics	Females' performance (but not males') varied directly with differential rewardings.

a. IRC = individual reward contingency; GRC = group reward contingency; IC = individual competition; GC = group competition.
SOURCE: Michaels (1977: 94).

wine in new bottles, and will not really achieve our aim of reaching the harder-to-reach students who are not motivated by conventional techniques. Perhaps our games ought not contain a great deal of Individual Competition in order to be effective with them. Again, we must learn *who* learns most from games, not just overall impacts.

In addition, Michaels notes that both IC and IRC structures are relatively ineffective in strengthening such group process variables as collaboration and coordination, interpersonal attraction, and positive attitudes toward achievement. Group Competition and Group Reward Contingencies both have better success in these. That may be cause for some pleasure to us, since many games employ students in group situations, and thus we should be able to hypothesize possible gains in these areas.

But it is not that simple. While, as I have urged earlier, game designers have often built in small groups as elements in their games, it seems to me that these groups are usually in competition. In other words, the Group Competition reward structure is most typical. Furthermore, although groups are often in competition—for example, to get the most policies passed—their competition is not only based on the usual questions of different inabilities and efforts, but is further based on the differential resources of their simulated roles. For example, my group may consist of smart people who try hard, but we are playing ghetto residents and have far fewer resources than does the group playing the taxpayers' association. They are bound to get more policies passed, no matter what we do; thus, we are bound to lose in the competition.

The reason I worry about this is because several studies have concluded that the positive group relations outcomes mentioned above may derive not simply from group effort, but from the outcomes of the group cooperation, particularly whether there is success. Blanchard, Adelman, and Cook (1975: 1026) report that

> members of successful, face-to-face cooperating groups liked and respected their group-mates more than did members of similar but failing groups. . . .
> The satisfaction generated by group success (and the rewards accompanying success) is associated with those who are involved in the group activities. This reward generalization, or spread of affect, results in increased intermember attraction.

Furthermore, there was a *lowering* of respect and liking that occurred when members felt there was group failure.

These researchers suggest that in conditions of enforced desegregation in schools and industry, where interracial or interethnic groups are assembled, the degree of liking and respect versus dislike and diminished respect that results may depend upon whether groups that cooperate experience success or failure as a result of their efforts. We must take the same evidence and ask about the results for interpersonal and interethnic relations if we put students in games emphasizing group competition with only one group winning and others losing.

In another important paper, Weigel, Wiser, and Cook (1975) begin by noting that the results from a number of studies suggest that cooperative contact seems to promote constructive interethnic relations, while competitive contact seems to hinder them. The problem, they suggest (1975: 222-223) is that American schools generally produce a classroom atmosphere that is heavily loaded in the direction of rewarding competitive as opposed to cooperative behavior. While participation in cooperative groups may lead to more favorable evaluation of ingroup performance and more liking of ingroup members (Ferguson and Kelley, 1964), intergroup competition may lead to negative ratings of other-group members, and may redirect friendship choices after the competition (Sherif et al., 1955, 1961; Diab, 1970; Sussman and Weil, 1960). Blake and Mouton (1962), examining adult workshop groups, found that other-group representatives were rated less favorably than they had been earlier on traits like intelligence and maturity; this was only true, however, for ratings by members of the losing groups. To the extent, then, that we design games in which group competition is a major factor, we must be alert to these possible outcomes.

Weigel, Wiser, and Cook (1975) also asked about the effects of formation of groups which were not in competition with one another, but which approximated Michaels's conditions of Group Reward Contingencies—that is, where the standard was outside rather than relative, and thus several groups could experience success. They found that cross-ethnic hostilities were lower in classes with cooperative rather than competitive learning. More significantly, cross-ethnic helping was much higher. Thus, the experience led to a significant change in interethnic interaction (though not in interethnic attitude of friendship) even though the experimental group spent only a small portion of the day in such cooperative enterprises.

It seems to me that there are several ways we, as game designers, can utilize these findings. First, by knowing this, we can be more specific in our instructions to operators for postplay discussion. We must point out this possible effect of group competition, and strongly urge that they focus on these feelings in a debriefing session.

Second, where our concerns are with fostering better relations between students, we may wish to reduce the degree of intergroup competition in our games. One way to do this is to include multiple measures of success. For example, we could have students and operators judge success not simply in terms of whether a group won an election or passed more policies, but also on whether they argued effectively, made the best use of the resources that they had available, and so on. In such a fashion, more students and more groups might emerge from the experience with a sense of having been successful, and thus not taking on the positions and feelings typical of those who feel their efforts have led to failure. If success has consequences for self-esteem and intergroup relations, perhaps by creating more success we can foster more of those other elements.

A third possibility open to us is to stress far more the overall cooperative character of the class' simulation participation. We can emphasize the cooperative character of the enterprise, highlighting to students after play that while they may have competed with one another in their simulated roles, they have cooperated in making the simulated system "work." Perhaps the parallel is to a theatrical performance in which people have different parts to play. We can note that because some people experienced the frustration of inadequate resources or lesser power and acted on this in the way real-world persons act, we were able to reenact in the classroom a scenario that takes place all the time in the real world. Thus, a cooperative goal—making the game work, the simulation operate—could be emphasized over the competitive subgroup or individual goals within the game itself. This perhaps would undo some of the potential negative effects of individual and group competition and create greater cohesion in the class, which as one large group could feel successful.

Finally, we can strive to design more games in which groups work in tandem, rather than in competition. The frame games Dick Duke and I designed—*Impasse?, At Issue,* and *The Conceptual Mapping Game* (Duke and Greenblat, 1979)—are examples of games that operate by principles of Group Reward Contingencies.

In summary, if competition in the game frequently results in a sense of failure for most students, and if a sense of failure is counterproductive with regard to promoting attraction and favorable attitudes toward others, then we must find procedures which assure many winners rather than many losers if we wish positive interpersonal outcomes.[1]

Finally, let me briefly mention the problem of personal consequences of participation in games. In Chapter 13 I noted the following:

> Where involvement is high and manifested by severe frustration, anger, depression and so on, are these "costs" to students that must be weighed against the gains? And how do these costs compare to those stemming from the frustration, anger, and depression created when students are "talked at," kept still and obedient, and the like in the regular classroom?

While I still believe this is a real and important question, I think there is another side to it. In the traditional classroom students can keep much of their feelings and attitudes private. One can reveal as much or as little as one wants, unless the teacher calls upon one to answer a question (and several studies have suggested that—at least at the college level—faculty generally do not call on students unless they volunteer). In a game, however, one must reveal much more. In some games, one is asked to reveal one's own values and attitudes; in others, one is given a role profile and asked to argue and act in terms of values and attitudes that are spelled out.

Eliezer Orbach (1977: 356) has argued that this is a salient characteristic of games designed to create attitude change. Urging that for attitude change games must have high degrees of role play, he continues: "What is an adequate set for role play simulation then? I suggest that an adequate set up is one that ensures the expression of personal opinion and feelings on the part of all game participants." Thus, in *The Marriage Game* (Greenblat et al., 1977) players are asked to express their personal values; in other games they are told that they should play to maximize certain values such as keeping the neighborhood free of "undesirable elements," increasing their own power, or keeping women in subservient positions.

But recall my urging that before, during, and after play players are students in a class. We are forced, I believe, to ask what costs they may pay by making these revelations. Is it an invasion of privacy? May the things they reveal about their "real selves" jeopardize their relations with classmates? We may argue that "openness" and "honesty" and "truth" are important, but do students have the right to decide how much openness and honesty and truth they want in their friendship and associational groups? What if these revelations are later used against them? I tried to highlight this problem (Greenblat, 1979) in describing the game that Linda Rosen, John Gagnon, and I designed to deal with adolescent sexual decision-making. There we assigned values that were known from research to be typical of adolescent males and females rather than asking players to set the values themselves. This design decision was made to avoid players—especially females—later being subject to pressure from others because they had revealed the relative importance of sexual gratification in their heterosexual relations.

But assigning roles with built-in values may not altogether deal with the problem. Can others always distinguish the "real person" from the one played, especially where the player has fine thespian talents? The better the player plays the role, the more difficult it may be to disassociate the student from the performance when it is over. Do you really know I am liberal and not the bigoted conservative I played? Do I really know you think women should be given equal rights even though you expounded highly chauvinist views for two hours according to the game designer's instructions?

I am not urging that students should not have to engage in these revelations or role plays. It is these very dimensions of breaking with the psychological isolation of the traditional classroom that may be most responsible for growth and learning. Unless students have to put more of themselves "on the line," have to take positions, have to negotiate and bargain and debate with others, they are unlikely to learn and grow as individuals. The educational process is, or should be, more than an accumulation of facts and principles. It should also include the development of judgment, a stronger understanding of oneself and one's views, openness to divergent opinions and new information—and all these require that they participate more fully than they do in the lecture format.

What I *am* urging is that when we ask students to pay these costs by relinquishing some privacy, we must be prepared to help them deal with the consequences. They must be protected from overrevelation and guided in the postplay discussion to new insights into themselves and others that make the costs worthwhile.

I do not have any easy answers to do this, but I think we must pay attention to the problem, both in the design of the games themselves and in the instructions to operators about leading a postgame discussion.

As I began writing this, I talked about some of the ideas with a friend who has considerable familiarity with gaming. She said, "I think they are important points you are raising. But how can designers deal with them, and how can researchers measure those possible outcomes to know if they are really problems in games?" I responded to her that writing the "first paper" is the easiest job; one needs to point out the problems. The subsequent papers are much harder, for one must then deal with possible solutions. I hope to return to ISAGA and hear some of the participants offer more concrete advice than I have been able to give about how we can better meet our responsibilities to those individuals and groups who participate in the games we design.

NOTE

1. Following presentation of the paper, there was active discussion of this section. The counterposition has been well expressed in a note from Henk Becker, a sociologist at the University of Utrecht, who comments as follows:

> One afterthought dealt with games that lead to one or more persons winning all the time and one or more other persons losing all the time. Winning always bores the winners in the end. In practice this leads to the introduction of handicap-formulae especially to keep the winner interested in the game. To give an example. When I taught my daughters how to play chess, we started with a handicap for me. I played without Queen and without two Knights. When the skills in playing of the daughters increased, the handicap was reduced, ultimately to zero. A kind of positive discrimination of the potential loser might be one solution in gaming in general with regard to unbalanced power of participants in the context.

In the second place, a number of us thought it advisable for you to discuss the potential function of a number of games to teach participants how to lose gracefully and without harm to their ego. Business games, war games, and training in the Peace Corps are rough and have to be rough. Only excessive roughness is wrong.

I am grateful to Professor Becker and his colleagues for these comments, and have encouraged him to write a "Comments" paper elaborating upon his points.

CHAPTER SIXTEEN

GAMING-SIMULATION AS A TOOL
FOR SOCIAL RESEARCH

CATHY STEIN GREENBLAT

In previous sections, the available research on learning, attitude change, and so forth, resulting from participation in gaming-simulations, has been reviewed. In the present section, the focus shifts from research on games to games for research—that is, to the question of what utility gaming-simulations may have for the social researcher.

Despite some early articles containing arguments that games might be useful to the social researcher (see, for example, Coleman, 1969), little has been written to explain just what the promise of these materials is. A perusal of the literature reveals a sprawl of ideas—some from work done, some speculative—but little in the way of organized thought outlining or describing modes of utilization. In this chapter, an exploratory outline for the researcher is attempted. The framework derives from combinations of responses to the questions: (1) What is the researcher's purpose? (2) What kind of gaming-simulation is employed? (3) What is the researcher's role? (4) What is the participant's role? These yielded four basic research modes, each with two variations based on the type of game used. These are illustrated in Figure 16.1 and are listed below. The body of the chapter will include a more detailed explanation of each type, including real and hypothetical examples.

The eight modes of doing social research using gaming-simulations are listed below. The researcher:

I A. operates an existing game with "player-subjects," and counts or measures behavioral or verbal units to generate data to test hypotheses set up in advance.

I B. designs a new game and operates it with "player-subjects," and counts or measures behavioral units to generate data to test hypotheses set up in advance.

II   A. designs a new game and operates it with "player-subjects," and observes and abstracts from the behavior and verbal messages and uses this to refine a theory.

II   B. operates an existing game with "player-subjects," and observes and abstracts from the behavior and verbal messages and uses this to refine a theory.

III   A. guides experts in designing a new game, and synthesizes their contributions. The product represents a specification of the system by experts.

III   B. guides experts in redesigning a frame game, and synthesizes their contribution. The product represents a specification of the system by experts.

IV   A. guides respondents in the redesign process of a frame game to create a game about some system of which they are a part, and counts or measures the elements they include. The data thus generated are phenomenological—they represent the system as the respondents view it.

IV   B. guides respondent-designers in the process of designing a new game about some system of which they are a part, and counts or measures the elements they include. The data thus generated are phenomenological—they represent the system as they view it.

Let's now see what these entail.

RESEARCH MODE I

In form A, the researcher has a set of hypotheses to be tested. An existing game is operated in a laboratory-like setting in which players serve as "subjects." The researcher counts or measures behavioral or verbal units to generate data to test the hypotheses. The basic procedure followed is familiar to the social psychologist, except that a game is the basis of the activity that takes place in the laboratory environment.

The variables to be investigated or manipulated may be social-psychological or social-systemic. For example, the researcher may investigate sex-role differences in problem-solving style, the relationship between personality characteristics and behavioral styles, bargaining methods, coalition formation, types of leadership patterns, and so on. In such a laboratory setting, such things as the effects of alternative social structures on individual behavior in the situation by altering communication patterns, forms of social organization may be examined. Through this systematic alteration of game parameters or the variation of player characteristics, causal hypotheses can be investigated.

The game-laboratory thus involves the creation of a social environment more natural than that in the usual laboratory experiment, yet less complex than the "real world." The complexity of the stimuli is greater than in the traditional laboratory, so one can observe more complex interactions; participants' motivations are likely to be higher; and players-subjects' actions may be more "natural" than the actions of traditional "subjects."

> It is true that subjects may perceive the rules or the content of the simulation game as unrealistic or unrepresentative. However, due to their experience with other games in which certain aspects of reality have been modified, suspended, or ignored, it is felt the subjects in simulation game experiments will be less likely to respond to the experimental situation as if it were meaningless. Thus simulation games exploit the subjects' willingness to suspend disbelief in game-like situations, a willingness that appears not to be present in subjects in more traditional types of psychological experiments [McFarlane, 1971: 155].

> The combination of the game and the simulation aspects allows the subjects to justify their actions after the fact in either serious or unserious terms; that is, the subjects can always say afterward 'it was only a game' *or* 'it was a very meaningful experience' [McFarlane, 1971: 154-155].

Gaming-simulations in the laboratory-type mode of use allow researchers to

> (1) abstract only the processes in which they are interested; (2) replicate many times social systems which are alike or different along specified dimensions; (3) speed up or compress time; (4) safely investigate potentially dangerous or costly situations; and (5) provide a situation for players which offers its own rewards for participation [Dukes, 1973b: 4].

Comparing simulation games to both participant observation and to traditional social-psychological laboratory methods, McFarlane (1971: 150) cites as advantages of the gaming:

> (1) an optimum combination of control and structure versus freedom and innovation with respect to experimental control of the subjects' actions; (2) a setting more likely to be perceived as "realistic" by the subjects participating in the experiment; and (3) a setting which allows the researcher more information with respect to complex, mutually contingent sequential interactions upon which he can perform his analysis.

Examples of studies done in this mode include the works of Vinacke (1959), a study by Clarice Stoll and Paul McFarlane (1969) and one by Stoll and Inbar (1970); some projects described by Raser (1969); and work by Terhune and Firestone (1970), Hermann (1969), Burgess and Robinson (1969), and Druckman (1968) in international relations. In several papers, Richard Dukes has described utilizations and potential utilizations of STAR-POWER as a research tool (1973a and 1973b), and Coplin (1970) presents a general discussion of games as experimental devices to study human behavior in complex environments.

Form B of Research Mode I is very similar to form A; here, however, the researcher designs a NEW game, rather than employing an existing one. The same procedure is then followed: again the researcher counts or measures behavioral or verbal units to generate data to test hypotheses specified in advance. The gaming-simulation thus again serves as the base for a social-psychological laboratory-type experiment.

Little is reported in the literature of attempts by researchers to create new games to test hypotheses. Among the only available examples are studies done by Murray Straus, who has designed a series of simple games for his research on family interaction patterns. He has had family units, for example, play a game in which success rates for children and parents are manipulated, degrees of conflict and competition varied, and the ways in which these were dealt with by the family are observed and analyzed. In this way, hypotheses regarding cross-class and cross-national differences have been tested. A clear example of the technique used in these studies can be found in "Methodology of a Laboratory Experimental Study of Families in Three Societies" (Straus, 1970).

RESEARCH MODE II

A look at Figure 16.1 will reveal the basis of the major difference between Modes I and II: the purpose in the latter is theory construction rather than hypothesis-testing. This mode is for more exploratory research studies in which the researcher is not seeking precise, prespecified data, but rather is interested in interactions which yield insights to help refine theoretical formulations. Rather than counting or measuring the game behaviors, therefore, the researcher observes them and abstracts from them; subsequently it may be possible to use the resultant insights to generate hypotheses for testing in a real-world situation. The game thus serves as a heuristic device in theory-development.

In form A, the researcher designs a new game based on a theory, turning postulates into rules. After the initial design period, the researcher finds players, observes their interactions, and abstracts from these. Often the game is redesigned or some of the parameters altered, and the procedure of observation and abstraction is repeated until the researcher has succeeded in generating a set of outcomes which replicate the outcomes seen in the real world.

This methodology contrasts to other techniques commonly employed by the theoretician-researcher. James Coleman, in "Games as Vehicles for Social Theory" (1969: 3), summarizes some of the differences as follows:

In contrast to survey research and observations in natural settings, it depends on the creation of special environments, governed by rules that are designed precisely for the study of the particular form of organization. In contrast to experiments with their experimental probe or stimulus and the consequent response, the principal element in game methodology is the construction of the rules which can elicit a given form of social organization.

A large number of topics can be examined using this procedure, including elements of social order and social organization, system linkages, the devel-

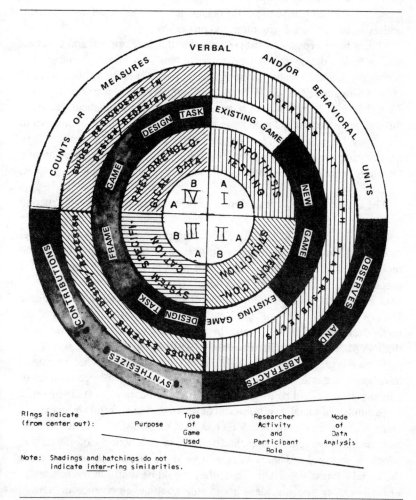

FIGURE 16.1   Four Basic Research Modes Using Gaming-Simulations

opment of norms, social-psychological processes, and possible outcomes of alternative strategies. Some such uses have been described. For example, William Gamson (1975) describes his attempts to understand major elements of social order through design of SIMSOC and subsequent modification upon modification of it due to initial lack of congruence between player behavior in the game and behavior in the real world. In "Collective Decisions," James Coleman (1964a) illustrates how social theory can be translated into a gaming-simulation, and then observation of the play of the game may lead to refinements which are fed back into the theory. Philip Ennis's (1975) description of his experiments with a simulation of the artistic system demonstrates the creative use of the design methodology to refine theoretical understanding of social structures and processes.

Others have expounded suggestions that the development and observation of a simulation might lead to better insights into what *might* be. Smoker's "Social Research for Social Anticipation" (1969) and Boguslaw et al.'s "A Simulation Vehicle for Studying National Policy Formation in a Less Armed World" (1966) demonstrate such creation of hypothetical situations through game design and parameter manipulation. Questions of concern to social psychologists, such as processes in the development of consensus or the construction of shared perceptions, might be examined by creation of a "multiple realities" game and careful analysis of behavior in it (Greenblat, 1975).

The advantage of this procedure over other modes of theory construction is that the researcher is forced to be explicit about assumptions and to be concrete, yet is able to avoid the semantic precision needed for a verbal model and the quantitative precision needed to construct a mathematical model. Such precision may be *emergent* from the model rather than a precursor to its development. Additional strengths are described by Druckman in "Understanding the Operation of Complex Social Systems: Some Uses of Simulation Design" (1971). Some of the costs and rewards of the method are described by Coplin in "Approaches to the Social Sciences through Man-Computer Simulations." (1970)

Form B is the same as A, with the exception that the researcher, instead of *developing* a game, employs an existing one. Any of a large number of existing games could be used as is or with modifications to study any of a large number of social-psychological or social-systemic factors in an exploratory fashion. For example, METRO-APEX, SIMSOC, STARPOWER, and several other games present fruitful and rich sources of interaction which, if observed and analyzed, could yield abstractions about behavior in the social context simulated. Thus, they would be useful in the attempt to formulate more specific ideas about role conflict, emergence of norms, leadership patterns, relative deprivation, exchange mechanisms, and so on. Bredemeier (1973: 77) suggests such a style of usage in urging:

Rawls deals with the matter of procedures for realizing the principles of justice in a provocative, if necessarily thin, discussion of some 200 pages comprising the middle of the book. There he discusses such matters as 'toleration of the intolerant,' civil disobedience, the branches of government and their functions, majority rule and 'participation,' among other institutions. . . . Are those the principles all rational persons with the qualities Rawls postulates would choose? The question might be nicely explored. Let students play the simulation games 'SIMSOC' or 'STARPOWER.' Let them experience the travails, restrictions on liberties and inequalities ordinarily experienced in those game settings. Then, stop the game and announce that it will be resumed later, with roles to be allocated all over again by lot. We now have a not-bad simulation of 'the original position.' Let the weeks (months) in the meantime be spent by the players in devising basic principles that will govern the game-playing when it is resumed. Will they arrive at Rawls' Principles? Without reading Rawls and the Utilitarians? With reading them? Under other experimental-pedagogical conditions?

Hypothetical conditions could similarly be investigated. The manual for THE MARRIAGE GAME, for example, includes instructions for the alteration of parameters concerning equality of the sexes, sexual freedom, and so forth. Play with such altered parameters should aid the researcher in generating fruitful hypotheses dealing with such conditions.

The "yield" from Research Mode II utilizations might take any of a number of forms, including lists of possible factors, consequences, obstacles. For example, an undergraduate student of mine with little prior knowledge of educational systems played the basic version of POLICY NEGOTIATIONS and generated the following list of impediments to educational change:

(1) opposition to change by some system members;
(2) tactical difficulties in bringing about change;
(3) large amount of time required to implement proposed changes;
(4) lack of verbalization of intended outcomes, leading to misunderstanding;
(5) failure to understand sources of past failures;
(6) lack of understanding of sources of power and points of leverage;
(7) lack of understanding of change processes.

She planned to follow these leads by looking at real-world school systems to see if the same impediments blocked effective change.

As yet, little research of this sort has been done, although those interested in international relations have done a number of such investigations using Guetzkow's "Simulations in the Consolidation and Utilization of Knowledge about International Relations" (1972).

MODE III

A look at Figure 16.1 will reveal that there is a basic split between Research Modes I-II and Research Modes III-IV, for a number of the defining parameters of the research modes change as one goes from the righthand side of the figure to the lefthand side. In addition, the first two modes of utilization have been discussed in the literature, albeit in a limited fashion, and examples of them can be found. The latter two modes of doing research utilizing gaming-simulations are more speculative; to the best of my knowledge they have not been employed and have not been described in the literature. The examples offered here, therefore, are hypothetical and simply indicative of the *types* of research problems that could be dealt with using gaming-simulation in these ways.

In Research Mode IIIA, the researcher's purpose is to gather from experts in a field their perceptions of the major dimensions of a system. Rather than interviewing them utilizing a standard questionnaire or interview guide, they are turned into game-designers and, under the guidance of the researcher, asked to express their ideas in the format of a game. If the system of concern is a prison, the experts would be penologists, and they would be asked to build a gaming-simulation of a prison; if the system of interest is an educational institution, scholars in the field of education would be called upon to serve as expert designers creating a school or university game. The researcher's additional task is then to synthesize the definitions of the roles, goals, resources, constraints, and contingencies of the system as specified by the experts. The game-design task thus functions somewhat as an in-depth interview guide; it is a set of questions (see Duke, 1974, and the design section of this volume). If joint work sessions can be arranged, it may also serve as a vehicle to permit the equivalent of a "group interview" with experts. The task will generate dialogue and confrontation, for the game design process inevitably entails arguments and debates among designers about what the system is *really* like. The advantage of this technique over more traditional modes of interviewing of experts derives from the fact that to design a game the experts will of necessity be confronted with the need to be specific about assumptions, to deal on various levels of abstraction, and so forth.

In order to understand Research Mode IIIB, we must introduce a new concept—that of the "frame game." Probably the simplest example is the crossword puzzle. Its basic framework consists of a matrix of black and white squares, a numbering system, a set of clues, and a feedback mechanism in the form of answers for the player who wishes to check on success or learn what has been missed. Once the basic framework is understood, different examples can be created by varying the content.

There are a number of gaming-simulations available which, like this, have standard frames into which content can be loaded. (See Duke and Greenblat, 1979). They consist of a framework, a sample set of content (often called a "priming game"), and instructions for redesigning the game to make it content-specific to the user's needs. These have been widely used for teaching purposes and for training, but their potential as "questionnaires" to gather system-specification data from experts has not been exploited.

Such frame games as IMPASSE?; AT ISSUE; and the CONCEPTUAL MAPPING GAME; NEXUS; POLICY NEGOTIATIONS; and COMMU-NITY DISPUTES provide frameworks of varying degrees of complexity and embodying different types of models into which content can be loaded. If one of these (or another frame game) embodies an appropriate model, the researcher will find that the process of loading content into an existing frame proves far easier and less time-consuming than the process of starting from scratch to design a new game. It may, therefore, be more plausible to think of getting experts to take the time to engage in this process rather than in the full design procedure.

The prison system has been offered as simply one example of what could be done in the way of research in this mode. IMPASSE? versions have already been designed to deal with such issues as environmental and ecological problems, urban planning, health care delivery systems. NEXUS versions deal with issues such as local authority finance problems, fire department operations, developing countries. POLICY NEGOTIATIONS has been redesigned to deal with hospitals, social work agencies, and so on. For Research Mode III purposes, however, the versions must be designed by those who are experts in the field rather than by game-designers with more limited understanding of the content area.

Figures 16.2 and 16.3 show (in reduced scale) the framework for IM-PASSE?, the simplest of the frame games mentioned above. Figure 16.2 presents an example of the game materials loaded to deal with assessment of the impact of introduction of a rapid transit system, and Figure 16.3 presents the empty frame elements. Using IMPASSE?, for example, those concerned with a prison system could ask experts to put into the large wheel the variables of a prison system that should be taken into account in assessing any potential or proposed policy or action. Next they would be asked to outline a series of changes, actions, or proposals that might be brought to bear in such a system; and finally the experts would be asked to indicate on the small wheels ("serial evaluators") their assessments of the impact of the given policies on the system parameters. Whether or not the resultant game(s) were ever used (that is, played), they would present statements of the system specifications as seen by these experts and hence be of value for research-theory building.

NEXUS employs a somewhat similar recording device for indicating the variables that characterize a system. The NEXUS center card is filled in with system variables and indications of the effects of various actions on each of the variables. These cards are later laid in the center of a board composed of scales for recording the cumulative changes in the state of the system resulting from the sequential actions. (The similarity between IMPASSE? and

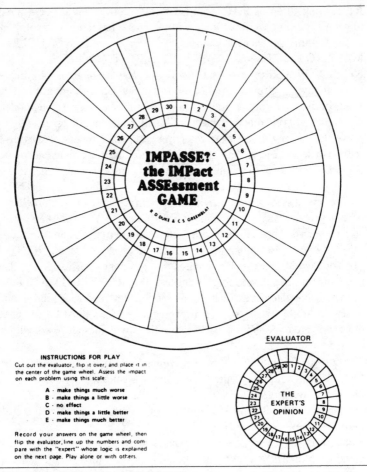

FIGURE 16.2   The Basic IMPASSE? Frame

NEXUS derives from their common ancestry in Olaf Helmar's FUTURES
GAME.) Experts could be asked to program the NEXUS cards in order to
elicit their views of the system.

If a more interactive model were needed, the researcher could locate
several experts and have them engage in the steps of redesign of POLICY
NEGOTIATIONS. As will be noted, the steps require a quite elaborate set of
system specifications.

The type of data collected by Olaf Helmar and Dennis Little via Delphi
techniques to develop (respectively) the FUTURE STATE OF THE UNION
GAME and STAPOL (State Policy Simulation) would be extremely useful

"RAPID TRANSIT" IMPASSE?

1:(E) Improved viability of the central business district would result in higher land values.

2:(D) More active business climate would result in higher tax derived from business.

3:(E) A successful, advanced rapid transit system will spawn other projects requiring federal aid.

4:(A) Basic changes in transportation capability will result inevitably in secondary costs for roads, sewers, etc.

5:(C) Some welfare recipients will be better off, but others will arrive to replace them.

6:(B) The existing tendency of industry to decentralize will be encouraged.

7:(B) Populations will shift as land use patterns adjust to transit capability, affecting wards.

8:(E) The very magnitude of a rapid transit system requires discussions, perhaps agreement?

9:(B) The existing tendency of the middle class to leave the city will be encouraged.

10:(B) Populations will inevitably shift; construction will intrude on existing neighborhoods.

11:(E) A viable rapid transit system inevitably makes a city a more viable "central place".

12:(A) Many actual improvements (low-cost transport, new jobs) will be offset by new migrants.

13:(B) Construction side effects, as well as improved mobility will result in shifting populations.

14:(A) A more active, viable central area will discourage street crime.

15:(D) Better transit gives better access, more opportunity to reach a variety of facilities.

16:(B) Construction of this magnitude inevitably causes damage, some of which is permanent.

17:(E) Improved mobility brings a greater area of access to residents, more people moved in a given space.

18:(E) Existing pressures for change will have a better chance for success.

19:(E) No rapid transit system will inevitably lead to more sprawl and deterioration of the city

20:(D) Entrepreneurial response to a new transport system is dramatic, perhaps too dramatic

21:(E) The new transport mode will make large areas more accessible to the city.

22:(E) In the long run, more dense land uses will locate near the terminals. A more European pattern will result.

23:(E) Assuming proper integration (!) more people will commit to public transport

24:(C) Some improvement is to be expected, however the auto is always with us.

25:(D) A rapid transport system is a major component in regional growth permitting improved planning.

26:(E) Growth can be expected to concentrate at the terminals of the rapid transit system.

27:(E) New shopping centers can be expected at the nodes or transit terminals.

28:(A) The central business district will be more readily accessible and therefore more viable

29:(E) Growth will be channeled by the transit system, planning decisions will be more orderly.

30:(E)

Our "expert," for this game, is Dr. William Drake, Assoc. Dean for Research, School of Natural Resources, the University of Michigan. Dr. Drake is director of the Ann Arbor Transportation Authority, which has successfully pioneered in the use of "Dial-a-Ride" mini-buses.

Should your perceptions differ (either with regard to the problems in the impasse wheel, the "expert's" values as assessed, or both) an explanation of his choice) should a note to the editor marked "Rapid Transit Impasse"

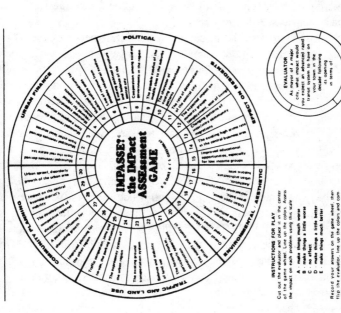

FIGURE 16.3 An Example of a Loaded IMPASSE? Game

THE EXPERT'S OPINION

EVALUATOR
As mayor of a major city, what impact would you expect an advanced rapid transit system to have on your town in the decade following its opening in terms of:

INSTRUCTIONS FOR PLAY

Cut out the evaluator and place it in the center of the game wheel. Line up the colors. Assess the impact on each problem using this scale

A make things much worse
B make things a little worse
C no effect
D make things a little better
E make things much better

Record your answers on the game wheel, then flip the evaluator, line up the colors and compare with the "expert" whose logic is explained on the next page. Play alone or with others.

199

to a researcher. These games could be used as frame games by wiping out the figures given by Helmar's and Little's respondents and having experts present their assessments of impacts. Again the game would serve as a sort of "questionnaire." In summary, then, the frame game in Research Mode IIIB is used as a device to elicit ideas of experts on the characteristics of complex systems: constituencies, roles, issues, impacts, problems, constraints, contingencies, and so forth.

MODE IV

The fourth Research Mode using gaming-simulations again involves utilization of a frame game. Here, however, our designers are not scholar-experts, but people who *live* in the system in question and thus serve as respondents to the games' questions, providing phenomenological data. In form A, for example, we would ask prisoners to design a prison version of POLICY NEGOTIATIONS rather than asking penologists to do this. The resultant model would reflect the biases inherent in the perceptions of those in one role in the system, but as such it would be a sound reflection of the prison system as seen by prisoners.

In this mode, then, the researcher guides designer-respondents in the redesign process of a frame game to create a game about some system of which they are a part. Having thus elicited the data, the researcher counts or measures the elements they include. The data thus generated are phenomenological as they represent the respondents' views of the system.

Again IMPASSE? could be used in a variety of ways: A predesigned version could be played by a group (such as prison inmates) and their assessments tabulated and analyzed like survey data. Inmates or staff of a prison could be asked to define the elements that should be included in the large wheel to make a PRISON IMPASSE? game. The researcher's task would be to determine the frequency with which various aspects were mentioned. Students might be asked to express their views of their university by creating a version of POLICY NEGOTIATIONS reflecting their university. They would be guided through the steps of redesign by the researcher who would derive a picture of their views from the new games they created. In a more elaborate research design, students, junior faculty, senior faculty, and administration at the institution might be asked to engage in the redesign process. Comparisons could be made on a series of game parameters (such as amount of influence allocated to each of the major constituencies, impact of passage of particular policies) to compare the perceptions of those in differing roles in the system.

Form B is almost the same as form A. It involves, however, the creation of a new game rather than the redesign of a frame game. Here the researcher guides designer-respondents in the design process of a new game. For example, prisoners would be guided in the design of a prison game, students in the design of a university game, and so on. In this manner, they would again present their perceptions of the system, generating phenomenological data for the researcher to count, measure, or otherwise analyze.

CONCLUSION

The utilization of gaming-simulation for social research has largely been ignored in methods texts and guides. Those that refer to the technique at all discuss only computer simulation or refer only to what is here described as Research Mode IA: utilization of an existing gaming-simulation for hypothesis testing in a social-psychological laboratory (Phillips, 1971: 171-190.) Those in the infant field of gaming have also neglected in their writings the research potentials of the technique. It is hoped that in the future the ideas and suggestions offered here will be more fully explored and essayed to learn more of the potential contribution of gaming to the research endeavors of social scientists.

PART IV

PUBLIC POLICY APPLICATIONS

CHAPTER SEVENTEEN

PUBLIC POLICY APPLICATIONS:
Using Gaming-Simulations
for Problem Exploration and Decision-Making

RICHARD D. DUKE

THREE USES FOR GAMING-SIMULATION

The primary use of gaming-simulation for the past quarter-century has been in an academic context. Immediately following World War II, various schools of business administration adopted the technique (borrowing it largely from the war gamers) and incorporated it into their curricula. Significantly, many special uses were employed for the "adult-education" of businessmen in the field, in a variety of short-course formats. Both on and off campus, "real-world" business managers were given the opportunity to run some mythical corporation. Much in vogue during this era were arguments, pro and con, about possible effects that might be transferred from the game to the operation of a real firm. Since some of the business games were fun for well-established businessmen under very exotic conditions, the question of carryover was not entirely academic.

Schools of education and then of the various social sciences were close on the heels of the business schools in their adoption of use of gaming-simulation, resulting in a profusion of games, covering a wide variety of subject matter and technique. Their range of sophistication is enormous, and their correspondence to reality ranges from the purely abstract to the iconic. There are at least three published catalogs which attempt to document these materials.

Inevitably, these gaming-simulations, like the earlier business games, found their way helter-skelter into nonacademic use (although almost without exception, the gaming instruments were originally prepared in some academic context). And again, questions were raised about their potential carryover effects.

There appear to be three central circumstances in which gaming-simulation can be successfully employed:

(1) for pedagogic purposes;
(2) as a communications device by an interdisciplinary team engaged in sophisticated research;
(3) for some direct public policy purpose—specifically to influence the decision-making of the voter, the civil servant, or the elected and/or appointed official.

Of these three purposes, only the first two have been pursued very assiduously. Attempts in the third area have been largely hit-or-miss forays spawned by the opportunity of the moment, using the resources at hand, with little attempt at measuring the impact of the effort. The question remains: Can gaming-simulation be effectively employed in actual public policy applications?

A positive response would seem to be justified; the historic use of gaming-simulation by the military is a case in point, as is the use of gaming-simulation in certain foreign policy applications. But can gaming-simulation be employed in less exotic settings? Both military and diplomatic considerations are sufficient to justify expensive technique. As the scale becomes less global, the problem more specific, the audience less sophisticated and more fleeting . . . is there a pragmatic, day-to-day potential for the technique?

Probably so, at least in the management of our urban centers, and these, of course, have a profound impact on the daily life of most Americans today.

THE AUDIENCES DEFINED

There are three applications in the urban arena for the productive use of games: first, directly with the voter; second, with the hired, appointed, or elected individuals who act for the citizen in the management of urban affairs; and third, with those individuals whose private actions have a profound impact on urban development—bankers, real estate men, large landholders, and other people in business. It is useful to distinguish among the three as potential targets for the gaming technique because the circumstances of application vary considerably.

The citizens (for brief definitional purposes defined here as those eligible to vote) viewed as a gaming target may exist as individuals, members of loose coalitions, or members of a permanent or semi-permanent organization dedicated toward specified goals. However they may be found, they are generally motivated toward questions of public policy on an *issue* or *problem* basis. As the problem or issue emerges, coalitions form in response; as this issue is resolved, the coalition dissolves, to be replaced by another formed to meet the next crisis. The membership overlaps from group to group, and some stalwarts are to be found as more or less permanent fixtures in the process of societal dialogue. But in large part the citizen is a fleeting target for the gaming-simulation technique.

This implies that gaming-simulation will be successfully employed with the citizen only if certain conditions can be met:

—simple game devices are employed; emphasis will be on frame games, where the basic format can be assimilated, but content can be readily changed;

—the instrument is used in narrow, problem-specific applications; this implies new material being developed issue by issue;

—the gaming instruments are simple, requiring neither exotic paraphernalia nor trained personnel to either develop or to run the exercises;

—the central theme of the gaming exercise will be to convey the "big picture" at least to the extent that a correlation can be made for the citizen regarding the issue at hand and the central factors impinging on a knowledgeable decision.

If gaming-simulation is effectively employed, it will increase the power of the citizens, making them more knowledgeably effective in public affairs and less dependent on the actions of either their appointed/elected/hired representatives or the decision makers of the business community.

The second target group—the hired/elected/appointed—requires a different mode of operation for the successful application of gaming-simulation. This group is much smaller in number, more specifically defined in terms of responsibility and perspective (role) in community affairs, and considerably more knowledgeable than the average citizen, at least about their specific area of interest. Further, although their mode of decision-making is basically issue to issue, they are charged with a broader responsibility in at least two dimensions: they are obliged to consider not only a given issue or problem, but an array of these as appropriate at a given moment; further, they are obliged to consider the impact of any given decision through time (for example, the impact on the municipal budget ten years from now). Given these considerations, the gaming-simulation vehicle(s) employed must meet several constraints:

—they must be reasonably complex; they must be sophisticated enough to meet the linkage of many dimensions of urban life;

—they must be valid; they must include or provide reasonable access to specific data sources as required;

—they must provide for the perspective of the major urban roles, either by accommodating real-world decision makers directly in the game and/or through the inclusion of stereotypes in the gaming model;

—they must permit the thoughtful review of a given issue or problem in terms of both its own merits and its impact on other issues.

If gaming-simulation is effectively employed to increase communication among elected/appointed/hired urban decision makers, at least three advantages should occur: the quality of decisions on individual issues should be improved; the impact of individual decisions on future time should be less destructive; and, finally, the inevitable conflict between departments should be minimized or at least rationalized.

Finally, the major decision makers in the private sector are a different audience. They are, first of all, profit-oriented. They are reasonably expert in their area of interest. They are narrowly oriented toward a particular project or interest. They cannot be expected to respond to "community interest" or considerations beyond the scope of their private interest, except perhaps, to pay lip service. Gaming-simulation, to be effective with this group, must be:

—problem-specific; each gaming situation must explore a particular circumstance where tangible private interests are at stake;

—sophisticated in technique; the presentation must be at a level appropriate to an expert audience;

—focused on tangible considerations; municipal, law, the power of the electorate, administrative power must be stressed rather than ethereal notions of the public good;

—designed to permit an exchange, a dialogue, between experts representing both private and public interests.

Gaming-simulation of this style may be employed to obtain a better integration of projects by trading off private self-interest against the public interest and the clout of an informed electorate.

SOME RECENT APPLICATIONS

Gaming-simulation efforts to date for municipal policy purpose can be conveniently divided into the use of simple and complex exercises. For this discussion, "complex" implies the use of a computer.

To date, "simple" games devised for academic purposes have been employed for use with citizen groups. These include, but certainly are not limited to, a variety of field applications for STARPOWER, CLUG, METROPOLIS, POLICY NEGOTIATIONS, and many others. The use of these games has generally been with citizen groups with some degree of cohesion (such as the League of Women Voters) and in a mode that comes closer to "adult education" than to a precise use of gaming for bona fide public policy purposes (that is, actual decision-making).

A second use of simple games has been the development of special problem-specific games for explicit public policy use. A variety of public agencies have developed such games. One of the more recent examples is WALRUS, developed by Allan Feldt for use in Traverse City, Michigan, to improve public understanding of the activities conducted under the Michigan Sea Grant Program. Although quite successful, this game does not go the full route on the continuum of public education-public policy game use. That is, WALRUS is probably most effective in conveying a general situation; it is of limited value to decision makers in dealing with a variety of specific issues which might emerge in the region.

A third context for "simple" games is programmatic use. This implies the deliberate effort to employ gaming as one tool for public dialogue on an emergent issue basis. One example known to me is in the Monterey Bay region of California (some of the materials being prepared are being used elsewhere). The Association of Monterey Bay Area Governments and the Council of Monterey Bay, under funding from the National Science Foundation, had a project to develop gaming for programmatic citizen use. A series of frame-games has been developed (IMPASSE?; AT ISSUE!; and CONCEPTUAL MAPPING . . .) for active local use.

Complex (computer) games are less in evidence, partly because they are more cumbersome to use, but largely because of the expense involved. There are several such exercises in existence and fairly widespread use. In almost all applications, they are prototypical; their primary purpose (in nonacademic usage) is to illustrate the ultimate potential of the technique.

METRO-APEX

METRO-APEX is one well-known example commissioned by the Tri-County Regional Planning Commission of Lansing, Michigan, under Housing and Home Finance Administration funding; it was originally intended as a device for familiarizing the various commissioners with the dynamics of the region. Originally completed in 1968, it has subsequently undergone more or less continuous revision and is now in use at many American universities. METRO-APEX has served as a prototype to researchers in several other countries (the game has been translated from English and now "speaks" German, French, and Spanish). While METRO—APEX is prototypical of sophisticated gaming for public policy purpose, its use to date has not generally been in a "real-world" context.

METRO-APEX serves as a vehicle for both urban management training and urban policy research. It is a micro-environment for decision makers in which an abstracted, simulated metropolitan area is represented via gamed roles and in-computer models and data systems. There are a variety of uses for METRO-APEX: teaching of professional urbanists, social scientists, planners, and administrators; research on a wide range of computer-oriented urban models calibrated to a common data base; and research on political and/or planning decision-making in a realistic small group laboratory setting.

METRO-APEX is still evolving; the current version stresses training of adult groups in problems inherent to "comprehensive" and fiscal planning to urban areas. Policy problems are represented in a condensed time frame, to give rapid feedback of consequences of decisions.

New policy problems, such as air and water pollution, public health, transportation, have been incorporated for particular occasions of use. METRO-APEX attempts to synthesize a coherent view of the city as a whole, to replace a narrow technical perspective with a broadened world view capable of grasping problems in their entirety. METRO-APEX starts with a *behavioral* as opposed to a technical model of urban systems, with bargaining emerging as a central phenomenon.

Perhaps the key distinguishing characteristic of METRO-APEX—in contrast with conventional urban simulations—is the stress on integrating a whole family of models (of only moderate complexity individually) to give a comprehensive representation of urban structure, rather than the progressive refinement and elaboration of specialized models.

The critical problems of urban regions are the ways in which decisions are made, with different views of the world leading to conflict, bargaining, and transactions. Too little is known or understood about these processes, so gaming instruments will always require continuous refinement. Playing out complex decision processes in gaming is the only device available for representing them, for either teaching or research, for mathematical models are a long way from handling the complexity (and the enormous permutational variety) they generate—even simple games have alternate solutions expressed in googols. The interaction of sets of decisions by players in multiple roles is the unique contribution of gaming-simulation to sensitizing researchers and future decision makers to the possibilities that can emerge in typical situations. Since all possibilities can never be evaluated, such devices are all that we have to develop, or to prepare for the developing of, contingency plans and strategies of intervention to promote plans.

THE LABORATORY COMMUNITY

Even more futuristic is the concept of the "Laboratory Community." The idea is to have a continuing three-way interaction between modeling (which generates ideas for *what* to measure, as well as where solutions to problems may lie) and data collection and analysis (which may significantly alter our concepts and theories, as well as give parameter estimates for models) and public policy proposals (which will force the above two to be more realistic and less purely academic). One may conceive of the whole process as a spiral of increasing refinement of models, and of data collection and measures, and, hence, of policy ideas, over time. The Laboratory Community concept thus envisions work by a team of researchers from many disciplines in a single metropolitan area, over perhaps a decade. The attempt would be to estabish a long-term study monitoring a broad spectrum of urban process for a single urban area, to generate time-series data that will be fed into and modify interdisciplinary policy-oriented urban models.

The research effort would be integrated through the development of a new METRO-style gaming-simulation of the Laboratory Community— with far more sophisticated data and models than now exist for any urban area. The next generation METRO, built around a Laboratory Community, would be sophisticated and detailed enough to really aid policy makers in a specific urban area in making better decisions. It would thus serve as an efficient device for disseminating the results of the Laboratory Community to both researchers and policy makers.

General advantages accruing from the development of the Laboratory Community would be that:

—it would be valuable to guide data collection for urban research by explicitly formulating models;

—it would serve as an integrative device for research; at the moment data and theories from different cities, different time periods, and different disciplines are very difficult to integrate into a common set of urban models;

—it would provide a better understanding of urban dynamics and of the real leverage points in the social structure.

The Laboratory Community is further defined in the next chapter by Miller and Duke; new hope for its fruition is on the horizon as a result of the microprocessor explosion.[1]

NOTE

1. See Chapter 19 in this volume, "Introducing Science and Technology at the Community Level: The Role of Gaming-Simulation," by Duke.

CHAPTER EIGHTEEN

GAMING:

A Methodological Experiment

ROY I. MILLER
RICHARD D. DUKE

INTRODUCTION

Just five years ago, government officials in nonmilitary agencies would shudder in disbelief at the prospect of using "games" in an applied (decision-making) context and would grimace with skepticism at proposals to use "games" in an instructional setting. Two years ago, this skepticism was replaced by curiosity as two major governmental agencies (HUD and DOT) circulated RFPs (requests for proposals) for the construction of gaming-simulations for training purposes. During this past year, the number of gaming-simulations under construction increased dramatically and the number of people using games, especially in educational institutions, skyrocketed. Yet, it is fast becoming apparent that government expectations were not met, as much of the early curiosity has reverted to a healthy skepticism (try to fund research in gaming with federal resources). As with so many other innovative approaches to social system problem-solving (such as, PPBS), enthusiasm for gaming-simulation appears to be going full circle—first none, then too much, and then none again. This should be neither surprising nor depressing. Rather, it should be a signal to people in the field to reassess their efforts and place them in a proper perspective. This chapter is an attempt to do just that. It is the major thesis of this chapter that, like those other innovative methodologies, gaming-simulation will find its place in society if it is allowed to mature and develop in the proper way. Furthermore, the impact of gaming-simulation on the political process can and will be dramatic.

AUTHOR'S NOTE: This is a slightly revised version of a paper prepared for delivery at the 1972 Annual Meeting of the American Political Science Association, Washington Hilton Hotel, Washington, D.C., September 5-9.

WHAT IS GAMING-SIMULATION?

The temptation to launch a full-blown discussion of the nature of gaming-simulation is hard to resist. The ambiguity of the term in the literature and in government circles is great, and a new clarity of definition is needed. However, although we have tried and are still trying, we have found it difficult to arrive at the type of definition needed to add precision to the analysis and evaluation of gaming-simulation exercises.[1] Because a more standard and less precise definition will suffice for this chapter, we, too, will be fuzzy. Unfortunately, we will not offer the definitive statement by which one might measure the value or appropriateness of using a particular gaming-simulation. In fact, our definition may even fall short of providing help in determining whether some "thing" is or is not a bona fide gaming-simulation.

The gaming-simulation methodology is a merger or hybrid of two distinct techniques: gaming and simulation. Although many authors, game builders, and game users use the terms interchangeably, there are games that are not simulations and, similarly, there are simulations that are not games. Although we make this distinction to contribute to the clarity of our definitions, much of what is said later applies equally well to games and gaming-simulations.

Simulation is the attempt to abstract and reproduce the central features of a complex system for the purpose of understanding, experimenting with, and predicting the behavior of the system. Usually, the abstraction or simulation utilizes some model or representation of the structure of the system and some mechanism for re-creating the process by which the system operates. In modern social science, simulation often takes the form of a computer program; however, restriction of the term to computer modeling is overly constraining. Whereas one might resort to simulating river flows on a computer to predict the future state or gain understanding of the river system, so might one resort to simulating the flow of the river by building a small-scale physical model of the river and pumping water through it.

Games are more difficult to define. Simply, they are sets of activities performed by groups of people (groups of one are allowed) where a set of rules or conventions constrains or defines the limits of activity. The rules themselves may be dynamic and, therefore, subject to change during the play of the game. Generally, people playing roles perform the sets of tasks suggested by the rules. Interaction in the form of competition and/or cooperation is almost always required to enable players to perform those tasks. If this was the entire definition, practically any group activity could be called a game. In fact, some scholars have argued that all group activities can best be understood when viewed as games. Norton Long (1958: 3) argues

> It is the contention of this paper that the structured group activities that coexist in a particular territorial system [community] can be looked at as games.

We feel it necessary to restrict our definition to something that differentiates between "real-world," serious gaming and gaming for fun. In the latter case, people participate for fun and, when the activity becomes tedious, they quit. The characteristic of serious games that distinguishes them from fun games is that they are pursued even under adversity. The characteristic that distinguishes serious games from the real world (the characteristic that probably accounts for the regrettable selection of that particular word as a name for this type of serious activity) is that the outcome—the winners and losers— are not final, nor are the participants held accountable for their behavior outside the game environment. (One might argue that the money won by each man on a professional championship football team is serious and final and that football is fun; however, this apparent contradiction of the definition is easily explained by acknowledging that professional football is a business, but touch football is a game played for fun.)

Gaming-simulation combines the two techniques: simulation and serious gaming. The set of rules governing the play of the game and the scenario setting the game environment act to constrain behaviors in the game so that the game activity simulates some more complex system. Quite often, computer-simulations are meshed with human decision makers in gaming-simulations but, again, it is overly restrictive to limit the term gaming-simulation to such man-machine systems.

These definitions or concepts of simulations, games, and gaming-simulations are virtually content- or subject-free. As defined, simulations, games, and gaming-simulations can (and do) appear in any and all fields. In short, we have defined a methodology, a way of looking at many kinds of systems in a variety of ways. To illustrate these concepts, let us offer a few examples.

It is possible to distinguish between physical systems such as climatological or hydrological systems, social systems such as cities or political parties, and logical systems such as mathematics or grammar. A group of non-simulation games have been developed that do not abstract physical or social systems. Instead of re-creating a physical or social system in a gaming-model, these non-simulation games re-create a system of logic or body of abstract knowledge and transfer it to participants through the activity of play. The Resource Allocation Games designed by Layman Allen and others are examples of non-simulation games.

> When the resources to be allocated in such games are symbols representing the fundamental ideas of a field of knowledge, the resulting activity can be a powerful instructional interaction. A learning environment can be designed to emphasize interacting peers creating and solving highly individualized problems for each other. . . . Players have something to do with the ideas that they are engaged in mastering; they don't merely hear them or see them expressed in print [Allen, 1972: 2].

Examples of simulations that are not games are more plentiful. Probably the best known political science simulation is the Simulmatics Project conducted to enable the Democratic Party to estimate the probable impact of different issues on the public during the 1960 election campaign (Pool and Abelson, 1962). Here, actual data were used to simulate the response to key issues of carefully selected voter classes reacting to cross-pressures created by opposing religious and party affiliations.

Again from the political sciences we draw an example of a gaming-simulation—the INTER-NATION SIMULATION (INS) (Guetzkow, 1968) The INS represents intranational processes through a computerized simulation relating selected prototypic variables and introduces international processes through gaming. Thus, it is a man-machine form of gaming-simulation.

WHAT DOES A GAMING SIMULATION DO?

The three examples in the last section illustrate not only the distinction between games, simulations, and gaming-simulations but also the diverse range of application of *each* of these techniques. The Resource Allocation Games are primarily (if not entirely) education or training exercises. The Simulmatics model is used to make conditional predictions of election outcomes through pure simulation. The INS is most often thought of as a device to build theory or compare theories—that is, do research.

Quite frankly, we know of only a handful of vigorous scientific attempts to demonstrate that gaming-simulations do any of these things well—teach, predict, or coordinate research.[2] The claims of our colleagues are justifiable by example (all games have a stock of anecdotes to illustrate the wonders of games) or by intuition (all gamers argue that if you'll just try it, you'll like it). This lack of more scientific justification or proof of the efficacy of gaming-simulation should not be construed as a "cop out" or failure on the part of gaming-simulators. The simple fact is that games are attempting to replace or supplement conventional forms of teaching, speculation, and/or research by introducing new and intangible features to the more standard approaches; therefore, conventional modes of evaluation are inadequate. Furthermore, the single most important one of these features is the ability to "handle" complexity, a feature that is hardly understood and certainly not measurable.

To complicate matters further, many people in the field argue that the methodology can be applied in a fourth way—to aid decision makers by allowing such people to explore the present and/or the future through the play of gaming-simulations. This, of course, creates a new set of problems for proponents of the methodology and opens the door to a completely different type of skepticism on the part of its critics.

We feel that even though the uses of the methodology are varied (and, therefore, the forms gaming-simulation takes are many), there is a single common characteristic of games that helps clarify the field and aid in understanding its significance. The claims and counterclaims of the gamers and the skeptics might, at least, deal with the same substance if this characteristic is carefully identified. If people using games acknowledge this attribute of the methodology, the focus of application in each context (education, predictive modeling, research, decision-making) will sharpen, and the methodology will find its proper place in society. In short, *games communicate*.

METRO—AN EXAMPLE

Like so many of our colleagues, the logic of our position about gaming revolves around example and anecdote. With our colleagues at the Environmental Simulation Laboratory, we have worked on the METRO gaming-simulation for eight years.[3] METRO is a complex, computerized man-machine gaming-simulation of an urban area. Players take on the roles of key decision makers: politicians, planners, land developers, industrialists, environmental control officers, and news media specialists. They run a city for a period of five to ten years by making annual decisions that parallel those of their real-world counterparts. The decisions are fed to a series of simulations of natural and artificial phenomena (for example, an air mass model and a land market model) to determine the immediate effect of each year's decisions. The decision-making process is repeated on the basis of the new computer printout (status of the city) for each year in the five- to ten-year period.

The project has been "finished" at least twice only to be restarted again with fresh funding and new personnel. As with so many other major projects beset by funding problems and the associated discontinuities of thought and action, the emphasis and direction of the development of METRO has shifted several times to accommodate the most recent funding agent or client group. Yet, METRO has been nothing more or less than a vehicle to communicate the nature of the urban system to students, policy makers, citizen groups, and anyone else who "wanted to know." We quote from the Phase I report—a document published in January 1966, even before the first computer program had been written.

> The METRO project will attempt to close this gap [between the urban "plan-makers" and the decision makers they attempt to serve], utilizing operational gaming techniques to develop a plan effectuation instrument. The instrument will have the capacity of demonstrating to appropriate human decision-makers the consequences of alternative decision chains on metropolitan growth patterns. This will be accomplished through the use of a simulated abstracted environment, employing a reduction of time span and dynamic inter-play of current decisions with fixed policies. The instrument is intended to simulate growth patterns which should occur naturally and enable their comparison with planned growth patterns.

This technique will introduce a dynamic quality into urban "plan-making" activities and allow for a structured interplay between those concerned with plan design and the "decision-makers" upon whom the plan's ultimate implementation depends [Urban Regional Research Institute, 1966: 5].

Although METRO has become known as a training tool, it was initially thought of as a dynamic supplement to conventional planning to further communication among decision makers, planners, and citizens involved in planmaking. As with *all* other large-scale simulations, METRO suffers from some major gaps and inaccuracies in the data and some weaknesses in the theoretical foundations of some of its components. Unlike some other supporters of simulation, the designers of METRO recognize these weaknesses and, therefore, emphasize the training use of the exercise.

As a result, in 1972, when we spoke of METRO as a prototype for a more sophisticated gaming-simulation to be used as a methodology for "dynamic urban planning," the response was that gaming-simulations are teaching tools or, at best, research vehicles. Yet, from the outset, our pioneering work in gaming-simulation has been moving toward a new planning concept— one that will upset the traditional political as well as planning processes. Our hope is to launch this planning concept in some city or region and demonstrate that it can, in fact, work. We call this anticipated first attempt the Laboratory Community.

THE LABORATORY COMMUNITY

Following the almost perverse penchant of people in gaming to select poor titles (witness the horror of the uninitiated at the thought of using games for serious purposes), we selected the title Laboratory Community for our vision. The intent is to provide a community with a set of gaming-simulation devices to be used in a laboratory by people in the community, in which they can register, explore, and play out their problems prior to any actions in the "real world." Unfortunately, too many people hear our title and think of some poor community being used as a laboratory by hard-hearted scientists out to prove they know how to run the world. Despite this, we exhibit the stubbornness and near fanaticism of our gaming-simulation colleagues and retain this title.

In our more fanciful moments, we envision some city procuring a series of gaming-simulation devices and setting them up in a large room in the basement of city hall.[4] In much the same way that the military chiefs in the movie "Dr. Strangelove" used their war room to thrash out key tactical and strategic problems, decision makers would use this "game room" to explore tactical and strategic problems for their city. Thus, the game room becomes the new political forum; however, it is a forum in which decisions are not final and the participants are not held accountable for their behavior when they go upstairs to council chambers. But when they do go up to council chambers, they will have a better understanding of the problems and a better feeling for the nature of the arguments for and against assorted policy options.

In order to appreciate how this game room might work we must explore the types of gaming-simulation tools that would be made available in the laboratory of the Laboratory Community. Each tool is there for a purpose and that purpose must be to further the communication to someone, from someone, or between groups and individuals.

The basic tool would be the METRO-style computerized gaming-simulation. This would be a sophisticated and accurate set of models to estimate the impact of key decisions on the urban system. The data base would be a living (easily updated), viable resource for the community to be used as part of the simulation and also as an independent entity. The purpose for building such an expensive and cumbersome gaming-simulation (we estimate that it would take our staff ten years at $500,000/year plus the strong support of the jurisdiction being simulated) is not so much to predict the future as to foster nonsophomoric discussion of the key current issues in the community. After all, the predictions generated by such a model would be conditional on many ceteris paribus assumptions no matter how complete the simulation; but, with the aid of the model, the discussion on the issues could take on substance and quality.

For example, consider the generally accepted principle that the fate of the city of Detroit rises and falls with the fate of the auto industry. So many decisions are made in Detroit with the impact on the auto industry serving as a prime argument for or against particular action. Yet, the actual magnitude of the effect the auto industry has on the economy is probably exaggerated, as is suggested by the recent failure of a boom in the industry to cure Detroit's unemployment.[5] Only in-depth exploration of the facts surrounding assumptions such as these can improve the quality of decision-making, and (only?) gaming-simulation will make the results of that exploration understood.

A second tool would be a NEXUS-type gaming-simulation questionnaire to communicate the opinions and feelings of citizens' groups to the decision makers and to communicate the professional expertise of the technician to both citizen groups and decision makers (Armstrong and Hobson, 1970). NEXUS is an information-generating and information-disseminating gaming-simulation that combines aspects of the DELPHI technique and survey research in a single gaming-simulation exercise. Players are asked to comment on (or estimate the magnitude of) the impact of various decisions on carefully selected quality of life indicators from the vantage point of their real-life role or some other assigned role. When specialists or "technocrats" play, the resulting consensus (if there is one) on impact represents expert opinion. When citizens play, the resulting consensus (or lack of it) indicates the intensity and direction of public opinion. When combinations of people play, these "consensus agreements" can be juxtaposed and fought over.[6]

As an example of how this tool might work in practice, consider the current method of resolving a request for a rezoning for a given parcel of land. Such a request would be announced in highly technical and unintelligible articles in the local newspaper. A public hearing is held in which citizens get five or ten minutes each to verbalize their feelings to Common Council. The planners present their recommendations to Council at the hearing and/ or in a special report. Pressure groups might contact particular politicians to assert their influence. At no time is a clear statement of the impact of the rezoning and the reasons behind the decisions made on the request made clear. Suppose that all persons concerned had systematically responded to a uniform questionnaire via a gaming-simulation device. The results could be tabulated and analyzed routinely if the process of administering the game-like questionnaire was ritualized. The outcome of the play would not necessarily alter the advocacy process in any way but would substitute a uniform method of argument for a haphazard battle of words.

Other types of problem-oriented gaming-simulations would be available through the Laboratory Community. For example, a gaming-simulation might be designed to teach people how to purchase housing, or how to interpret a budget. These are educational devices—but what is education but a form of communication? Similarly, gaming-simulations might be built to solve the problems of communication between the police and the youth of a community[7] or the blacks and the whites in the community.[8] In fact, the possibilities are limitless, subject, of course, to the constraints set by our own imaginations and willingness to experiment.

In sum, the combination of gaming-simulation techniques made available in the laboratory would serve the larger community in the following ways:

(1) Help decision makers identify new and potentially troublesome issues at the earliest possible moment (NEXUS-type game).
(2) Let competing groups reformulate and restate the issues to suit their perspective (NEXUS-type game).
(3) Help decision makers gain reasonable input from technocrats and citizen groups with regard to the probable impacts of decisions on key issues (NEXUS-type game).
(4) Allow concerned people (such as decision makers, technicians, citizen groups, interest groups, students) to systematically explore the primary, secondary, and tertiary ramifications of select policy options in the urban or regional system (NEXUS- or METRO-type game).
(5) Bring the power of the computer, a large data base, and related technical aids to those responsible for governing our urban and regional centers as well as to concerned citizens in those centers (METRO-type game).

(6) Provide the mechanism for creating a dynamic, living plan (through the games) to replace the standard maps of the "Comprehensive Plan" used today.

THE IMPLICATIONS OF THE LABORATORY COMMUNITY

The implications for the world of politics (and, hence, political science) of establishing and institutionalizing the Laboratory Community are many. The last section of this paper made repeated reference to multiple sources of input (such as technicians, citizens) to the planning and decision-making processes. Of course, these processes are highly political and bound up in tradition but, nevertheless, political obstacles to broadening the base of decision-making and planning must be overcome by today's establishment. James Q. Wilson (1968: 223) made this point quite clear.

> Citizen participation in urban renewal [or other urban programs], then, is not simply (or even most importantly) a way of winning popular consent for controversial programs. It is part and parcel of a more fundamental reorganization of American local politics. It is another illustration—if one is needed—of how deeply embedded in politics the planning process is.

Donald N. Michael (1968: 1190) suggests that the widespread use of computers with legally enforced citizen accessibility provisions may be the method for reorganizing local politics to accommodate such participation.

> For those who want to participate in the political process, the opportunity to challenge the system or to support it on basis of knowledge *as* the government develops its own position and then to monitor and criticize *continuously* the implementation of whatever policy prevails should be a heady incentive for extensive use of such computer facilities. . . . But the approach proposed here involves no casual laying-on of minor modifications in the conduct of urban government. Opening up the information base of political decision-making would be one of the most painful wrenches conceivable for conventional styles of government.

Although the Laboratory Community as described here is a somewhat different concept than Michael's open-access, multiterminal, computerized information system, it will achieve the same end and, of course, pose the same threat to the conventional political process. We submit that one of the most serious potential impediments to the Laboratory Community concept arises out of this threat. Politicians and decision makers may well be afraid of the Laboratory Community.

There are several sources of fear, some healthy and others disturbing. First, policy makers are afraid of being replaced by the "machine." If a simulation were devised that could make accurate and objective predictions of future states given policy alternatives, this fear might prove to be partially valid. However, somebody must still design alternatives and evaluate future states of society—the policy maker. Realistically, the design of such a powerful simulation is highly unlikely. At best, simulation and gaming-simulation will give a feeling for the possible configuration of future states and allow people to communicate their fears and opinions about those states, but the policy makers will still have to interpret the validity and consequences of the assumptions underlying the gaming-simulation when making their decisions.

A second source of fear is the widespread citizen input needed to make the game room viable and, if that input is secured, the consequences of grassroots decision-making. The expense and inefficiency of maintaining the capability to mingle with citizens in the gaming-simulation environment is a legitimate concern—legitimate, but not wise. The political system in this country must find a way to systematically get a grassroots solutions to the problems, whatever the cost. Failure to do so is an invitation to social upheaval even more severe than that already experienced by our larger cities. Furthermore, once the cost of initiating the Laboratory Community has been met, the cost of maintenance in time and money should not be too great if the process is routinized. The fear of the consequences of grassroots decision-making has even less foundation. The elitist view that technocrats know best has been proven wrong. Technology has run away from the reins of society and must be balanced by citizen control.

A third source of fear is the most depressing from the perspective of the advocate of the use of gaming-simulation in a public policy context. A scientific gaming-simulation Laboratory in the basement of city hall, open to all, will erode the power base of those who currently have the information and clout and return the bureaucracy to a position of service rather than dominance. We argue that this erosion must take place despite the fear and opposition of the bureaucracy to such erosion, and, because gaming-simulation has the potential for causing that erosion to begin, it ought to be pursued.

NOTES

1. This problem is treated in detail in a paper presented at the Eleventh Symposium of the National Gaming Council at Johns Hopkins University, Baltimore, Maryland, in October, 1972.

2. Possibly the best attempt to perform controlled experimentation on the teaching capability of games is reported by Margaret Monroe (1968). Other research concerned with the validation of games (as opposed to evaluation) is going on at the University of Southern California (Russell, 1971; Boocock, 1972b).

3. A full set of manuals and the computer program for METRO-APEX, the most recent version of the game, are now available from several sources including the Environmental

Simulation Laboratory of the University of Michigan, the COMEX Project at the University of Southern California and the Office of Manpower Training of the Environmental Protection Agency.

4. As far-fetched as this may sound, we are currently working with the University of Wisconsin at Milwaukee in setting up such a game room on their campus. Although the room is going to serve students at the university in the early stages of the program, the intention is to include citizens' groups and the establishment in the operation of the Laboratory as the gaming-simulations housed therein begin to pertain more directly to the problems faced in Milwaukee.

5. See the News Analysis by Ralph Orr entitled "Auto Sales Soar, But Not the Jobs" in the Sunday edition of the Detroit *Free Press* of June 25, 1972 for some comments on the impact of the auto industry on Detroit.

6. We had hoped to report on our experiences with this technique more fully in this paper; however, our time schedules for experimentation have been set back by funding delays. To date, we have prepared a NEXUS-type game, POLICY PLAN, to study housing problems in Rochester, N.Y., but have not finished testing this particular exercise. POLICY PLAN was designed by Larry Coppard and Mary Kay Naulin of our staff.

7. One such game, POLICE COMMUNITY RELATIONS or, more popularly, THEY SHOOT MARBLES, DON'T THEY, has been designed by Fred Goodman of the School of Education at the University of Michigan.

8. Several games have been designed on this theme. One of the better ones is URBAN DYNAMICS, designed by the staff of Urbandyne in Chicago.

CHAPTER NINETEEN

INTRODUCING SCIENCE AND TECHNOLOGY AT THE COMMUNITY LEVEL:

The Role of Gaming-Simulation

RICHARD D. DUKE

Systems analysis, computer science, data processing, operations research, simulation, and similar social science techniques are new to the local level of government since World War II. There have been waves of effort by universities, foundations, and public agencies at the state and national level to propagate these new techniques to improve the processes of local government. These efforts have been more or less successful dependent on the techniques, the timing, the locality, and the problem addressed. The most notable achievements have been the transformation of normal administrative processes from hand to computerized operations; unfortunately, these are the most mundane activities and least likely to justify funds for scientific inquiry.

The failures during this period have largely been in those areas dealing with prediction, strategy, planning, policy formulation, and sophisticated modeling of systems; failures which can be traced in almost all cases to several common problems. The first problem is that of a given new scientific technique being promulgated by enthusiasts who oversell the advantages while simultaneously underestimating the difficulties associated with applying the technique. The second major difficulty has been the more or less random appearance of these new methodologies in a sequence which is not logical in terms of the evolution of local skills towards their intelligent utilization. Still another difficulty has been the limits to computing power and data processing equipment; it is only in the very recent past that machine capability and cost have become adequate to a point where they do not limit the user. Finally, and most important, these techniques have failed because they are a new vernacular; they are basically foreign to the experience and the ability of local officials. For that reason, even the potential successes have failed because the local authorities were not able to comprehend the nature of the process and, therefore, they were unable and unwilling to give credence to the product of these new efforts.

It goes beyond the purpose of this chapter to give a complete documentation of the activities alluded to above. However, several major developments should be noted by way of illustrating these points. For example, urban "Data Banks" were very much in vogue in the late 1950s and early 1960s. Almost without exception, these were failures representing considerable loss of public funds and perhaps more important, a loss of goodwill on the part of urban officials who had been hoodwinked into supporting these activities. These early data bank efforts failed for several reasons. First, they were premature in that no rational, coherent urban theory existed to guide their articulation and development; second, no models, simulations, or similar processes were in existence which could benefit from the data; third, no suitable hardware and/or software existed for the proper reduction of this data for public policy issues; and finally, there was no experience with the communication interface between public officials and quantitative data of this type. Worse yet, most of these data bank efforts were ill-conceived in their basic management, underfunded, far too optimistic in terms of completion schedules, and plagued with inaccuracies so frequent and so great as to make any results suspect to even the casual observer. As can be expected, early advocates of data bank development did not outdo one another in public candor concerning these difficulties. To this day, the data bank concept is suspect in the majority of its applications on the urban scene.

At about the same period in history (the early 1960s) there was a significant effort, largely on the part of commercial concerns, to distribute hardware to municipalities. These were the so-called "second-generation" computers; by and large, the failure rate of these efforts in their initial application was quite high. Fortunately, they frequently led to an evolutionary process where equipment was customized to a particular municipality to meet basic administrative needs. The long-term results have been remarkably successful. Most American communities today have more computing capacity and more technical knowledge concerning that capacity than many Third World nations have at the national policy level. The reason for this evolutionary success stems from two basic facts. The first is that communities were growing rapidly and administrative processes were becoming increasingly complex, and therefore the pressure to automate was high. This, of course, was coupled with the routine nature of this demand which permitted a solution, once achieved, to be utilized on a continuing basis. On the other side of the coin, we had a very active commercial development of hardware and a major competitive effort by manufacturers to deliver hardware with ever-increasing capacity at ever-lower cost. We stand, at the moment, on the threshold of an entirely new era of computer development where the introduction of micro-processors and very large scale integration (VLSI) of circuitry will result in truly astonishing changes in hardware over the next decade. This will be addressed later.

More or less simultaneously with the emergence of data banks and computing equipment came models and simulations for urban management purposes. These were initially traffic models prompted by the development of the Interstate Highway System but they soon grew into increasingly more complex simulations and model sets sold to communities to solve a variety of policy ills. The success rate of these efforts has been remarkably poor; perhaps their only effective use has been by consultants who developed a "Black Box" which was used in city after city in the evolution of transportation plans, but even these can be the subject of legitimate criticism. Certainly the linkage between the data banks and the transportation models never came close to fulfilling the promise implied in the many expenditures of public funds.

The more complex model sets which have been reported in the literature and tried in several cities failed on several accounts. First, there was a lack of coherent and tested theory to guide their development. As a consequence they proceeded on an ad hoc and experimental basis. As these model sets emerged their defined data needs were, in many cases, not met by the existing data banks which has been prepared in an anticipation of the models (the classic "cart before the horse" situation) and the result was often that data were pieced together at the last moment in an ad hoc and estimated fashion. These models, in their complexity, quickly outran the available computing power for practical purposes, and they were soon restricted to use by university groups and others who had an interest in their scientific development. *Finally, and most significantly, those efforts which did reach some technical success failed almost completely in their public policy mission because local politicians put little or no faith in the product.* The exceptions, of course, were the transportation models which were often manipulated to give results suitable for some local political need. The results, of course, were then quickly adopted for local purposes under the guise of being "scientific."

Perhaps the final dissemination effort that should be mentioned is the various analytic techniques which have found their way into communities in the past quarter century. These include, but are not limited to, such methods as critical path network, queuing theory, statistical methods, PERT, systems analysis in several forms, demographic models. These have had limited but growing success. One of the serious limitations to the introduction of many of these techniques was the lack of adequately trained personnel. In the past decade, universities have produced many young professionals coming from a variety of programs who have much greater capacity to deal with these techniques. Interestingly enough, most of these techniques have found their way into specific applications which deal with applied problems in the workaday world of the community. These become very important examples since they have a payoff that is perceived at the local community level. One can assume that in the coming decade similar analytic techniques will find their way into the community as each new crop of university students emerges into the working world.

In summary, then, a quick look at the history of the last 25 years reveals a number of discouraging failures and many continuing difficulties in the application of science and technology to public policy at the local level; however, on balance, the successes far outweigh the failures with the result that the fruits of science and technology are now ubiquitous; they can be found at the applied level in communities across the land. Furthermore, this is likely to be a self-fulfilling process carried by its own weight; that is, we can expect to see the more aggressive communities put into application the latest technique, method, and theory only to be copied by other communities in a relatively short time. Please note, however, that these successes have been and will continue to be of a pragmatic nature as a way of improving on processes which are now routinely conducted.

The challenge of the next decade, then, lies in bringing the strength of science and technology to the local community so that it can be applied to strategic thinking in a way which will permit leaders to anticipate change in the community and to plan for an evolutionary process which takes into account the many aspects of community development.

THE SIGNIFICANCE OF THE MICROPROCESSOR EXPLOSION

At one point in time it was common to speak of computers in terms of their "generation": in this system of accounting, the Illiac and Mistic machines were viewed as first generation, the first wave of commercial machines was viewed as the second generation, and so on. At best these were approximate terms and the distinction was often blurred by the rapid evolution of the equipment. Certainly if one were to continue the use of these descriptors the advent of the microprocessors would have introduced us into the most recent "generation" of machines. More significantly, we stand on the threshold of yet another "generation" of machines which takes advantage of very large-scale integration (VLSI). The microprocessors have brought powerful and inexpensive machines into use by individuals on a personal basis; in an explosive development still rapidly underway, the VLSI development promises to increase the power of machines by several orders of magnitude.

The evolution of the hardware (and the associated software) has been so swift and so dramatic that we sometimes fail to recognize its significance. It has been very difficult for university personnel to stay abreast of hardware and software developments, and certainly impossible for communities. As a consequence, as we talk about science and technology finding its way into the community, we must recognize that it is normal to see a very spotty pattern of evolution governed to some degree by the chance acquisition of hardware by one community or another. In any given locale, this evolution is likely to proceed in a very sporadic and irregular way, largely because the purchase or other commitment to a new computer installation tends to be of many years' duration (because of the change-over cost).

Virtually all communities are still operating largely on a batch processor mode with one centralized facility. It is not difficult to predict that the new microprocessors, particularly as they are supplemented by VLSI technology, make it probable that within five years the typical community will have many small computer installations, each customized to some specific departmental or other functional activity. One can expect that this development will be fought by those who have a vested interest in the existing batch processor machines, but their battle will prove futile since the new equipment will move inexorably onto the scene.

Microprocessors are ubiquitous. The rate of production of the most popular models has not been officially revealed, but speculation exists that perhaps a quarter million units per year are entering the market. Significantly, these units have a long half-life, not yet determined; that is, the equipment tends to be easy to maintain. It is modular, with the possibility of adding new chips to upgrade the equipment as the technology advances; therefore, the additional units each year will tend to be cumulative for some time into the future. Significantly, an entire generation of college students is beginning to emerge which feels completely at home with the use of this equipment. Also of great importance, software packages are evolving at a rapid rate and a variety of exchange media have emerged. It is now common to find retail outlets for microprocessors in cities of even modest size and remote location within the United States.

In our attempt to understand the impact of science and technology on public policy in the public sector in the community in the post-World War II period, we have identified hardware and related software as being a significant controlling variable. That is, only as the hardware emerged was it possible for communities to begin to make effective application of scientific knowledge. We now are entering into a dramatic new period when the hardware/software will take a quantum jump. This shift will be significant in at least two dimensions: first, communities will be released from the constraints of batch processing; and, second, the new microprocessor machines which will soon be found in abundance in every community will be significantly greater in capacity and much more convenient than the existing batch processing machines.

Here we should pause and look at a phenomenon that has been associated with computers since their first introduction. That is, before one has access to the machine, one is not certain of its application. However, once a machine is made available, the user invents problems which can be solved. We now have an urban environment into which a new class of technocrats is entering from the university community to discover a new generation of hardware waiting to be put to use. *Clearly this is a remarkable opportunity for public intervention towards the orderly transfer of scientific knowledge and the speedy dissemination of the latest developments into the field.*

FIVE QUANDARIES WHICH INHIBIT EFFECTIVE DISSEMINATION OF SCIENCE AND TECHNOLOGY

In the late 1950s, Stanford Optner developed a series of articles and monographs dealing with the "City as a System." In these documents he envisioned the time when municipal leaders would use the full power of science and technology not only in a day-to-day, pragmatic level of management but also in a more powerful sense to develop strategies for the logical evolution of the community through time. More than two decades later, this prophetic work is still a promise, not a reality. However, many of the preconditions to this evolution have been met: better theory, better hardware and software, appropriate data technology, greater public acceptance, and better techniques for communicating along the man-machine interface. Major scientific projects at the national level have repeatedly demonstrated the feasibility of planning at the strategic level using sophisticated modern science and technology (the space program serves as an excellent example). Before we can expect similar successes in strategic development at the community level, there are several major difficulties which must be met. I have identified these as the "five quandaries":

(1) *Urban problems, by and large, can only be solved in the long run; but politicians seek solutions in the short term measured against their next election* (usually two years away). Virtually any significant urban problem, whether it is housing, the economy, air pollution, unemployment, transportation, or the like, represents complexity and emerging trends which must be perceived as long-term developments if any effective local strategy is to be employed. Politicians are notorious in dodging the logical long-term results of their actions (the budget crisis in New York City came as no surprise to most analysts, nor to most politicians, even though year after year they were party to policy decisions which made the result inevitable).

(2) *Science requires explicit knowledge in a coherent, predictive model, whereas politicians frequently seek to hide and obfuscate.* Science survives on the logic that truth must be obtained and recognized and that progress is achieved through the evolutionary linkage of bits and pieces of knowledge through time. Politics deals with very fuzzy attitudinal matters where Truth is hard to discern (and even harder to remember after election day). Therefore, when science and technology are applied to the local community, one can expect politicians to react negatively if Truth interferes with their freedom of political action.

(3) *Science takes time and politicians cannot wait.* The nature of scientific inquiry is such that results must wait on the accumulation of knowledge which justifies a conclusion; political reality dictates that decisions must be made now on the basis of whatever fragmentary knowledge may be at hand. Science cannot be hurried and politics are conducted under an imperative.

(4) *Science seeks Truth for its own sake and politics views itself as the art of the possible.* This reality explains why the two approaches are significantly different. Science, in seeking Truth, pursues each component in more detail and as a consequence scientists normally feel comfortable speaking only to a microcosm on which they have data. Politicians inevitably must deal with a macrocosm in which all things are happening simultaneously with many linkages implied but unknown—consequently they demand that scientists speak to this macrocosm if they are to be heard on policy issues.

(5) *There is a contempt for politics by scientists and a contempt of science by politicians.* The scientific community prefers to remain aloof from the day-to-day world of the community. There is a different reality, a different vernacular, in the two worlds. This credibility gap is pervasive and accounts for the failure of science and technology in public policy at the municipal level even in those instances where technique is sufficient.

There is a growing need to reevaluate the role of science and technology vis-à-vis public policy decisions. Two circumstances contribute to the need for reevaluation of the role of science/technological activities (Michael, 1969):

> There is a growing appreciation that societal survival requires a system perspective, an ecological perspective, a holistic perspective. This appreciation is greatly reinforced by other changes in images of self and social condition but, certainly, it grows especially from recognition of the interactiveness of all important processes especially as they are netted together through the impact of technologies and their infrastructures. A bits and pieces, disjointedly incrementalist approach simply won't do, though that message, while increasingly recognized in principal has been excruciatingly slow to be realized in practice.

> Increasing demands by citizens for participation in decisions affecting their destiny. On the one hand, this demand for participation has also increased the demand for information about proposed technologies so the participants can judge their implications. On the other hand, in the dynamic of participation there is a tendency toward splintering and autonomy, toward group proliferation. And each group demands recognition of its entitlement to influence decisions regarding the destiny of a proposed technological development.

Demands for participation plus proliferation of groups complicates the application of a systems perspective but it also stimulates attention to a wider variety of scenarios about the impacts of the new technologies.

Because of the interconnectivity of today's world it has probably never been more urgent to improve the quality of public policy decision-making. Although one might logically assume that science is the handmaiden of policy, or that the scientist and the policy maker would share a professional respect for the other's ability, the evidence is strongly to the contrary. The painful character of this dichotomy is reflected repeatedly in the literature. A 1977 article by Kenneth F. Watt, entitled "Why Won't Anyone Believe Us?", serves to illustrate the current dilemma. Dr. Watt describes his eight-year participation in developing large-scale computer simulation models at the University of California at a cost of several million dollars. This work was supported by the Ford Foundation, the United States National Science Foundation, the Subcommittee on Energy and Power of the House of Representatives, as well as the East-West Center in Honolulu. He states:

> A primary goal of the project has been and is to influence decision makers, a goal which we pursued aggressively. But by any objective standards, all of our efforts have had no impact whatsoever on public policy. Furthermore, many recent studies and surveys show that modeling and simulation have had virtually no effect on public policy, despite world-wide expenditures in this area of perhaps half a billion dollars.

Dr. Watt then goes on to analyze the reasons behind this circumstance and arrives at essentially the same conclusions that appear in other studies: The world of the decision maker is sufficiently different from the world of the scientist/modeler that communication is essentially nonexistent. While the behavior/posture of both groups is logical and defensible to their peers, each is openly cynical toward the other. Witness the following quotation:

> When we began, some of us assumed that legislators making critical policy decisions for society would have professional-level understanding of the subjects about which they make decisions, which may have huge financial implications (as in transportation systems). Therefore, we assumed that it would be relatively easy to communicate to them the results of our simulations so as to aid them in forming public policy. We have discovered to our chagrin, as any political scientist or politician could have told us, that legislators do not make decisions on the basis of expert knowledge about enormously important problems, but rather by responding to influence from powerful constituencies. Thus, the very language in which our output data was expressed often came as a complete surprise to legislators. . . . In short, a modeling group which has been funded to have a useful impact on public policy discovers that, after the simulation is complete, it must engage in an exhaustive program (which may last for years) to educate the electorate and the legislators.

The politician's response to such a statement might be equally hostile in expressing doubts about the validity of developing alternatives predicated on exclusively quantifiable data. The politician "knows" that many nonquanti-fiable variables ("soft data") exist and affect the issue at hand. The politician knows intuitively that science fails at dealing with these subjective and value-laden issues.

And so the two persist in isolation chambers and the continued existence of this false dichotomy, although recognized time and again, remains the root obstacle to improved public policy decision-making. In the summary to his article, Dr. Watt itemizes the failure of past efforts and provides a list of eight changes that he believes are essential to improved impact of science on public policy decisions. Providing graphic evidence to his analysis of where the problem lies, and what must be done to solve it, the final argument is that most of the budget of any simulation project must be *"devoted to communi-cating research findings to policy makers and the public in language that they will understand"* (emphasis mine).

The objective of this chapter is to propose methodologies which can improve communications on the science/public policy interface. As the proliferation and specificity of scientific research increases, the need for communicating these findings to the policy maker becomes more difficult, creating the need for a new mode of communication. Gaming-simulation, appropriately conceived and executed, is the most promising method to provide this interface. Decision makers, aware of the usefulness of models but uninitiated in computer use, become the natural clients for such a game.

ROLE OF GAMING/SIMULATION

During the evolutionary period described above, one of the several tech-niques which has emerged is gaming-simulation as a communications tool for improved understanding between scientists and public officials. Actually the origins of gaming-simulation as a scientific tool of serious purpose predates these other developments by several hundred years. First employed in a rudimentary form by the Prussians as a military training device during the 1800s, gaming was the exclusive domain of military strategists until the end of World War II. Business schools adopted the technique for training purposes, and these developments were quickly followed by political scien-tists, who modified the technique to explore evolving global political pat-terns. Close on the heels of the political scientist came many other social scientists finding ways to introduce gaming into the educational arena. By the early 1970s, gaming was finding its way into actual applied situations as a predecision tool of public policy. This operational use of gaming in the urban policy area moved rapidly throughout the States and into Europe; in recent years it has become widespread in Third World nations as well.

Gaming-simulation is a dynamic, interactive, communication mode that has been developed by professionals into a rigorous methodology serving as a hybrid man-machine link; a situation-specific tool. Recent developments of the methodology contribute to its capacity to serve as a communications interface or link between the world of the scientist and the world of the decision maker. As was previously established, the root of the problem is poor communications between scientists and policy makers; this flows from several difficulties:

(1) *The basic objectives of the scientist and policy maker are very different.* The scientist seeks replicable "Truth" and the logical pursuit of its consequences. The public policy maker operates in a world of reality and hopes through coalition formation to achieve "the art of the possible."

(2) This first characteristic derives in part from a second basic difference. *The scientist needs quantifiable, replicable data;* the politician works with non-quantifiable, nonreplicable imagery that derives from a political sense.

(3) The first two difficulties in turn contribute to a third, which is the *impediment of jargon.* Kenneth Watt's article cited above provides ample evidence.

(4) *The scientist and policy maker operate on different time horizons.* The scientist focuses on horizons appropriate to scientific data; the politician focuses on horizons of strictly political significance.

(5) *The two frequently operate from a different scope or perspective in terms of definition of the problem.* There is no inherent reason why micro and macro perception need to be at variance; however, as a practical matter, the scientist and politician are at different ends of the continuum.

(6) *The two groups operate with conflicting reward structures and peer group imagery.* The scientist will tend to be much more concerned with the elegance of the mathematical model while the politician will take a jaundiced view until its pragmatic value in political terms has been revealed.

This list of difficulties derives from differing perceptions of the decision process: the perception of scientists that decision is a logical process which contrasts markedly from the political reality of decision as a gestalt event. If the exchange of information across the science/public policy interface is going to improve, new styles of communication must be suited to this need.

Gaming/simulation has become a disciplined activity subject to careful professional use. It is a problem-specific technique, where the particulars will vary from problem to problem but with a process, procedure, and rules of application that can be consistently followed (Duke, 1974).

There are many advantages to using gaming-simulation as a science/public policy interface tool. The most significant is that it turns the "cold" processes of science into "warm" activities of the game that a politician can identify with and understand. Further, it gives the politician a hands-on opportunity with the scientific instrument, but in a context and a vernacular that are familiar. This reduces the dependence of the politician on a technician or other scientific intermediary; or, worse yet, the dependence on technical data in the form of a listing which is incomprehensible and/or recommendations from scientists that give one or more options without the supporting logic being clear.

Another significant use of gaming-simulation is to serve as prototype for specific kinds of scientific activity; such prototypes are very useful for training purposes of several kinds. They can be used to train specific techniques that are being disseminated, they can be used to train in particular substantive areas, and, most significantly, they can be used to acquaint participants with the character of the system with which they are dealing. In this fashion they meet the constraints of one of the five quandaries stated earlier in that a good game/simulation can be an effective blending in hybrid form of the known as drawn from science and the unknown or partially known that can be drawn from the world of social science.

Gaming-simulation can also serve as an effective device for introducing the microprocessor itself to community officials. It is far more interesting to explore the capability of a piece of equipment using an example which mimics one's own reality than it is to use strictly scientific examples. This can be equated with the phenomenon of learning the game Monopoly by simply joining in someone else's ongoing game rather than trying to begin by reading the detailed rules (a process few enjoy).

Games can serve as a predecision tool to link a more complex model to the real world. In this case we are talking about a "model of a model" which is somewhat analogous to the architect's use of a physical model to illustrate what a building might look like when it is completed. The architect has a detailed plan, but it is incomprehensible to the layman. Similarly the scientist's understanding, when expressed in the vernacular of scientific papers, is generally incomprehensible to the layman. It can, however, be abstracted into an effective game/simulation which serves the same function as the architectural scale model. This permits the layman to communicate to the scientist through the game in an effective manner, again analogous to the layman looking at the architectural model and requesting modification to the design of the ultimate building.

CHAPTER TWENTY

URBAN GAMES FOR THE 1980s:

The Introduction of Microprocessors into Local Decision-Making

RICHARD D. DUKE
JAN RENEE GRAF

INTRODUCTION

The previous chapter presented the case for a new generation of urban policy games based on the expanded abilities provided by the microprocessor. This chapter describes a recent example of a game/simulation developed in response to this new technology.

Early urban games were of two types: manual or computer. Manual games were most popular, especially for training purposes; however the logistics of hand operation required that they be kept simple, hindering their policy use. The utility of computer games was limited because the input was batch-processed. This slow process required that games be presented in a discontinuous mode; presenting a serious barrier to communication among players. Errors, both human and machine, were inevitable in the process and could not be corrected except by way of "historical" explanation. As a consequence, only the most dedicated operators were successful with these computer games.

Microprocessors changed this dramatically due to their low cost (an entire system—computer, printer, disk drives, CRT—costs about the same as an hour of computer time on a large batch machine of the mid 1960s) it is now possible to have a dedicated system for the immediate and exclusive service of the game. This provided several dramatic advantages:

(1) The game design and the computer configuration can be matched at the outset; the technology is governed by the problem rather than the reverse.
(2) Once acquired, the system remains constant in its response (large batch processing systems are under constant revision and modification requiring the game user to invest heavily in time and money to adapt the game program to the new technical mix).

(3) The system is portable and fully dedicated. It goes wherever the game is played, permitting instant turnaround on player decisions and immediate correction of errors (of which there are far fewer).

(4) Many refinements are possible because of the capabilities of the new equipment. Batch processing imposed severe constraints of sequentiality; microprocessors permit interruption and flash-forward or flash-backward to other parts of the model, as may be required. Color graphics are available, as well.

(5) The game operator is not required to have any technical knowledge, the presentation can be entirely in conventional language. This is in contrast with early uses which required that the operator have full technical knowledge of the program to insure success.

THE OKLAHOMA CASE

The Oklahoma Department of Economic and Community Affairs was recently charged with training municipal officials in the characteristics of new state legislation which modified municipal budget practice. The new law provides an alternative to the present system of adopting and administering city budgets. It establishes fiscal practices, requires greater financial disclosure, and allows municipalities to implement generally accepted standards of financial management. The primary difference between the two laws is that the new law places the decision-making power solely in the hands of the municipal governing body, whereas the old law required review of the budget by the county excise board. The greatest single need of the new process is the accurate projection of revenue by the city manager and council.

Because this law differs in its particulars from the existing law, it is necessary to train municipal officials in the new act. Further, in the normal course of events, there is a relatively high turnover of municipal officials (newly elected politicians representing somewhere between 25 percent to 30 percent of elected officials in the average year). All of these individuals must be introduced to the new law.

The new budget procedures represent a continuous process with dynamic linkage to many facets of the community. This process can best be shown by some form of simulation because of the complexities involved; gaming-simulation was selected as the most effective technique for use in training newly elected politicians.

The objective of the client was to develop a gaming-simulation of the municipal budgeting process for a mid-sized Oklahoma city; the completed exercise was to serve as the core of a training exercise to be conducted by the staff of the Department of Economic and Community Affairs for the benefit of elected officials at the local community level. It is expected that the "ODECAS" exercise will be used to supplement the short course on municipal budgeting currently offered by the Oklahoma Department of Planning and Economic Development. ODECAS will also be used as a "stand alone" training exercise for municipal officials; its function in both instances is to highlight the relationship between municipal budgeting activity and community planning.

The game is played in a series of cycles, each cycle representing one budget year and repeating a sequence of decisions. These decisions are made in an environment which changes due to player's actions and outside factors. The player's responsibility is to respond to the situation shaping community change in order to create some desired objective. Certain variables act as indicators of transitions in the status of wards, others of city conditions, and still others of the status of a role. This exercise is expected to take about five hours to complete (it is possible to have shorter or longer exercises).

What is ODECAS About?

ODECAS demonstrates the budgetary and fiscal management processes of a small community. In order to achieve this, an abstraction of both the budgetary process and other appropriate urban processes are combined with role playing by actual decision makers. The community and the roles are described below to give a flavor of the game; details of the budgetary process are omitted from this discussion, but the process is represented in the game in great detail.

ODECAS, population 17,000, is a small city with slow but steady growth. The city has significant minority, low income, elderly populations. The government is a weak major-manager/council type. A council representative is elected from each of the 4 wards, which are nearly equal in population. ODECAS is at the crossroads of two rivers and two rail lines; in addition major roads bisect the city: one from north to the south; and three from east to west. The area surrounding the city consists of farms and ranches. The city's economic health depends largely on its four primary employers; this has made city officials eager to diversify the economic base, protecting the city from high unemployment. New commercial growth is beginning along major roads at the edges of the city, including a shopping center. ODECAS has a sizeable stock of older homes, but the condition of its housing stock varies greatly, as does the condition of its infrastructure. The older industrial areas are along the rail lines.

The city is represented in the game by four wards. Ward 1 is experiencing much of the new residential growth. The residents are mostly singles and young families, a majority of which are Caucasian; both their education levels and their incomes are higher than the city average. The most vocal and organized part of the city, they demand a high level of public services. They are seeking revitalization and expansion of the city.

Ward 2, along the river front, is both the oldest and most beautiful residential section in the city. Many of the long-standing families live in this ward; they are primarily both Caucasians and conservatives. Although the homes are old, they have a higher than average value and a low percentage of deterioration among them.

Ward 3 is the old core of the city, containing many of the major industries, government buildings, the downtown, and the oldest residential sections. It has been allowed to deteriorate greatly over the years. Much of the housing stock is substandard and overcrowded. Its residents have income well below the average; there is a high percentage of unemployment and retirees as well. The ward's population is predominantly Black and Indian.

The fourth ward is a middle income, blue collar, strongly conservative section of the city. The ward centers around the school; the community's large families reside here. The Black and Indian population is strong in this ward, and is the most vocal. The unemployment here fluctuates greatly with the city's economy. The ward is bounded on three sides by light industrial and commercial development.

The Roles

All participants are given the opportunity to vote using their existing clout in the community leaders' opinion poll each cycle. Many events or issues are presented to the players requiring their decision. Some examples include the creation of a city income tax which would remove the uncertainty of revenues by reducing the dependency of utility fees for revenues (which would fall primarily on low-income residents); the enforcement of the building code which would leave many low-income residents unable to afford a home; industrial rezoning harming the quality of life but improving the city's economy; annexation of a township which increases the tax burden and service demands; and so forth.

The roles act as a framework into which each individual can impute goals; they mirror the key actors in this decision and the computer acts for the residents of the community.

The city manager is responsible for the administration of the budget process, the only administrative role in the game. The manager is indirectly responsive to the public through the hire/fire power held by the city council (the last decision to be made at the annual council meeting). The manager takes the first cut at the budget, making estimates of the revenues, revenue distribution to funds, and fund distribution for departmental expenditures. This player prioritizes capital improvement projects based on the inputs of planners, the opinion poll, and the public's preference as indicated in the newspaper. During the council meeting the manager presents a brief budget message summarizing the city's condition and the proposed budget, and, finally, acts as a technical expert on all budget issues at the meeting. The main difference between the politician and the city manager is that the manager's assessment of the current needs is more citywide in orientation. These goals may or may not be similar to those of the politician.

ODECAS is played with either 3 or 5 politicians (council persons); one of these is always elected at large in the city and designated as the mayor. The remaining 2 or 4 players are elected from a specific ward and are responsive to their constituencies. The primary function of the politician is to set the city's operational budget including capital improvement projects, under the advice of the city manager, and considering the demands of pressure groups and the population as found in the newspaper. The amount of discretionary funds the politicians have available to pay for capital projects is rather small after the deduction of departmental operations, maintenance, and personnel expenses.

These players set the utility rate structure and millage rates by which the city generates its revenue. They review and approve all plans, zoning changes, and utility/road expansions. They may fire and hire the city manager. The politicans will have to decide their own goals and what measures might be used to assess progress toward those goals. A politician may be seen to do right for the poor of the city; success being measured by the amount of influence exerted on the other players. The politician might have nonpersonal goals, such as a rapid increase in employment in the city or equity of public expenditures; or personal goals, such as remaining in office or maintaining clout.

The number of realtors will range between one to five dependent on the number of players participating in any play of the game. The realtors are sequentially numbered and color coded to indicate their holdings and transactions on the board. Each realtor will also receive a holding sheet at the end of the predecision phase which keeps track of the individuals total assets and changes in those assets. The realtors play the role of the land developer/ speculator; buying land with the hope it will appreciate in value. They keep an eye on the issue in the opinion poll to determine which of the three wards is likely to be the most profitable. It may prove beneficial to try to influence the vote of other roles to achieve a favorable outcome, or at least a nonharmful one. In addition to deciding where to invest (any of the four wards), the realtor must also choose between various land uses and building development types. (There are 28 types of investments to be made.) This choice may include one, any combination, or all of these to invest in, given sufficient funds. A decision to make any one of these investments may require a rezoning or improvements. The realtor receives income from the operation of holdings and must pay both utilities and taxes. Profits and rate of profit increase are obvious measures of the realtor's success; individual players may find other measures of satisfaction.

The planners' main concern is with planning the city in order to prevent haphazard development by speculative interests. Their concern includes the community's economic health, a major problem of American cities today. Since their authority is generally limited to recommendations, the planners' power rests in their ability to persuade the other roles. The actions in which they are active include zoning changes, land use planning, policy plans, and capital improvements projects. Consideration of goals are very important to the planner's role; possible goals may include no growth, industrial revitalization, low density, or increased recreational emphasis.

There are three pressure groups, any number of which may be presented in any cycle of the game. The three pressure groups are Minority Council; Friends of the Court; Chambers of Commerce. Clout is designated to each specific pressure group and each player gauges success by the additional clout given for a favorable resolution of an issue according to the stance of the group.

There is one city clerk, who is also the game operator. It is the primary function of this role to process all player inputs for the computer and designate board changes at the proper time. All land transactions, clout counts, budget decisions and recommendations must be recorded on the computer. Therefore, players must return all forms to the clerk after the necessary portions are completed.

Technical Description

In the past, games have relied on traditional techniques for sequencing and accounting functions. The sophistication of gaming, computers, and the budgeting process suggested the need for an advancement in those techniques. With the introduction of the microprocessor into the policy game, new bounds and limits were set: increased level of detail and complexity, improved access to data and reduced processing time, and increased attention to synchronizing cycling of both game and computer processing.

ODECAS is a game which mirrors both the budgetary process of a city and the larger municipal decision-making environment. The preparation of a budget is not an isolated act; it is at best only half the task. Foremost, budgeting requires targeting funds to community needs, with fiscal and management control to assure those funds are spent as allocated. Here the larger community forces become of concern; the public at large and special interests influence politicians as to the needs which ought to be addressed. These forces are represented in the ODECAS game both by the roles and within the accounting mechanisms of the microprocessor.

ODECAS did not discard the traditional accounting and sequencing techniques but rather combined the two. The traditional visual techniques contain many important symbols which can be more closely focused on since the accounting burden has been reduced for the players. In addition, the use of the microprocessor in the game eases the uncomfortable feeling many have with using computers.

Pacing of a game has been dependent on its cycling structure, the speed of the players, accounting operations, and the steps of play (see Figure 20.1). The microprocessor introduces a new, faster pace to the game, restoring the "hubbub" factor often lost in past games because of detailed processing requirements. The program sequence indicates the processing order. Figure 20.1 demonstrates the impact that processing has on game sequencing since the computer actions are going on as the player decisions are being made. In addition, players are spurred on by the output produced. The

Player Actions	*Computer Actions*
PRE-DECISION	BUDGET PROCESSING PHASE
—election	—CIP entered; voter response for all
—clop issues; collect clout	bonds and millage; purge file
—distribute newspaper	—update infra index by cell
—computer update	—rev. generation
—distribute budget print out	—property tax
—distribute players print out	—utility fee
	—input new millage and utility rate
	—revenue by funds
	—expenditures spread by departments
	—bonding deficit automatic
DECISION PHASE	CLEAN UP PHASE
—CM estimates revenue expenditures	—property reassessment routine
by department	—dept. CIP random generation
—Pol. selects ward specific CIP; QOL;	—infra. index depreciation
review zoning and utility changes	—Quality of Life
—Dev. buy; builds; zone; improve; sell	
—planners CIP rec'd; land use plan;	ISSUE PHASE
review zoning changes; policy plan;	—election routine
utility plan	—clop; goal, employment
—Pressure groups lobby	
—Clerk changes board as required	
COUNCIL PHASE	DECISION PHASE
—dispense clout; mayoral election	—process realtors decisions
—budget message	—process planners decisions planners
—politician CIP approval; budget	CIP file; realtors holdings and rental
approval, millage approval; utility rates;	algorithm realtor tax and utility
plan approval; fire/hire CM	assessment
	—clout calculation

FIGURE 20.1

DATA FOR CELL

A	LAND USE	Q	INFRASTRUCTURE IDX
B	ZONING CODE	R	POLK VAR 1
C	HOUSE TYPE 1	S	POLK VAR 2
D	HOUSE TYPE 2	T	POLK VAR 3
E	HOUSE TYPE 3	U	POLK VAR 4
F	HOUSE TYPE 4	V	POLK VAR 5
G	UTIL CONN CODE	W	POLK VAR 6
H	VACANCIES	X	POLK VAR 7
I	BLDG QUANTITY	Y	ENVIR VAR 1
J	BLDG QUALITY	Z	ENVIR VAR 2
K	OWNERSHIP	1	LAND VAL/ACRE
L	LAND VALUE 000S	2	ASSESSED VAL 000S
M	CIP CARRIED CYCLE	3	CIP VALUE 000S
N	HOLD CAPACITY	4	POPULATION
O	BUS UNITS	5	# OF JOBS
P	BLDG TYPE	6	BLDG VALUE 000S

FIGURE 20.2

computer facilitates storage of information, especially where more than one decision is required for action. Game storage consists of cell data (see Figure 20.2 for description of cell) permanent storage, temporary storage, and constants:

(1) Cell data: contains all parameters describing a particular cell.
(2) Permanent storage: Files used for entire game. This provides a permanent record of the game and thus comparison of various fiscal scenarios is possible, such as quality of life, number of buildings, number of jobs.
(3) Constants: permanent data without added variables (such employment matrix, building density, inflation index).
(4) Temporary storage: store value until a new value is input or the value is printed (such as realtor's transactions).

This glimpse at the storage system indicates the detailed level of accounting which is programmed into the microprocessor. Human manipulation of the data would be cumbersome and the fast-paced atmosphere of the game would be lost. However, to use the computer solely would result in mistrust by the participants; the combined use of the board with the printouts, supplemented by the processor's graphic display, enhances the understanding that could be achieved by any one technique.

The gaming-simulation was developed as a man-machine exercise using a 48K Apple microprocessor with 5-inch floppy disk input and line printer output. The computer program is written in Apple basic language and transmitted on a diskette; this and accompanying player operator manuals and playing board constitute the complete exercise.

The board, a traditional accounting mechanism, consists of a grid (10x28). Each cell in that grid represents one city block or 20 acres and has a data bank of 30 some variables, 13 of which are graphically represented on the board. The power of the visual symbols blocks for buildings, dotted lines for rails, and colors for ownership becomes readily clear, and a glance allows the player to access changes which may occur. The graphics on the computer allow a first order approximation of the relative position of each cell for all of the variables.

Forms and wall charts used in traditional games have gained in sophistication; the wall charts now come "hot off the press." The forms have a dual accounting system and require coding for operator input. The key is the coordination of the two in sequencing, processing, and operating. The game and the microprocessor enjoy a symbiotic relationship with an enormous potential for expansion of tools for policy decision-making. The game gives the microprocessor access to an audience previously reluctant to accept and use it. The microprocessor enhances the game storage, accounting, and policy comparison capabilities.

Field Use of the Exercise

At this writing the exercise has been delivered to the client and all training of staff is complete. Although field use is just getting underway, several observations are possible. The first concerns ease of use. The training staff was able to handle the computer operation literally from the first effort; as a consequence, attention could be focused on the use of the exercise. The hardware, which was purchased for the dedicated use of this exercise, already has serious competitive use. Staff have "invented" a variety of uses which now keep the equipment in constant use; these inevitably lure them further into this new technology. A variety of other uses have shown an interest in the technique and will secure the program to serve as an example to prompt interest in the equipment as well as the gaming technique.

Appendix A
Guidelines for Recording
Game Information

Users of gaming-simulation often have difficulty communicating with one another about the critical components and characteristics of the materials of interest to them. The "Gaming-Simulation Record Sheet" presented here is meant to serve as a form for keeping records of new and old gaming-simulations: their major characteristics and the evaluations of the user.

GAMING-SIMULATION RECORD SHEET*

TITLE: _____

Designer:
Date of construction: Present stage of development:
Subject matter:
Purpose:
Intended use:

Related games: ancestors or descendants

PRAGMATICS
  Availability:
      Cost:
      Source:

  Space and paraphernalia:
      Space requirements:
      Computer requirements:
      Other media required (not provided in kit):

  Kit paraphernalia:
      Materials and quantities needed:

      Standard/custom-made:
      Documentation:

  Personnel requirements:
      Number of operators needed:
      Operator roles and skills:

Player characteristics:
  Number of players:
  Age range:
  Prior knowledge or sophistication required
      or recommended:
  Desired degree of homogeneity:

Time parameters:
  Preparation time:
      Operator training:
      Player preparation:
  Duration of play:
      Introduction:
      Flying time:
      Critique:

DESIGN AND OPERATING CHARACTERISTICS:

Steps of play and plot outline:

Player organization:
  Individual/team/coalition:

  Number of players/role or team:

OTHER NOTES:

Appendix B
A General Framework For Evaluation

In addition to recording evaluation of gaming-simulations, a user may wish to elicit the evaluations of participants and to collect information on what transpired. Appendix B presents a very skeptical evaluation form that might be employed for such purposes. It is deliberately sufficiently general to be used with almost any gaming-simulation. Specific questions relevant to a particular gaming-simulation can be added by the user who wishes more detailed feedback from players.

GAMING-SIMULATION EVALUATION FORM
FOR PARTICIPANTS

Name of simulation: _____

Date of simulation: _____

Group (if more than one session run simultaneously): _____

1. What was your individual or group identity in the game? (e.g., city politician, "circle," "green")

2. If your role changed during the session, please give later roles played:

3. If there were formal leaders in your group, please indicate the position you had by circling the appropriate number:
   1 leader
   2 participant
   0 not applicable

4. If there were no formal leaders, please indicate how you would describe your participation in the decision-making process. Would you say you were:
   1 a "leader"
   2 an active participant (i.e., vocal in expressing your ideas)
   3 a passive participant (i.e., followed the deliberation but contributed little)
   4 physically present but uninvolved
   0 not applicable

5. Please describe *your group* in terms of each of the dimensions listed. These are obviously subjective evaluations, so yours may differ from that of other group members. In each case 1 = low, 2 = medium, and 3 = high.

	Low	Medium	High	Inapplicable
a. degree of activity of group	1	2	3	0

	Low	Medium	High	Inapplicable
b. broad participation by group members (e.g., everyone participating)	1	2	3	0
c. group cohesion	1	2	3	0
d. degree of cooperation	1	2	3	0
e. ability to reach concensus despite disagreements	1	2	3	0
f. quality of leadership exercised by formal or informal leaders	1	2	3	0

6. Which three people do you feel had the *most effect,* for better or for worse, on what happened in the course of play? If you think they had a positive effect, put a + sign after the name; if you think they had a negative effect, put a − sign after the name.

_____   _____   _____

7. Please describe each of the following dimensions of your personal participation by using the scale below. Again, 1 = low, 2 = medium, and 3 = high.

	Low	Medium	High	Inapplicable
a. interest in the session(s)	1	2	3	0
b. enjoyment of the session(s)	1	2	3	0
c. learning about the system or topic simulated	1	2	3	0
d. development of empathy for those who play your role in real life (i.e., understanding of their problems, tasks, etc.)	1	2	3	0
e. development of empathy for those who in real life play other game roles	1	2	3	0
f. self-awareness, self-understanding	1	2	3	0
g. getting to know others in the group or class	1	2	3	0

8. How would you rate the simulation in general as a learning/communication experience? Would you rate it:
   1 Very good or excellent
   2 Good
   3 Fair
   4 Poor
   or 5 Terrible

9. What did you find the most valuable about this experience?

10. What did you find the least valuable about participating?

Please use the back of this page to give us any general comments.
Thank you for your assistance.

Appendix C
A Checklist for Evaluation

Basic Information

Title
Designer
Date
Description-Subject
Purpose
Intended Use
Space Requirements
Computer Requirements
Other Media Required

Kit Availability

Kit paraphernalia

Cost
Source
Portability
Standard or custom-made
Documentation
Materials and quantities

Participants

Age range
Homogeneity
Prior knowledge
Sophistication
Number

Player involvement

Player organization (team, coalition, individual)
Emotional/Intellectual
Active/Passive

(Continued on next page)

251

Time	Duration of play	
	Preparation Time	
Content	Playability	Introduction
		Inertia
		Flying
		Critique
		Player
		Operator
		Steps of play and plot outline
Dynamics of play	Flexibility	Level of Abstraction
		Gaminess
		Complexity, number of variables, interactions, decisions, supersymbols, models, decision-makers
		Alternative scenarios
		Issue generation
		Changing subject matter (frame game)
		Observability
Evaluation	Does the conceptual map correspond to reality?	Is the conceptual map explicit, implicit or integral?
		What is the theoretical or empirical basis?
		Is the game message acceptable?
		Is the game message valid?
	Was the translation into a game successful?	Is the message appropriate to game's purpose?
		Were valid construction procedures employed?
		Were appropriate gaming techniques applied?
		Is the system gestalt clear?
		Is the system responsive to player actions?
	Is the product acceptable?	Is the conceptual map conveyed as intended?
		Are there adequate challenge provisions?

Appendix D
Periodicals on Gaming-Simulations

AMERICAN BEHAVIORAL SCIENTIST
has devoted several entire issues (for example October 1966, November 1966, July-August 1969) to simulation and games. Copies available from Sage Publications, 275 South Beverly Drive, Beverly Hills, CA 90212.

ISAGA NEWSLETTER
is published 6 times a year by the International Simulation and Gaming Association (ISAGA), and is provided to members. It contains short articles and Association news. Occasional special issues focus on special topics or on developments in a particular region of the world. Available in the United States from Dr. Cathy Greenblat, U. S. Secretariat for ISAGA, Dept. of Sociology, Rutgers University, New Brunswick, NJ 08903; and out of the United States from Dr. Jan Klabbers, ISAGA European Secretariat, University of Nijmegen, Dept. of Psychology, Box 9104, 6500 HE Nijmegen, The Netherlands.

JOURNAL OF EXPERIENTIAL LEARNING AND SIMULATION (JELS)
is a relatively new academic journal which regularly includes articles on gaming and simulation, with particular attention to applications in business and business education. JELS is published by Elsevier North-Holland, Inc., 52 Vanderbilt Avenue, New York, NY 10017.

SIMGAMES
is a brief, informal Canadian publication which includes short articles, news, game reviews, and book reviews. It is published quarterly by Simgames, Champlain Regional College, Lennoxville Campus, Lennoxville, Quebec, Canada J1M 2A1.

SIMULATION/GAMES FOR LEARNING
is published by the Society for Academic Gaming and Simulation in Education and Training. In addition to articles and game and book reviews, a review of other journals' offerings, conferences, and other news items are regularly reported. The SAGSET journal has consistently published articles on controversial topics and editorials which deal with current issues. Available from the Secretary, SAGSET, Centre for Extension Studies, University of Technology, Loughborough, LEICS LE11 3TU.

SIMAGES
is the official publication of the North American Simulation and Gaming Association (NASAGA). It was first published two years ago, following the demise of

Simulation/Gaming/News, and represents an attempt to preserve the tone and style of S/G/N. Emphasis is on short articles, news items, simple games, and hints for designers and users. Available from Dr. Tom Nichols, Secretary-Treasurer, NASAGA, Box 100, Westminster College, New Wilmington, PA 16142.

SIMULATION AND GAMES: AN INTERNATIONAL JOURNAL OF THEORY, DESIGN, AND RESEARCH,
is designed to provide a forum for theoretical and empirical papers related to man, man-machine, and machine simulations of social processes. The journal publishes theoretical papers about new gaming techniques. Each issue includes book reviews and simulation reviews. Published quarterly by Sage Publications, 275 South Beverly Drive, Beverly Hills, CA 90212.

SIMULATION-GAMING-NEWS,
now defunct, was published five times during each school year, beginning February 1972, by Don Coombs. S/G/N was published in tabloid format and tended toward the informal. Back issues may be available from Simulation-Gaming-News, Box 3039, University Station, Moscow, ID 83843.

STRATEGY AND TACTICS
provides a ready-to-play conflict simulation, a feature article dealing with the same subject, other feature articles, and game and book reviews and comments. Subscriptions are available from Simulations Publications, Inc., 44 East 23rd St., New York, NY 10010.

References

Abelson, Robert P. (1968) "Simulation of Social Behavior," in Gardner Lindzey (ed.) Handbook of Social Psychology, vol. II. Cambridge, MA: Addison Wesley.

Abt Associates, Inc. (1965) Games, Learning and Disadvantaged Groups. Cambridge, MA: Abt.

Abt, Clark (1967) "Education is Child's Play," pp. 123-155 in Werner Z.Hersch et al., (eds.) Inventing Education for the Future. San Francisco: Chandler.

——— (1970) Serious Games. New York: Viking.

Adair, Charles H. and John T. Foster, Jr. (1972) A Guide for Simulation Design, Tallahassee, FL: Instructional Simulation Design Inc.

Adams, Dennis (1973) Simulation Games: An Approach to Learning. Columbus, OH: Charles A. Jones Co.

Alexander, Robert (1977) "Life, Death, and Creativity." Simulation and Games (March): 111-120.

Alser, C.F. (1963) "Use of the Inter-Nation Simulation in Undergraduate Teaching," pp. 150-189 in H. Guetzkow et al. (eds.) Simulation in International Relations: Developments for Research and Teaching. Englewood Cliffs, NJ: Prentice-Hall.

Allen, Layman E. (1972) "RAG-PELT: Resource Allocation Games: Planned Environments for Learning and Thinking." Presented to the International Conference on Simulation and Gaming, July, Birmingham, England.

Allen, Layman E., Linda M. Bangert, and Mitchell J. Rycus (1979) "To Enhance Learning: The Snuffing Version of EQUATIONS." Simulation and Games 10 (September): 257-264.

Allen, Layman E., Gloria Jackson, Joan Ross, and Stuart White (1978) "What Counts is How the Game is Scored: One Way to Increase Achievement in Learning Mathematics." Simulation and Games 9 (December): 371-392.

Alley, R., and S.C. Gladhart (1975) "Political Efficacy of Junior High Youth: Effects of a Mayoral Election Simulation." Simulation and Games 6 (March): 73-83.

Allport, G. (1954) The Nature of Prejudice. Reading, MA: Addison-Wesley.

Alschuler, Alfred, Gerald Weinstein, Judith Evans, Roy Tamashiro, and William Smith (1977) "Education for What? Measuring Self-Knowledge and Levels of Consciousness." Simulation and Games 8 (March): 29-47.

American Bar Association (1975) Gaming: An Annotated Catalogue of Law-Related Games and Simulations. Chicago: American Bar Association.

Anderson, C.R. (1970) "An Experiment on Behavioral Learning in a Consumer Credit Game." Simulation and Games 6 (March): 43-54.

Andes, John (1977) "In-Basket Simulation: Conceptual Framework, Scoring, and Analysis." Simulation and Games 8 (December): 505-513.

Armstrong, R.H.R. and Margaret Hobson (1969a) "Games and Urban Planning." Surveyor 31 (October): 32-34.

———— (1969b) "Models for Life." Education 5 (September).

———— (1969c) "Planning Games Are More than Just Fun." Municipal and Public Services Journal 2089 (November).

———— (1970) "The Use of Gaming-Simulation Techniques in the Decision Making Process." Prepared for the United Nations Interregional Seminar on the Use of Modern Management Techniques in the Public Administration of Developing Countries, August, Washington D.C.

———— (1975) "Introduction to Gaming-Simulation Techniques," in C. S. Greenblat and R. D. Duke (eds.) Gaming-Simulation. New York: Halsted.

Armstrong, R. H. R., and John L. Taylor [eds.] (1970) Instructional Simulation Systems in Higher Education. Cambridge, England: Cambridge Institute of Education.

Associated Public School Systems (1957) 57 Games for Learning. New York: Columbia University, Teacher's College, Institute of Adminstrative Research.

Attis, J. C. (1967) "Use of Games as a Teaching Technique." Social Studies 58 (January): 25-29.

Attiyeh, Richard (1976) Computer Simulation Policy Games in Macroeconomics. Iowa City: CONDUIT.

Avant, G., and K. Avant (1979) "Preparing Ethics Learning Materials for Students in Professional Disciplines." Presented at NASAGA, 18th Annual Conference, Austin, Texas, October 9-13.

Avedon, E., and B. Sutton-Smith (1971) The Study of Games. New York: John Wiley.

Averch, H. A., S. J. Carroll, T. S. Donaldson, H. J. Kiesling, and J. Pincus (1972) How Effective is Schooling? Santa Monica, CA: Rand Corporation.

Ayal, Isal, and Jehiel Zif (1978) "R & D Marketing: A Management Simulation." Simulation and Games 9 (December): 429-443.

Babb, E. M., A. Leslie, and M. D. Slyre (1966) "The Potential of Business Gaming Methods in Research." Journal of Business 39, 4: 465-472.

Back, K. W. (1963) "The Game and the Myth as Two Languages of Social Science." Behavioral Science 8 (January): 67-71.

Baker, E. (1968) "A Pre-Civil War Simulation for Teaching American History," pp. 135-142 in S. S. Boocock and E. O. Schild (eds.) Simulation Games in Learning. Beverly Hills: Sage.

Baldwin, John D. (1969) "Influences Detrimental to Simulation Gaming." American Behavioral Scientist 11 (July-August): 14-20.

Barker, Clive (1979) Theater Games. New York: Drama Book Specialists and Publishers.

Bartlett, Robin L., and Timothy I. Miller (1981) "Evaluating the Federal Open Market Committee Simulation: A Complimentary Teaching Technique." Simulation and Games 12 (March): 29-49.

Barton, Richard F. (1970) A Primer on Simulation and Gaming. Englewood Cliffs, NJ: Prentice-Hall.

———— (1980) "Creating and Controlling Simulated Industries for Verisimilitude." Simulation and Games 11 (December): 441-450.

Bavelas, A. (1950) "Communication Patterns in Task Oriented Groups." Journal of the Acoustical Society of America 22: 725-730.

———— and D. Barrett (1951) "An Experimental Approach to Organizational Communications." Personnel 27: 336-371.

Becker, Henk A. (1980) "The Emergence of Simulation and Gaming." Simulation and Games 11 (March): 11-25.

———— and H. M. Goudappel [eds.] (1972) Developments in Simulation and Gaming. Utrecht, Netherlands: Boom Meppel.

Becker, Howard (1950) "Sacred and Secular Societies." Social Forces 28: 361-367.

———— (1963) Outsiders: Studies in the Sociology of Deviance. New York: Free Press.

———— (1964) The Other Side: Perspectives on Deviance. New York: Free Press.

Belch, Jean (1973) Contemporary Games: Vol. 1—Directory. Detroit: Gale Research Co.

———— (1974) Contemporary Games: Vol. 2—Bibliography. Detroit: Gale Research Co.

Bell, David C. (1975) "Simulation Games: Three Research Paradigms." Simulation and Games 9 (September): 271-287.

Bell, Irene Wood, and J. E. Wieckert (1979) Basic Media Skills Through Games. Littleton, CO: Libraries Unlimited, Inc.

Bell, Robert, and Joan Coplans (1978) Decisions, Decisions: Game Theory and You. New York: W. W. Norton.

Benjamin, Stanley (1968) "Operational Gaming in Architecture." Ekistics 26 (December): 525-529.

Beres, Mary E., Barbara M. Koehler, and Gerald Zaltman (1975) "Communication Networks in a Developing Science: A Simulation of the Underlying Socio-Physical Structure." Simulation and Games 6 (March): 3-38.

Berger, Edward, Harvey Boulay, and Betty Zisk (1970) "Simulation and the City: A Critical Overview." Simulation and Games 1 (December): 411-428.

Berger, P. and T. Luckmann (1966) The Social Construction of Reality. Garden City, NY: Doubleday.

Best, John (1978) "Possible Difficulties in the Interpretation of Simulation Outcomes." Simulation and Games 9 (December): 445-460.

Biggs, William D. (1978) "A Comparison of Ranking and Relational Grading Procedures in a General Management Simulation." Simulation and Games 9 (June): 185-200.

———— and Paul S. Greenlaw (1976) "The Role of Information in a Functional Business Game." Simulation and Games 7 (March): 53-64.

Blake, R.R., and J. Mouton (1962) "The Intergroup Dynamics of Win-Lose Conflict and Problem Solving Collaboration in Union-Management Relations," in M. Sherif (ed.) Intergroup Relations and Leadership. New York: John Wiley.

Blanchard, F.A., L. Adelman, and S.W. Cook (1975) "Effects of Group Success and Failure upon Interpersonal Attraction in Cooperating Interracial Groups." Journal of Personality and Social Psychology 31: 1020-1030.

Bligh, D. (1972) What's the Use of Lectures? London: Penguin Hammondsworth.

Bloomfield, L.P., and N.J. Padelford (1959) "Three Experiments in Political Gaming." American Political Science Review 53 (December): 1105-1115.

Boguslaw, Robert, Robert H. Davis, and Edward B. Glick (1966) "A Simulation Vehicle for Studying National Policy Formation in a Less Armed World." Behavioral Science 11 (January): 43-61.

Bonham, G. Mathew, Michael J. Shapiro, and George J. Nozicka (1967) "A Cognitive Process Model of Foreign Policy Decision-Making." Simulation and Games 7 (June): 123-152.

Boocock, Sarane S. (1963) Effects of an Election Campaign Game in Four High School Classes. Research Program on the Effects of Games with Simulated Environments in Secondary Education. Report 1. Baltimore: Johns Hopkins University Department of Social Relations.

———— (1966a) "An Experimental Study of the Learning Effects of Two Games with Simulated Environments." American Behavioral Scientist 10 (October): 8-17.

———— (1966b) "Games with Simulated Environments in Learning." Sociology of Education 39 (Summer).

———— (1966c) "Toward a Sociology of Learning: A Selective Review of Existing Research." Sociology of Education 39 (Winter): 1-45.

———— (1967a) "Games Change What Goes on in the Classroom." Nation's Schools 80 (October): 94-95.

_____ (1967b) "LIFE CAREER Game." Personnel and Guidance Journal 46 (December): 328-334.

_____ (1970) "An Innovative Course in Urban Sociology." American Sociologist 5 (February): 38-42.

_____ (1971) "Instructional Games," in Encyclopedia of Education. New York: Macmillan.

_____ (1972) An Introduction to the Sociology of Learning. Boston: Houghton Mifflin.

_____ (1972b) "Validity-Testing of an Intergenerational Relations Game." Simulation and Games 3 (March): 29-40.

_____ and J. S. Coleman (1966) "Games With Simulated Environments in Learning." Sociology of Education 39 (Summer): 215-236.

Boocock, Sarane S., and E. O. Schild (1968) Simulation Games in Learning. Beverly Hills: Sage.

_____ and C. S. Stoll (1967) Simulation Games and Control Beliefs. Center for Social Organization of Schools, Report No. 10 (ERIC 016-736). Baltimore: Johns Hopkins University.

Bottari, A. (1980) "Gaming for Urban Studies and Planning: Some Concepts Behind Practice." Presented at the Eleventh Annual ISAGA Conference, Geneva.

Boulding, Kenneth E. (1968) "General Systems Theory: The Skeleton of Science," in Walter Buckley (ed.) Modern Systems Research Behavior for the Behavioral Scientist. Chicago: Aldine.

Bower, E. M., K. Bersamin, A. Fine, J. Carlson, et al., (1974) Learning to Play, Playing to Learn. Berkeley: Emotional Learning Program, School of Education, University of California.

Boydell, T. (1976) Experiential Learning. Monograph No. 5, University of Manchester.

Bracken, Paul (1977) "Unintended Consequences of Strategic Gaming." Simulation and Games 8 (September): 283-318.

Bradsher-Fredrick, H. R. (1980) "Gaming-Simulation: A Mode for Communicating the Research Embodied in the Mesarovic-Pestel World Model to Policy Makers." Ph.D. dissertation, University of Michigan.

Brams, S. J. (1975) Game Theory and Politics. New York: Free Press.

Brand, Charles F. (1980) "Learning from Simulation Games: Effects of Sociometric Grouping." Simulation and Games 11 (June): 163-186.

Braskamp, L. A., and R. M. Hodgetts (1971) in K. Edwards, Student Evaluations of a Business Game As a Learning Experience. Bethesda, MD: ERIC Document Reproduction Service (ED 058 142).

Bredemeier, Harry C. (1973) "Justice, Virtue and Social Science." Society (September-October): 76-83.

Bredemeier, M. E. (1978) "Providing Referents for Sociological Concepts: Simulation Gaming." Teaching Sociology 5 (July): 409-421.

_____ (1981) "Simulation Games in Counselor Training." SIMAGES 3 (Spring).

_____ and C. S. Greenblat (1981) "The Educational Effectiveness of Simulation Games: A Synthesis of Recent Findings." Simulation and Games 12 (September)

Brenenstuhl, Daniel C. (1975a) "Cognitive Versus Affective Gains in Computer Simulations." Simulation and Games 6 (September): 303-311.

_____ (1975b) "An Experiential Study of Performance in a Basic Management Course." Proceedings of the Second Annual Conference of the Association for Business Simulation and Experiential Learning (April): 83-91.

_____ and Richard O. Blalack (1978) "Role Preference and Vested Interest in a Bargaining Environment." Simulation and Games 9 (March): 53-65.

Brent, Edward E., Jr., and Richard E. Sykes (1980) "The Interactive Bases of Police-Suspect Confrontation: An Empirically Based Simulation of a Markov Process." Simulation and Games 11 (September): 347-363.

Brewer, Garry D. (1976) "Documentation: An Overview and Design Strategy." Simulation and Games 7 (September): 261-280.

——— (1978) "Scientific Gaming: The Development and Use of Free-Form Scenarios." Simulation and Games 9 (September): 309-338.

Brim, O. G., Jr. (1955) "Attitude Content-Intensity and Probability Expectations." American Sociological Review 20 (February): 68-76.

Brodbelt, Samuel (1969) "Simulation in the Social Studies: An Overview." Social Education 33 (February): 176-178.

Bruner, Jerome (1961) The Process of Education. Cambridge, MA: Harvard University Press.

——— (1966) Toward A Theory of Instruction. Cambridge, MA: Harvard University Press.

Bruner, J. and S. Bruner [eds.] (1976) Play: Its Role in Development and Evolution. New York: Basic Books.

Buabeng, Osafa William (1977) "United Nations International Workshop of the Training of Human Settlement Managers." Tedeco 2 (Tema, Ghana).

Buckley, Walter (1968) "Society as a Complex Adaptive System," in Walter Buckley (ed.) Modern Systems Research for the Behavioral Scientist. Chicago: Aldine.

Burgess, Philip (1966) "Political Science Gaming in Teaching and Research." Ohio State University, Fall WOSU Faculty Lecture Series.

——— (1969) "Organizing Simulated Environments." Social Education 33 (February): 185-192.

Burgess, P., and James A. Robinson (1969) "Alliances and the Theory of Collective Action: A Simulation of Coalition Processes," pp. 640-653 in James Rosenau (ed.) Foreign Policy and International Politics. New York: Free Press.

Byrd, Jack, Jr. (1976) "A Conceptual Approach to the Use of Simulation Gaming in Technology Assessment." Simulation and Games 7 (June): 209-218.

Callois, Roger (1961) Man, Play and Games. New York: Free Press.

Campbell, D. T., and R. F. Boruch (1975) "Making the Case for Randomizing Assignment to Treatments by Considering the Alternatives: Six Ways in Which Quasi-Experimental Evaluations in Compensatory Education Tend to Underestimate Effects," in A. Lumsdaine and C. A. Bennet (eds.) Evaluation and Experience: Some Critical Issues in Assessing Social Programs. New York: Academic Press.

Cangelosi, Vincent E., and William R. Dill (1965) "Organizational Learning: Observation Toward a Theory." Administrative Science Quarterly 10 (September): 175-203.

Carlson, Elliot (1967) "Games in the Classroom." Saturday Review (April 15): 62-64, 82-83.

——— (1969) Learning Through Games. Washington, DC: Public Affairs Press.

Carranza, E. (1974) "An Assessment of the STARPOWER Game." Simulation and Games 5 (June): 219-221.

Castillo, Rodolfo F. (1971) A Survey of Simulation and Gaming. Austin: University of Texas.

Center for War-Peace Studies (1972) Curriculum Materials on War, Peace, Conflict and Change: An Annotated Bibliography with a Listing of Organizational Resources. New York: Author.

Certo, Samuel [ed.] (1976) Sourcebook of Experiential Exercises: Interpersonal Skills. Terre Haute: Bureau of Business Research, Indiana State University.

Chapman, Katherine (1974) Simulation Games in Social Studies: A Report. Boulder, CO: ERIC Clearinghouse for Social Studies-Social Science Education (available from Social Science Education Consortium).

——— J. E. Davis, and A. Meier (1974) Simulation Games in Social Science: What Do We Know? Social Science Education Consortium Publication 162, Boulder, CO: Social Science Education Consortium.

Chapman, T. (1974) Simulation Game Effects on Attitudes Regarding Racism and Sexism. Research Report, University of Maryland Cultural Study Center.

Charles, Cheryl L., and Ronald Stadsklev (1973) Learning With Games: An Analysis of Social Studies Education Games-Simulations. Boulder, CO: Social Science Education Consortium, Inc.

Chartier, Myron R. (1972) "Learning Effect: An Experimental Study of a Simulation Game and Instrumented Discussion." Simulation and Games 3 (June): 203-218.

_____ (1973) Some Current Games as Learning Devices: A Summary of Empirical Findings and Their Implications for the Utilization of Games in Instruction. Bethesda, MD: ERIC Reproduction Document Service.

Cherryholmes, Cleo H. (1966) "Some Current Research on Effectiveness of Educational Simulations: Implications for Alternative Strategies." American Behavioral Scientist 10 (October): 4-7.

Church Center for the United Nations (1972) A Bibliography of Educational Simulations. New York: National Council of Churches.

Clements, I. (1970) "The Development of a Simulation Game for Teaching a Unit on the Use of Consumer Credit." Ph.D. dissertation, Oklahoma State University.

Coch, L. and J. R. F. French, Jr. (1948) "Overcoming Resistance to Change." Human Relations 1: 512-532.

Cohen, A. (1964) Attitude Change and Social Influence. New York: Basic Books.

Cohen, B. S. (1962) "Political Gaming in the Classroom." Journal of Politics 24 (March): 367-381.

Cohen, Kalmen J., and Eric Rhenman (1975) "The Role of Management Games in Education and Research," pp. 263-269 in C. S. Greenblat and R. D. Duke (eds.) Gaming-Simulation. New York: Halsted.

Cohen, K. J., et al. (1964) The Carnegie Tech Management Game: An Experiment in Business Education. Homewood, IL: Irwin.

Cole, Richard L., and Stephen J. Wayne (1980) "Predicting Presidential Decisions on Enrolled Bills: A Computer Simulation." Simulation and Games 11 (September): 313-325.

Coleman, James S. (1964a) "Collective Decisions." Sociological Inquiry 34 (Spring): 166-181.

_____ (1964b) "Mathematical Models and Computer Simulation," pp. 1027-1062 in R. E. L. Faris (ed.) Handbook of Modern Sociology. Chicago: Rand McNally.

_____ (1966) "Introduction: In Defense of Games." American Behavioral Scientist 10 (October): 3-4.

_____ (1967a) "Game Models of Economy and Political Systems," pp. 30-34 in Samuel Klausner (ed.) The Study of Total Societies. New York: Anchor Books.

_____ (1967b) "Academic Games and Learning." Presented at the Invitational Conference on Testing Problems, Educational Testing Service, Princeton, New Jersey.

_____ (1967c) "Learning Through Games." National Educational Association Journal 56 (January): 69-70.

_____ (1968) "Social Processes and Social Simulation Games," pp. 29-51 in S. S. Boocock and E. O. Schild (eds.) Simulation Games in Learning. Beverly Hills: Sage.

_____ (1969) "Games as Vehicles for Social Theory." American Behavioral Scientist 12 (July-August): 2-6.

_____ (1970) The Role of Modern Technology in Relation to Simulation and Games For Learning. Bethesda, MD: ERIC Document Reproduction Services (ED 039 704).

_____ (1971) "A Decade of Gaming-Simulation," Symposium address to the Tenth Annual Meeting of the National Gaming Council, Ann Arbor, MI.

Coleman, James, S. A. Livingston, G. M. Fennessey, K. J. Edwards, and S. J. Kidder (1973) "The Hopkins Game Program." Educational Researcher 2 (August): 307.

Coleman, James, et al. (1961) The Adolescent Society. New York: Free Press.

———— (1966) Equality of Educational Opportunity. Washington, DC: U.S. Department of Health, Education and Welfare.

Conway, M. Margaret, David Ahern, and Eleanor Feldbaum (1977) "Instructional Method, Social Characteristics, and Children's Support for the Political Regime." Simulation and Games 8 (June): 233-254.

Coombs, Don H. (1976) Simulation and Gaming: The Best of Eric. Stanford, CA: ERIC Clearinghouse on Information Resources, Stanford Center for Research and Development in Teaching, School of Education, Stanford University.

Coplin, William D. (1966) "Inter-Nation Simulation and Contemporary Theories of International Relations." American Political Science Review 60 (September): 562-578.

———— (1968) Simulation in the Study of Politics. Chicago: Markham Publishing.

———— (1970) "Approaches to Social Sciences through Man-Computer Simulations." Simulation and Games 1 (December): 391-410.

Coppard, L., and F. Goodman [eds.] (1977) Urban Gaming-Simulation '77: An Ongoing Conference for Educators and Trainers. Ann Arbor: University of Michigan, Publishers Distribution Service.

Cousins, Jack (1977) "Simulation Games for Political Education." Simulation and Games 8 (September): 361-374.

Craft, C.J., J.M. Kibbee, and B. Nanns (1961) Management Games: A New Technique for Executive Development. New York: Reinhold.

Craig, Samuel C., and Lawrence A. Brown (1978) "Spatial Diffusion of Innovation: A Gaming Approach." Simulation and Games 9 (March): 29-52.

Cratty, Bryant J. (1971) Active Learning: Games to Enhance Academic Abilities. Englewood Cliffs, NJ: Prentice-Hall.

Cruickshank, D. (1970) "The Use of Simulation in Teacher Education: A Developing Phenomenon." Journal of Teacher Education 20 (Spring): 23-26.

———— (1977) A First Book of Games and Simulations. Belmont, CA: Wadsworth.

———— and F.W. Broadbent (1969) "An Investigation to Determine Effects of Simulation Training on Student Teaching Behavior." Education Technology 9 (October).

Cruickshank, D., and R. Telfer (1979) Simulation and Games: An ERIC Bibliography. Washington, DC: ERIC Clearinghouse on Teacher Education.

Curry, J. and R. Brooks (1971) "A Comparison of Two Methods of Teaching Life Career Planning to Junior High School Students." Denton: North Texas State University (ERIC ED 059 401).

Daniellan, Jack (1967) "Live Simulation of Affect-Laden Cultural Cognitions." Journal of Conflict Resolution 11 (October): 312-324.

Degnan, Daniel A., and Charles M. Haar (1975) "Computer-Assisted Simulation in Urban Legal Studies," pp. 220-232 in C.S. Greenblat and R.D. Duke (eds.) Gaming-Simulation. New York: Halsted.

DeKock, Paul (1969) "Simulation and Changes in Racial Attitudes." Social Education 33: 181-183.

DeKoven, Bernard (1978) The Well Played Game. Garden City, NY: Doubleday.

———— (1980) The Grasshopper. Toronto: University of Toronto Press.

DeLeon, Peter (1975) "Scenario Designs: An Overview." Simulation and Games 6 (March): 39-60.

DeNike, Lee (1973) "An Exploratory Study of Cognitive Style as a Predictor of Learning from Simulation Games." Ph.D. dissertation, Kent State University.

———— (1976) "An Exploratory Study of the Relationship of Educational Style to Learning from Simulation Games." Simulation and Games 7 (March): 65-74.

DeVries, David L. (1976) "Teams-Games-Tournament: A Gaming Technique That Fosters Learning." Simulation and Games 7 (March): 21-33.

Diab, L. N. (1970) "A Study of Intragroup and Intergroup Relations Among Experimentally Produced Small Groups." Genetic Psychology Monographs 82: 49-82.

Dickson, P. (1973) "Games People (Should) Play." Passages (Northwest Orient's Inflight Magazine) 4 (February): 13-17.

Diehl, B. J. (1979) "Current Simulation Gaming in Australia." Simulation and Games 10 (September): 265-274.

Dittrich, John E. (1977) "Realism in Business Games: A Three-Game Comparison." Simulation and Games 8 (June): 201-210.

Dooley, B. (1969) "Research on the Market Game," in G. Dawson (ed.) Economic Education Experiences of Enterprising Teachers, vol. 5. New York: Joint Council on Economic Education.

Dorner, D. (1979) "On the Difficulties People Have in Dealing with Complexity." Bambers University, West Germany. (unpublished)

Douglass, J. (1971) American Social Order: Social Rules in a Pluralistic Society. New York: Free Press.

Drabek, Thomas E., and J. Eugene Haas (1967) "Realism in Laboratory Simulation: Myth or Method?" Social Forces 45 (March): 337-346.

Druckman, Daniel (1968) "Ethnocentrism in the Inter-Nation Simulation." Journal of Conflict Resolution 12 (March): 46-58.

———— (1971) "Understanding the Operation of Complex Social Systems: Some Uses of Simulation Design." Simulation and Games 2 (June): 173-195.

Duke, Richard D. (1963a) "Gaming Simulation Studies in Urban Resource Allocation." Bulletin of the Association of Collegiate Schools of Planning 1, 3.

———— (1963b) Bibliography for Gaming in Urban Research, Bibliographic Series #5. East Lansing: Michigan State University, Institute for Community Development.

———— (1964) Gaming Simulation in Urban Research. East Lansing: Institute for Community Development and Services, Michigan State University.

———— (1965) "Gaming Urban Systems." (2 parts) Planning (April, June).

———— (1966a) "Urban Planning and Metropolitan Development in the Role of Technology," in Applying Technologies to Urban Needs, Vol. F. Technology and the American Economy, National Commission on Technology, Automation, and Economic Progress.

———— (1966b) "Operational Gaming in Urban Planning," in Selected Papers on Operational Gaming. Miscellaneous Paper No. 5. Ithaca, NY: Center for Housing and Environmental Study, Cornell University.

———— (1966c) "The M.E.T.R.O. Urban Game-Simulation—An Experiment in In-Service Training." Prepared for the 4th Annual Conference on Urban Planning Information Systems and Programs, University of California, Berkeley.

———— (1966d) "Can the Simulation Techniques of War Gaming Practices Revolutionalize Urban Problem Solving?" Presented at the 43rd Annual Congress of Cities, Las Vegas, December.

———— (1966e) Selected Bibliography of Publications Related to Operational Gaming. University of Michigan. (mimeo)

———— (1967) "Simulating Urban Environments." Archiv, Kommunalwissenschaftliches Forchungzentrum, Berlin, August.

———— (1968) "The Adaptation of War-Gaming to Urban Problem Solving," in New Concepts in Municipal Government. Proceedings of the 43rd Annual Congress of the National League of Cities, December.

———— (1971) "Systems Theory and Gaming Simulation," in Proceedings, 2nd International Gaming Conference, Utrecht, Netherlands, October.

———— (1972a) "Gaming-Simulation: A New Communication Form," in Proceedings, 3rd International Gaming Conference, Birmingham, England, July.

_____ (1972b) "The Language of Gaming," in Proceedings, 11th Annual Conference of the National Gaming Council, Baltimore, October.

_____ (1974) Gaming: The Future's Language. New York: Halsted.

_____ (1977a) "National Nutrition Planning in Developing Countries via Gaming-Simulation." Gaming-Simulation and Health Education, Health Education Monographs, Vol. 5.

_____ (1977b) "The Simulated Nutrition System, Phase I (SNUS)." Journal of Natural Resource Management and Interdisciplinary Studies, 2, 1.

_____ (1977c) "Gaming-Simulation and the Science-Public Policy Interface," in Proceedings, 8th International ISAGA Annual Conference, Birmingham, England, June.

_____ (1978a) "Gaming-Simulation as a Tool for Future's Research," in J. Fowles (ed.) The Handbook of Future's Research. Westport, CT: Greenwood Press.

_____ (1978b) "Gaming-Simulation as a Public Policy Tool," in Proceedings, 8th Annual ISAGA Conference, Lund, Sweden.

_____ (1979) "Nine Steps to Game Design," in Proceedings, 10th Annual International ISAGA Conference, Leeuwarden, Netherlands, August 8-11.

_____ (1980a) "Format for the Game—Logic or Intuition?" Simulation and Games 11 (March): 27-34.

_____ (1980b) "A Paradigm for Game Design." Simulation and Games 11 (September): 364-377.

_____ and Barton B. Burkhalter (1966) The Application of Heuristic Gaming to Urban Problems. East Lansing: Institute for Community Development, Michigan State University.

Duke, Richard D., and Robert Cary (1975) "Simulated Nutrition System—The F.A.O. Game." Ann Arbor, MI: Multilog, Inc.

_____ (1979) Railroad Deregulation—A Game/Simulation. Washington, DC: Consolidated Rail Corporation.

Duke, Richard D., and Cathy S. Greenblat (1979) Game-Generating Games—A Trilogy of Games for Community and Classroom. Beverly Hills: Sage.

Duke, Richard D., and Richard Meier (1966) "Gaming Simulation for Urban Planning." Journal of the American Institute of Planners 32 (January).

Duke, Richard D., Allen Feldt, and Hans Hansen (1977) Stadtenwicklung: Planspiel-Simulation Als Hilfsmittez fur die stadtebauliche Planing. Bonn, Germany: Datum E. V.

Duke, Richard D., et al. (1967) M.E.T.R.O.-Michigan (Urban) Effectuation, Training and Research Operational (Game), Description and Game Manuals. Washington, DC: U.S. Department of Housing and Urban Development.

_____ (1970) METRO-APEX: A Training Exercise in Air Quality Management Employing Computerized Simulations in the Context of Urban Regions (27 volumes). Washington, DC: U.S. Department of Health, Education and Welfare.

_____ (1973) A Trilogy of Urban Games. Final Report to the Council of Monterey Bay, Environmental Simulation Laboratory, University of Michigan.

_____ (1977a) Conference Book, Global International Gaming Conference. Nijmegen, Netherlands, July 9-13.

_____ (1977b) Handbook for the Organization and Design of Games. Paris: UNESCO (UNEP).

Dukes, Richard L. (1973a) "Learning Tools to Research Instruments: A Research Package for STARPOWER." Boulder: University of Colorado. (mimeo)

_____ (1973b) "Symbolic Models and Simulation Games for Theory Construction." Presented at the annual meeting of the American Sociological Association.

_____ and C. Seidner [eds.] (1978) Learning with Simulations and Games. Beverly Hills: Sage.

Dukes, Richard L., and Suzan J. Waller (1976) "Toward a General Evaluation Model for Simulation Games: GEM." Simulation and Games 7 (March): 75-96.

Dupuy, G. (1971) The Ideology of Urban Gaming. Paris: Beture.

Easterley, Jean L. (1978) "Simulation Game Design—A Philosophic Dilemma." Simulation and Games 9 (March): 23-28.

Edwards, Keith J. (1971a) The Effects of Ability, Achievement, and Numbers of Plays on Learning from a Simulation Game. Report 115. Baltimore: Center for Social Organization of Schools, Johns Hopkins University.

_____ (1971b) Student Evaluations of a Business Game as a Learning Experience. Bethesda, MD: ERIC Document Reproduction Service.

Elder, Charles (1975) "Problems in the Structure and Use of Educational Simulation," pp. 292-310 in C. S. Greenblat and R. D. Duke (eds.) Gaming-Simulation. New York: Halsted.

Elkin, Ed, and Kimberly McKell (1977) "A Jungian-Gestalt Approach to Self-Integration: Toward a Researchable Model." Simulation and Games 8 (March): 61-72.

Elliott, J., and R. McGinty (1975) Proceedings, 14th Annual NASAGA Conference, Los Angeles, October 23-25.

Emshoff, J. R., and R. L. Sisson (1970) Design and Use of Computer Simulation Models. New York: MacMillan.

Ennis, Philip (1975) "The Simulation of an Artistic System," pp. 410-417 in C. S. Greenblat and R. D. Duke (eds.) Gaming-Simulation. New York: Halsted.

Environmental Simulation Laboratory (1971) Proceedings, 10th Annual Symposium, the National Gaming Council. Ann Arbor, MI: Author.

Environmetrics, Inc. (1971) "The State-of-the-Art in Urban Gaming Models." Prepared for the U.S. Department of Transportation.

Enzle, Michael E., and Ronald D. Hansen (1976) "Effects of Video-Mediated Visual Contact on Observer's Attributions of Causality and Reciprocal Game Behavior." Simulation and Games 7 (September): 281-294.

_____ and Charles A. Lowe (1975) "Humanizing the Mixed-Motive Paradigm: Methodological Innovations from Attribution Theory." Simulation and Games 6 (June): 151-165.

Estes, J. E. (1980) "Research on Factors Affecting Learning Using a Computerized Simulation in the Basic Management Course." Simages 2 (Fall): 7-9, 19-21.

Evans, W. M. (1963) "Peer Group Interaction and Organizational Socialization." American Sociological Review 23: 436-440.

Feldbaum, Eleanor G., John J. Buckley III, and Morris J. Levitt (1976) "Students and Simulation: A Study of Effects of Simulation in State and Local Government Courses." Simulation and Games 7 June: 153-176.

Feldt, Allen (1966) "Potential Relationships between Economic Models and Heuristic Gaming Devices," in Vincent P. Rock (ed.) Policy Makers and Modelbuilders: Cases and Concepts. New York: Gordon and Breach.

_____ (1966a) "Operational Gaming in Planning Education." Journal of the American Institute of Planners 32 (January): 17-23.

_____ (1966b) Selected Papers on Operational Gaming. Ithaca, NY: Division of Urban Studies, Cornell University.

_____ (1972) "Operational Gaming in Planning Education." Journal of American Institute of Planners 22 (January): 17-23.

Fennessey, Gail (1973) Guidelines for Writing the Directions Manual for a Simulation Game. Baltimore, MD: Johns Hopkins University.

_____ and E. O. Schild (1974) User's Manual for Information: A Frame Game. Baltimore, MD: Academic Games Associates.

Fennessey, Gail M., Samuel A. Livington, Keith J. Edwards, Steven J. Kidder, and Alyce W. Nafziger (1975) "Simulation, Gaming, and Conventional Instruction: An Experimental Comparison." Simulation and Games 6 (September): 288-302.

Fennessey, James, and Shiro Horiuchi (1979) "Assessing the Accuracy of Teachers' Quantitative Judgments." Simulation and Games 9 (June): 139-166.

Ferguson, C. K., and H. H. Kelley (1964) "Significant Factors in Overevaluation of Own Groups' Product." Journal of Abnormal and Social Psychology 69: 223-228.

Fisher, C. W. (1975) "Value Orientations Implied or Encouraged by METRO-APEX (and Some Other Simulated Games) and a Suggested Change Technique," in Proceedings of the 14th Annual Conference of the North American Simulation and Gaming Association, Los Angeles: University of Southern California Press.

Fisher, Judith E. (1976) "Competition and Gaming: An Experimental Study." Simulation and Games 7 (September): 321-328.

Fletcher, Jerry L. (1971a) "The Effectiveness of Simulation Games as Learning Environments: A Proposed Program of Research." Simulation and Games 2 (December): 425-454.

_____ (1971b) "Evaluation of Learning in Two Social Studies Simulation Games." Simulation and Games 2 (September): 259-287.

Fluegelmen, A. (1976) The New Games Book. Garden City, NY: Doubleday.

Forster, E. M. (1964) Abinger Harvest. New York: Harcourt Brace Jovanovich.

Foster, John L., Allan C. Lachman, and Ronald M. Mason (1980) "Verstehen, Cognition, and the Impact of Political Simulations: It is Not as Simple as it Seems." Simulation and Games 11 (June): 223-241.

Fowlkes, Diane L. (1977) "Realpolitik and Play Politics: The Effects of Watergate and Political Gaming on Undergraduate Students' Political Interest and Political Trust." Simulation and Games 8 (December): 419-438.

France, William, and John McClure (1972) "Building a Child Care Staff Learning Game." Simulation and Games 3 (June): 189-202.

Friedenberg, Edgar (1963) Coming of Age in America. New York: Random House.

Fuller, Buckminster (1969) "The World Game." Ekistics 28 (October): 289-291.

Gagne, Robert, et al. (1962) Psychological Principles in System Development. New York: Holt, Rinehart and Winston.

Gamson, William A. (1975) "SIMSOC: Establishing Social Order in a Simulated Society." pp. 115-129 in C. S. Greenblat and R. D. Duke (eds.) Gaming-Simulation. New York: Halsted.

_____ (1973) SIMSOC. New York: Free Press.

_____ and Russell J. Stambaugh (1978) "The Model Underlying SIMSOC." Simulation and Games 9 (June): 131-157.

Garvey, Dale M. (1967) Simulation, Role Playing and Socio-Drama in the Social Studies. Emporia, KS: Emporia State Research Studies.

_____ and W. Seiler (1966) A Study of Effectiveness of Different Methods of Teaching International Relations to High School Students: Final Report. Emporia: Kansas State Teachers College (ERIC ED 010 007).

Gentry, J. W. (1980) "Group Size and Attitudes Toward the Simulation Experience." Simulation and Games 2 (December): 451-460.

Gibbs, G. I. (1974) Handbook of Games and Simulation Exercises. Beverly Hills: Sage.

_____ (1978) Dictionary of Gaming, Modeling and Simulation. Beverly Hills: Sage.

_____ and J. Wilcox (1975) "Perspectives on Academic Gaming and Simulation," in Proceedings of the 1975 SAGSET Conference.

Giffin, S. S. (1965) The Crisis Game: Simulating International Conflict. Garden City, NY: Doubleday.

Gilboa, E. (1973) "Educating Israeli Officers in the Process of Peacemaking in the Middle East Conflict." Journal of Peace Research 16: 155-162.

Gillespie, P. H. (1973) Learning Through Simulation Games. Paramus, NJ: Paulist Press.

Glazier, Ray (1970) How to Design Educational Games. Cambridge, MA: Abt Associates.

Goffman, Erving (1961) Encounters: Two Studies in the Sociology of Interaction. Indianapolis: Bobbs Merrill.

_____ (1969) Strategic Interaction. Philadelphia: University of Pennsylvania Press.

Gohring, Ralph J. (1979) "Publishing a Simulation Game." Simulation and Games 10 (September): 275-285.

Goldhamer, Herbert, and Hans Speier (1959) "Some Observations on Political Gaming." World Politics 12 (October): 71-83.

Goodman, Fred L. (1972) "Games and Simulations," in Robert Travers (ed.) Handbook of Research on Teaching. Chicago: Rand McNally.

Gordon, Alice Kaplan (1970) Games For Growth. Palo Alto, CA: Science Research Associates.

Gover, R. (1961) The $100 Misunderstanding: A Novel. New York: Grove.

Graham, R., and C. Gray (1969) Business Games Handbook. New York: American Management Association.

Granberg, Donald, J. Scott Stevens, and Sandra Katz (1975) "Effect of Communication on Cooperation in Expanded Prisoner's Dilemma and Chicken Games." Simulation and Games 6 (June): 166-187.

Greenblat, Cathy S. (1971a) "Le Developpement des Jeux-Simulations a l'usage du Sociologue." Revue Francaise de Sociologie 12 (avril-juin): 206-210.

_____ (1971b) "Simulations, Games, and the Sociologist." American Sociologist (May): 161-164.

_____ (1974a) "Gaming as Applied Sociology," in Arthur Shostak (ed.) Putting Sociology to Work. New York: David McKay.

_____ (1974b) "Gaming and Gaming-Simulation: An Overview for Teachers, Trainers, and Community Workers," in Marshal Whithed and Robert Sarley (eds.) Urban Simulation Design and Analysis. Netherland: Sitjhoff.

_____ (1975a) "Simulating Society." Society (July-August): 48-52.

_____ (1975b) "Gaming-Simulations for Teaching and Training: An Overview," pp. 180-195 in C. S. Greenblat and R. D. Duke (eds.) Gaming-Simulation. New York: Halsted.

_____ (1975c) "From Theory to Model to Gaming-Simulation: A Case Study and Validity Test," pp. 106-114 in C. S. Greenblat and R. D. Duke (eds.) Gaming-Simulation. New York: Halsted.

_____ (1975d) "Sociological Theory and the 'Multiple Reality' Game." pp. 148-161 in C. S. Greenblat and R. D. Duke (eds.) Gaming-Simulation. New York: Halsted.

_____ (1975e) "Teaching With Simulation Games: A Review of Claims and Evidence," pp. 270-284 in C. S. Greenblat and R. D. Duke (eds.) Gaming-Simulation. New York: Halsted.

_____ (1979) "Designing POMP AND CIRCUMSTANCE." Presented at the 1979 Annual Meeting of the International Simulation and Gaming Association, Leeuwarden, Netherlands, August.

_____ (1980) "Group Dynamics and Game Design: Some Reflections." Simulation and Games 11 (March): 35-58.

_____ and Richard D. Duke (1974) "A Demonstration of Urban Impasse?" in M. Whithed and R. Sarley (eds.) Urban Simulation Design and Analysis. Netherland: Sitjhoff.

_____ (1975) Gaming-Simulation: Rationale, Design, and Applications. New York: Halsted.

Greenblat, C. S., and John H. Gagnon (1975) "BLOOD MONEY: A Gaming-Simulation of the Problems of Hemophilia and Health Care Delivery Systems." National Heart and Lung Institute and the National Hemophilia Foundation.

_____ (1979) "Further Explorations on the Multiple Reality Game." Simulation And Games 10 (March): 41-59.

Greenblat, C. S., P. Stein, and N. Washburn (1977) The Marriage Game: Understanding

Marital Decision-Making. (rev. ed.). New York: Random House.

Greenlaw, P., L. Herron, and R. Rawdon (1963) Business Simulation in Industrial and University Education. Englewood Cliffs, NJ: Prentice-Hall.

Groome, A. J. (1975) "Interaction Effects in LIFE CAREER Simulation: Sex and Ability of Role and Participants." Simulation and Games 6 (September): 312-319.

Grunfeld, F. [ed.] (1975) Games of the World. New York: Holt, Rinehart, and Winston.

Guetzkow, Harold (1959) "A Use of Simulation in the Study of International Relations." Behavioral Science 4 (July): 183-191.

——— (1962) Simulation in Social Sciences: Readings. Englewood Cliffs, NJ: Prentice-Hall.

——— (1963) Simulation in International Relations: Developments for Research and Teaching. Englewood Cliffs, NJ: Prentice-Hall.

——— (1968) "Simulation in International Relations," in William Coplin (ed.) Simulation in the Study of Politics. Chicago: Markham Press.

——— (1972) "Simulations in the Consolidation and Utilization of Knowledge about International Relations," pp. 674-690 in Randall L. Schultz (ed.) Simulation in Social and Administrative Science: Overviews and Case Examples. Englewood Cliffs, NJ: Prentice-Hall.

Haefele, Donald L. (1976) "An Investigation of Factors Associated with a Teaching Problem Simulation." Simulation and Games (September): 311-320.

Hamilton, Lawrence C. (1980) "Political Kidnapping as a Deadly Game." Simulation and Games 11 (December): 387-402.

Harrison, Roger (1977) "Self-Directed Learning: A Radical Approach to Educational Design." Simulation and Games 8 (March): 73-94.

Harvey, Michael D., and Michael E. Enzle (1977) "Effects of a Dependent Other's Psychological Need on Subjects' Use of Power in a Simulation Game." Simulation and Games 8 (December): 405-418.

Hasell, J., and J. Taylor (1980) "Basic Simulation Guidance in the Study of Environmental Change and Development." Presented at the ISAGA Conference, Geneva.

Heap, James L. (1975) "The Student as Resource: Uses of the Minimum-Structure Simulation Game in Teaching," pp. 209-219 in C. S. Greenblat and R. D. Duke (eds.) Gaming-Simulation. New York: Halsted.

Hearn, J. (1980) "The Potential of Gaming and Simulation." Simulation-Games for Learning 10 (Spring): 21-25.

Heeren, J. (1970) "Alfred Schutz and the Sociology of Common-Sense Knowledge," pp. 45-56 in J. Douglas (ed.) Understanding Everyday Life: Toward The Reconstruction of Sociological Knowledge. Chicago: Aldine.

Heitzmann, U. R. (1974) Educational Games and Simulations: What Research Says to the Teacher. Washington, DC: National Education Association.

Helmar, Olaf (1972a) On the State of the Union. Middletown, CT: Institute for the Future.

——— (1972b) "Cross-Impact Gaming." Futures (June): 149-167.

Henderson, Bob G., and George Gaines (1971) "Assessment of Selected Simulation Games for the Social Studies." Social Education (May): 508-513.

Henderson, Thomas A., and John L. Foster (1976) "Teaching American Government With Games." Simulation and Games 7 (June): 177-192.

Hermann, C. F. (1967) "Validation Problems in Games and Simulations With Special Reference to Models of International Politics." Behavioral Science 12 (May): 216-231.

——— (1969) Crisis in Foreign Policy: A Simulation Analysis. Indianapolis: Bobbs-Merrill.

Hernandez, R. A., and R. G. Mochofsky (1974) "Notes on an Environmental Simulation Exercise: The Bariloche Case Study." UNESCO (July).

Heyman, Mark (1975) Simulation Games for the Classroom, Fastback 54. Bloomington, IN: Phi Delta Kappa Publications.

Hickman, James L., Michael Murphy, and Mike Spino (1977) "Psychophysical Transformations Through Meditation and Sport." Simulation and Games 8 (March): 49-60.

Higgins, J. L., and L. A. Sachs (1974) Mathematics Laboratories: 150 Activities and Games for Elementary Schools. Columbus: ERIC Information Analysis Center for Science, Mathematics and Environmental Education, Ohio State University.

Hine, Alison, et al. (1976) Environmental Modeling and Decision Making—The United States Experience. A report of the Scientific Committee on Problems of the Environment. New York: Praeger.

Hoffmeister, J. Ronald, and Nicholas J. DiMarco (1977) "Influence of Personality on Performance in a Financial Management Simulation." Simulation and Games 8 (September): 385-394.

Hollander, Patricia A. (1977) "The Uses of Simulation in Teaching Law and Lawyering Skills." Simulation and Games 8 (September): 319-340.

Holmes, C. A. (1980) "Some Ethical Implications of Game Model Behavior." Dept. of Philosophy, University of Prince Edward Island, Canada. (unpublished)

Horn, R., and A. Cleaves (1980) The Guide to Simulation Games for Education and Training (4th ed.) Beverly Hills: Sage.

Hounshell, Paul B., and I. Trollinger (1977) Games for the Science Classroom: An Annotated Bibliography. Washington, DC: National Science Teachers Association.

House, Peter (1974) The Urban Environmental System: Modeling for Research, Policy-Making and Education. Beverly Hills: Sage.

Huizinga, Johan (1955) Homo Ludens. Boston: Beacon Press.

Inbar, Michael (1966) "The Differential Impact of a Game Simulating a Community Disaster." American Behavioral Scientist 10 (October): 18-27.

—————— (1969) "Development and Educational Use of Simulations: An Example 'The Community Response Game' " International Journal of Experimental Research in Education 6 (January): 5-44.

—————— (1970) "Participation in a Simulation Game." Journal of Applied Behavioral Science 6 (Spring): 239-244.

—————— (1976) "Toward Valid Computer Simulations of Bureaucratized Decisions." Simulation and Games 7 (September): 243-260.

Inbar, Michael, and Clarice S. Stoll (1972) Simulation and Gaming in Social Science. New York: Free Press.

Ingraham, L. W. (1967) "Teachers, Computers, and Games: Innovations in the Social Studies." Social Education 31 (January): 51-53.

Isaacs, David I., and Susan G. Mooney (1977) "Mindgames: The Personal Control of Memory, Mental Speed, and Creativity." Simulation and Games 8 (March): 95-110.

Jackson, M. W. (1979) "An Antipodean Evaluation of Simulation in Teaching." Simulation and Games 10 (June): 99-138.

Johnson, G. A., and W. E. Stratton (1978) "Learning Style and Performance, Exploring Experiential Learning: Simulations and Experience Exercises," pp. 189-192 in the Proceedings of the 5th Annual Conference of the Association for Business Simulation and Experiential Learning, April.

Johnson, Marianne, and Thomas M. Nelson (1978) "Game Playing with Juvenile Delinquents." Simulation and Games 9 (December): 461-475.

Johnson, R., and D. Euler (1972) "Effect of the LIFE CAREER Game on Learning and Retention of Educational-Occupational Information." School Counselor 19: 155-159.

Joint Council on Economic Education (1968) Bibliography of Games—Simulations for Teaching Economics, and Related Subjects. New York: Joint Council on Economic Education.

Kadivar, S., J. Franzini, Paisley, and Dajani (1978) "The Potential of the Simulation-Gaming Model to Study Third World Development Planning Phenomena." Presentation at 9th International Simulation-Gaming Association (ISAGA), Lund, Sweden, July 19-22.

Kadivar, S., and J. Franzini (1977) "Sir Walrus—A Policy Decision Game." Presented at the Annual Meeting of NASAGA, Boston, October 12.

Kahan, James P., and Phillip Bonacich (1980) "Palette: A Resource-Free Experimental Paridigm for Studying Coalition Formation." Simulation and Games 11 (September): 259-278.

Kanin, F., and M. Kanin (1959) *Rashomon* (adapted from the stories of Akutagawa). New York: Samuel French.

Kardatzke, Howard (1969) "Simulation Games in the Social Studies: The Reality Issue." Social Education 33 (February): 179-180.

Kasperson, Roger E. (1968) "Games as Educational Media." Journal of Geography 62 (October):

Keach, E., and D. Pierfy (1972) The Effects of a Simulation Game on Learning of Geographic Information at the Fifth Grade Level: Final Report. Athens: University of Georgia (ERIC ED 168 889).

Kenen, P. B., and R. H. Kenen (1978) "Who Thinks Who's in Charge Here—Faculty Perceptions of Influence and Power in the University." Sociology of Education 51 (April): 113-123.

Keys, Bernard (1974) National Conference on Business Gaming and Experiential Learning. Oklahoma Christian College. (unpublished)

Kibel, B. M. (1972) Simulation of the Urban Environment. Washington: Association of American Geographers.

Kidder, Steven J. (1971a) Emotional Arousal and Attitude Change During Simulation Games Report III. Baltimore: Center of Social Organization of Schools, Johns Hopkins University.

———— (1971b) Simulation Games: Practical References, Potential Use: Selected Bibliography. Baltimore: Center for Social Organization of Schools, Johns Hopkins University.

Kidder, S. J., and H. E. Aubertine (1972) Attitude Change and Number of Plays of a Social Simulation Game, Report 145. Baltimore: Johns Hopkins University Center for Social Organization of Schools, December.

Kidder, S. J., and John T. Guthrie (1972) "Training Effects of a Behavior Modification Game." Simulation and Games 3 (March): 17-28.

Kinley, Holly J. (1966) "Development of Strategies in a Simulation of Internal Revolutionary Conflict." American Behavioral Scientist 10 (November): 5-9.

Klabbers, Jan (1976) "The Process of Model-Building and Analysis of Social Systems." Social Systems Research Group, Department of Psychology, Nijmegen, Netherlands, April.

Klabbers, Jan, Katy Hoefnagels, Gert Jan Truin, and Pieter Van Der Hijden (1980) "Development of an Interactive Simulation-Game: A Case Study of DENTIST." Simulation and Games 11 (March): 59-86.

Klietsch, Ronald G. (1969) An Introduction to Learning Games and Instructional Simulations: A Curriculum Guideline. St. Paul: Instructional Simulations, Inc.

Klietsch, Ronald, and Fred Wiegman (1969) Directory of Educational Simulations, Learning Games, and Didactic Units. St. Paul: Instructional Simulations, Inc.

Kohl, Herbert R. (1974) Math, Writing, and Games in the Open Classroom. New York: Vintage.

Kotler, P., R. L. Schultz, and H. Guetzkow (1972) Simulation in Social and Administrative Science. Englewood Cliffs, NJ: Prentice-Hall.

Kringen, John A. (1980) "Utility of Political Gaming: An Evaluation." Simulation and Games 11 (June): 139-148.

Kraft, Ivor (1967) "Pedagogical Futility in Fun and Games." National Educational Association Journal 56 (January): 71-72.

Laponce, J. A., and P. Shoker [eds.] (1972) Experimentation and Simulation in Political Science. Toronto: University of Toronto Press.

Lashutka, Sergius (1977) "A Cross-Cultural Simulation as a Predictor of Cross-Cultural Adjustment." Simulation and Games 8 (December): 481-492.

Laska, Richard M. (1972) "Games People Play Help Solve Urban Ills." Computer Decisions 4 (February): 6-10.

Lauffer, Armand (1973) The Aim of the Game: A Primer on the Use and Design of Gamed Simulations. New York: Gamed Simulations, Inc.

Lawrence, Roderick J. (1980) "The Simulation of Domestic Space: Users and Architects Participating in the Architectural Design Process." Simulation and Games 11 (September): 279-300.

Leavitt, H. J. (1951) "Some Effects of Certain Communications Patterns on Group Performance." Journal of Abnormal and Social Psychology 46: 38-50.

Leavitt, M. R. (1967) "Materials on an All-Computer Simulation Model of U.S. Foreign Policy at the Level of General Trend." for Comparative Policy Systems Program, Wayne State University. (unpublished)

Lederman, Linda Costigan, and Brent D. Ruben (1978) "Construct Validity in Instructional Communication Simulations." Simulation and Games 9 (September): 259-274.

Lee, Robert S., and Arlene O'Leary (1971) "Attitude and Personality Effects of a Three-Day Simulation." Simulation and Games 2 (September): 309-347.

LeGates, R. T. (1974) The AMCOG Game: A Regional Housing and Urban Development Policy Game. San Francisco State University.

Lemert, E. M. (1962) "Paranoia and the Dynamics of Exclusion." Sociometry 25: 2-20.

Lerner, Daniel (1958) The Passing of Traditional Societies. New York: Free Press.

Lester, James P., and Michael J. Stoil (1979) "Evaluating a Role-Specific Simulation." Simulation and Games 10 (June): 167-188.

Levin, Martin L. (1976) "Displaying Sociometric Structures: An Application of Interactive Computer Graphics for Instruction and Analysis." Simulation and Games 7 (September): 295-310.

Lewin, K. (1952) "Group Decision and Social Change," in T. Newcomb and P. Hartley (eds.) Readings in Social Psychology. New York: Holt, Rinehart, and Winston.

Lewis, Darnell, and D. Wentworth (1971) Games and Simulations for Teaching Economics. New York: Joint Council on Education.

Liggett, Helen (1977) "An Evaluation Instrument for Use with Urban Simulation Games." Simulation and Games 8 (June): 155-188.

Lim, Timothy, Dean Uyeno, and Ilan Vertinsky (1975) "Hospital Admissions Systems: A Simulation Approach." Simulation and Games 6 (June): 188-201.

Lindblad, S. (1973) "Simulation and Guidance: Teaching Career Decision-Making Skills in the Swedish Compulsory School." Simulation and Games 4 (December): 429-439.

Linden, G., and H. van Rooijen (1975) "Educational Gaming Simulation: An Example of an Application in an Urban and Regional Planning Course in the Netherlands." Presented at PTRC summer annual meeting, Warwick, England.

Lindsay, Sally (1972) "APEX." Saturday Review (May 13): 55-57.

Little, Dennis (1972) "Social Indicators, Policy Analysis and Simulation." Futures (September): 220-231.

Livingston, Samuel A. (1971) "Simulation Games and Attitudes Toward the Poor: Three Questionnaire Studies." Report 118. Baltimore: Center for Social Organization of Schools, Johns Hopkins University.

———— (1972) "Effects of a Legislative Simulation Game on the Political Attitudes of Junior High School Students." Simulation and Games 3 (March): 41-51.

———— and S. J. Kidder (1973) "Role Identification and Game Structure: Effects on Political Attitudes." Simulation and Games 4 (June): 131-144.

Livingston, S. A., and Clarice S. Stoll (1973) Simulation Games for the Social Studies Teacher. New York: Free Press.

Livingston, S. A., G. M. Fennessey, J. S. Coleman, K. J. Edwards, and S. J. Kidder (1973) The Hopkins Games Program: Final Report On Seven Years of Research. Report 155. Baltimore: Johns Hopkins University Center for Social Organization of Schools.

Long, Norton E. (1958) "The Local Community as an Ecology of Games." American Journal of Sociology 64 (November).

Lorsted, Mats (1978) ISAGA Conference Book, 9th Annual Conference, Lund, Sweden.

Louscher, David, and Robert Van Steenburg (1977) "Effectiveness of a Short-Term Simulation as a Teaching Device in Political Science Courses." Simulation and Games 3 (December): 439-460.

Lowenstein, Louis K. (1971) An Annotated Bibliography on Urban Games (Exchange Bibliography 204). Monticello, IL: Council of Planning Libraries.

Lucas, Henry C., Jr. (1929) "Performance in a Complex Management Game." Simulation and Games 10 (March): 61-74.

Lucas, L., C. Postma, and J. Thompson (1974) A Comparative Study of Cognitive Retention Using Simulation Gaming as Opposed to Lecture-Discussion Technique (ERIC ED 089 690).

Lucas, Robert C., and Mordechai Shechter (1977) "A Recreational Visitor Travel Simulation Model as an Aid to Management Planning." Simulation and Games 8 (September): 375-384.

Luce, D., and H. Raiffa, (1957) Games and Decisions: Introduction and Critical Survey. New York: John Wiley.

Lundgren, Terry D., and R. Michael Loar (1978) "CLUG: The Spirit of Capitalism and the Success of a Simulation." Simulation and Games 9 (June): 201-207.

Lyman, S. M., and M. B. Scott (1970) A Sociology of the Absurd. New York: Appleton-Century-Crofts.

Mahoney, Robert, and Daniel Druckman (1975) "Simulation, Experimentation, and Context: Dimensions of Design and Inference." Simulation and Games 6 (September): 235-270.

Maidment, R., and R. Bronstein (1973) Simulation Games: Design and Implementation. Columbus, OH: Charles E. Merrill.

Majak, R. Roser (1968) "Social Science Teaching with Inter-Nation Simulation: A Review." Social Studies 59: 116-119.

Manocchio, A. J., and J. Dunn (1970) The Time Game: Two Views of a Prison. Beverly Hills: Sage.

Mar, Brian W., and Jeff Wright (1978) "Exchange Mechanisms for Policy Analysis Games." Simulation and Games 9 (December): 393-412.

Martin, Patricia Yancey, and Marie Withers Osmond (1975) "Structural Asymmetry and Social Exchange: A Sex-Role Simulation." Simulation and Games 6 (December): 339-365.

Marts, John A. (1977) "Paying Your Way: The Development and Evaluation of a Personal Finance Simulation Game." Simulation and Games 8 (June): 189-200.

Maruyama, Magoroh (1968) "The Second Cybernetics: Deviation-Amplifying Mutual Causal Processes," in Walter Buckley (ed.) Modern Systems Research for the Behavioral Scientist. Chicago: Aldine.

McAleese, Ray [ed.] (1977) Perspectives on Academic Gaming and Simulation: The Proceedings of the 1977 Conference of SAGSET. New York: Nichols.

McFarlane, F., J. McKenney, and J. D. Seiler (1970) The Management Game: Simulated Decision Making. New York: Macmillan.

McFarlane, P. T. (1971) "Simulation Games as Social Psychological Research Sites: Methodological Advantages." Simulation and Games 2 (June): 149-161.

McGinley, K. (1980) "Use of Simulation in English for Special Purpose Courses in a Developing Country." Simulation-Games for Learning (the Journal of SAGSET) 10 (Spring): 10-20.

McGuire, C., L. Solomon, and P. Bushook (1977) Construction and Use of Written Simula-
    tions. New York: The Psychological Corporation.
McGuire, William J. (1969) "Theory-Oriented Research in Natural Settings: The Best of Both
    Worlds for Social Psychology," in Muzafer Sherif and Carolyn W. Sherif (eds.) Interdisci-
    plinary Relationships in the Social Sciences. Chicago: Aldine.
McHugh, P. (1968) Defining the Situation. Indianapolis: Bobbs-Merrill.
McInish, Thomas H. (1980) "A Game-Simulation of Stock Market Behavior: An Extension."
    Simulation and Games 11 (December): 477-484.
McKenney, James L., and William R. Dill (1966) "Influences on Learning in Simulation
    Games." American Behavioral Scientist 10 (October): 28-32.
McLaughlin, B. (1971) Learning in Social Behavior. New York: Free Press.
McLear, H., and M. Raymond (1976) Design Your Own Game. Lebanon, OH: The Simulation
    and Gaming Association.
McLeod, J. (1968) Simulation: The Modeling of Ideas and Systems with Computers. New
    York: McGraw-Hill.
McLuhan, Marshall (1964) "Games: The Extensions of Man," in Marshall McLuhan, Under-
    standing Media. New York: McGraw-Hill.
Mead, George H. (1934) "Play, the Game, and the Generalized Other," in G. H. Mead, Mind,
    Self, and Society. Chicago: University of Chicago Press.
Megarry, J. (1979) "Monitoring." Simulation-Games for Learning (Winter): 170-177.
Meier, Richard L. (1963) "Game Procedure in the Simulation of Cities," pp. 348-354, in L. J.
    Duhl (ed.) The Urban Condition: People and Policy in the Metropolis. New York: Basic
    Books.
———— (1967) "Simulations for Transmitting Concepts of Social Organization," pp. 156-175 in
    Werner Z. Hirsch et al. (eds.) Inventing Education for the Future. San Francisco: Chandler.
Meier, Richard, and Richard D. Duke (1966) "Gaming Simulation for Urban Planning."
    Journal of American Institute of Planners 32 (January): 3-17.
Merton, R. (1968) Social Theory and Social Structure. New York: Free Press.
Michael, Donald N. (1968) "On Coping with Complexity: Planning and Politics." Daedalus
    (Fall): 97-104.
———— (1976) "Technology Assessment in an Emerging World." Address to the Second
    International Congress on Technology Assessment, University of Michigan, October 25.
Michaels, J. (1977) "Classroom Reward Structures and Academic Performance." Review of
    Educational Research 47: 87-98.
Milgram, S. (1963) "Behavioral Study of Obedience." Journal of Abnormal Social Psychology
    (October): 371-378.
Miller, D., G. F. Snyder, and R. Neff (1973) Using Biblical Simulations. Valley Forge, PA:
    Judson Press.
Miller, Larry D. (1978) "The Modified Values Auction: A Data Analytic Classroom Game."
    Simulation and Games (September): 275-288.
———— (1979a) "Interaction Games: A Rationale and Model." Simulation and Games 10
    (December): 355-358.
———— (1979b) "The Perception Game: Understanding Self and Other." Simulation and Games
    10 (December): 419-428.
Miller, Roy I., and R. D. Duke (1972) "Gaming: A Methodological Experiment." Proceedings,
    American Political Science Association, Washington, DC, September.
Mize, J. H., and J. G. Cox (1968) Essentials of Simulation. Englewood Cliffs, NJ: Prentice-
    Hall.
Modelski, George (1970) "Simulations, 'Realities,' and International Relations Theory." Simu-
    lation and Games 1 (June): 111-134.

Monroe, Margaret Warne (1968) "Games as Teaching Tools: An Examination of the Community Land Use Game." M. S. dissertation, Cornell University.

Moore, Omar Khayyam, and Alan Ross Anderson (1975) "Some Principles for the Design of Clarifying Educational Environments," pp. 47-71 in C. S. Greenblat and R. D. Duke (eds.) Gaming-Simulation. New York: Halsted.

Moriarity, J. [ed.] (1973) Simulation and Gaming. National Bureau of Standards Special Publication 395 for Department of Commerce, National Bureau of Standards. Washington, DC: Government Printing Office.

Nagelberg, Mark (1970) Simulation of Urban Systems—A Selected Bibliography. Middletown, CT: Institute for the Future.

―――― and Dennis Little (1970) "Selected Urban Simulations and Games." Simulation and Games 1 (December): 459-481.

NASAGA (1979) 18th Annual Conference Book (Applications for Education and Training). Austin, Texas, October 9-13.

Naylor, T. H., and J. M. Finger (1967) "Verification of Computer Simulation Models." Management Science 14 (October): 97-101.

Naylor, T. H., J. L. Balintfy, D. S. Burdick, and K. Chu (1966) Computer Simulation Techniques. New York: John Wiley.

Nelson, Thomas M., Marianne E. Johnson, and Carol J. Laden (1981) "B-SAFE: Test of an Industrial Safety Contest." Simulation and Games (March): 51-66.

Nesbitt, William (1971) Simulation Games for the Social Studies Classroom. New York: Thomas Y. Crowell.

Newman, J. (1974) "The Effectiveness of an Educational Simulation in Teaching Ethnic Studies to High School Students." Ph.D. dissertation, Northern Illinois University.

Noel, Robert C. (1971) "Inter-University Political Gaming and Simulation Through the POLIS Network." Presented at the annual meeting of the American Simulation and Gaming Association.

―――― (1975) "POLIS Network: A System for Distributing Simulation and Gaming." Presented at the meeting of the North American Simulation and Gaming Association.

Noesjirwan, Jennifer, and Colin Freestone (1979) "The Culture Game: A Simulation of Culture Shock." Simulation and Games 10 (June): 189-206.

Norris, Dwight R., and Robert E. Niebuhr (1980) "Group Variables and Gaming Success." Simulation and Games 11 (September): 301-312.

Norton, Robert W. (1979) "The Coalition Game: Isolating Social System Subgroups." Simulation and Games 10 (December): 385-402.

O'Leary, Timothy J. (1980) "Simulating the Can of Worms." Simulation and Games 11 (June): 149-161.

Orbach, Eliezer (1977) "Some Theoretical Considerations in the Evaluation of Instructional Simulation Games." Simulation and Games 8 (September): 341-360.

―――― (1979) "Simulation Games and Motivation for Learning: A Theoretical Framework." Simulation and Games 10 (March): 3-40.

Osmond, Marie W. (1970) "Participating in a Simulation Game." Journal of Applied Behavioral Science 6: 239-244.

―――― (1971) "The Method of Simulation Games in Family Life Education." Presented at the 1970 National Council on Family Relations Convention (Bethesda, MD: ERIC Document Reproduction Service, ED 044 721-RIE April).

Paterson, Philip D., Jr., and Peter House (1969) "An Environmental Gaming Simulation Laboratory." Journal of the American Institute of Planners 35 (November): 383-388.

Pettegrew, Lloyd S. (1979) "The Paradox Game: Identifying and Overcoming Untenable Interactions." Simulation and Games 10 (December): 359-383.

Pfeiffer, J. W., and J. E. Jones (1979) A Handbook of Structured Experiences for Human Relations Training (vols. 1-7) La Jolla, CA: University Associates.

Philips, Bernard S. (1971) Social Research: Strategy and Tactics. New York: Macmillan.

Pierfy, David A. (1977) "Comparative Simulation Game Research: Stumbling Blocks and Steppingstones." Simulation and Games 8 (June): 255-268.

Pitts, Forest (1966) The Varieties of Simulation: A review and Bibliography. Philadelphia: Regional Science Research Institute.

Plummer, Charles M. (1976) "Dynamic Modeling of Alternative Futures Through Simulation-Gaming." Viewpoints, Bulletin of the School of Education, Indiana University, Bloomington.

Pool, Ithiel De Sola, and Robert Abelson (1962) "The Simulmatics Project," in Harold Guetzkow (ed.) Simulation in Social Science: Readings. Englewood Cliffs, NJ: Prentice-Hall.

Pool, Ithiel De Sola, Robert P. Abelson, and Samuel L. Popkin (1965) Candidates, Issues, and Strategies: A Computer Simulation of the 1960 Presidential Election. Cambridge, MA: MIT Press.

Postma, C. (1973) "Simulation in High School Social Studies: Students' Cognitive Retention and Pupil-Teacher Affective Perceptions." Ph.D. dissertation, Ball State University.

Pratt, Linda K., Norman P. Uhl, and Elizabeth R. Little (1980) "Evaluation of Games as a Function of Personality Type." Simulation and Games 11, (September): 336-346.

Prud'homme, Remey, Jean de la Brunetiere, and Gabriel Dupuy (1972) Les Jeux de Simulation Urbanistiques. Paris: Tema-Editions.

Ramey, James W. (1967) "Simulation in Library Administration." Journal of Education for Librarianship 8 (Fall): 85-93.

Rapoport, A. (1960) Fights, Games and Debates. Ann Arbor: University of Michigan Press.

Raser, John R. (1969) Simulation and Society: An Exploration of Scientific Gaming. Boston: Allyn and Bacon.

Raser, J. R., and Wayman J. Crow (n.d.) "A Simulation Study of Deterrence Theories." La Jolla, CA: Western Behavioral Sciences Institute.

Rausser, Gordon C., and S. R. Johnson (1968) "On the Limitations of Simulation in Model Evaluation and Decision Analysis." Simulation and Games 6 (June): 115-150.

Ray, Paul, and Richard D. Duke (1968) "The Environment of Decision-Makers in Urban Gaming Simulations," in William Coplin (ed.) Simulation in the Study of Politics. Chicago: Markham.

Redfield, Robert (1962) "Civilization as Things Thought About," pp. 364-391 in Margaret Park Redfield (ed.) Human Nature and the Study of Society: The Papers of Robert Redfield, Vol. 1. Chicago: University of Chicago Press.

Reese, Jay (1977) Simulation Games and Learning Activities Kit for the Elementary School. West Nyack, NY: Parker.

Reid, Norman (1979) "Some Affective Outcomes from Simulation Techniques in Secondary Education," pp. 146-156, in How To Build A Simulation Game. Vol. 1. Leeuwarden, Netherlands: Proceedings of the 10th ISAGA Conference.

——— (1980) "Simulation Techniques in Secondary Education: Affective Outcomes." Simulation and Games 11 (March): 107-120.

Remus, William (1977) "Who Likes Business Games?" Simulation and Games 8 (December): 469-480.

——— (1979) "Playing Business Games: Attitudinal Differences Between Students Playing Singly and as Teams." Simulation and Games 10, March.

——— (1981) "Experimental Designs for Analyzing Data on Games: Or, Even the Best Statistical Methods Do Not Replace Good Experimental Control." Simulation and Games 12 (March): 3-14.

Rhyne, R. F. (1975) "Communicating Holistic Insights," pp. 15-28 in C. S. Greenblat and R. D. Duke (eds.) Gaming-Simulation. New York: Halsted.

Rice, George H., Jr. (1980) "Economics of the Hidden Matrix." Simulation and Games 11 (June): 205-221.

Riesel, T. (1969) "A Comparative Study of Two Approaches to the Teaching of Economics in Suburban New Jersey Twelfth Grade Economics Classroom." Ph.D. dissertation, New York University.

Riley, Mathilda (1963) Sociological Research: A Case Approach. New York: Harcourt Brace Jovanovich.

Roberts, F. J. (1975) "Play Games in this Department: An Experimental Comparison of Conventional Lecture and Classroom Games Formats in the Introductory American Government Course." Teaching Political Science 2 (January): 123-143.

Roberts, Thomas B. (1977) "Education and Transpersonal Relations: A Research Agenda." Simulation and Games 8 (March): 7-28.

Robinson, James A. (1966) "Simulation and Games," in Peter Rossi and Bruce Biddle (eds.) The New Media and Education. Chicago: Aldine.

Robinson, James A., Lee F. Anderson, Margaret G. Hermann, and Richard C. Snyder (1966) "Teaching with Inter-Nation Simulation and Case Studies." American Political Science Review 60 (March): 53-64.

Robinson, J. N. (1978) "Are Economic Games and Simulations Useful? Some Evidence from an Experimental Game." Simulation and Games 9 (March): 3-22.

Romanos, Michael (1978) "Undergraduate Planning Curricula: Is Gaming the Answer?" Simulation and Games 9 (March): 89-106.

Rosen, David J. (1981) "METRO-APEX as a Course." Simulation and Games 12 (March): 15-21.

Rosenfeld, F. (1975) "The Educational Effectiveness of Simulation Games: A Synthesis of Recent Findings," pp. 285-291 in C. S. Greenblat and R. D. Duke (eds.) Gaming-Simulation. New York: Halsted.

Rosenthal, R. (1966) Experimenter Effects in Behavior Research. New York: Appleton-Century-Crofts.

Ruben, Brent D. (1973) "The What and Why of Gaming: A Taxonomy of Experience Based Learning Systems." Presented at the 12th Annual Meetings of the National Gaming Council and the 4th Annual Meeting of the International Simulation and Gaming Association.

——— (1977) "Toward a Theory of Experience-Based Instruction." Simulation and Games 8 (June): 211-231.

Ruben, B., and R. Budd (1975) Human Communication Handbook: Simulations and Games. Rochelle Park, NJ: Hayden.

Rubin, Herbert J. (1978) "A Note on PARIDIGM: A Simulation Model of the Competition of Ideas in Evolving Groups." Simulation and Games 9 (June): 173-184.

——— (1981) "Applied Simulations and Persuasion Campaigns: Designs in Rural Villages." Simulation and Games 12 (March): 85-98.

Russell, Constance (1971) "Validity Testing of a Social Simulation," in The Proceedings of the 10th Annual Symposium of the National Gaming Council. Ann Arbor, MI: The Environmental Simulations Laboratory.

——— (1972) "Simulating the Adolescent Society: A Validity Study." Simulation and Games 3 (June): 165-188.

Sanoff, H. (1979) Design Games. Los Altos, CA: William Haufman.

Sarason, Seymour (1971) The Culture of the School and the Problem of the Change. Boston: Allyn and Bacon.

Scheff, T. J. (1967) "Toward a Sociological Model of Consensus." American Sociological Review 32 (February): 32-46.

Schein, E. H. (1972) Organizational Psychology. Englewood Cliffs, NJ: Prentice-Hall.

Schild, E. O. (1971) "Simulation Review: BLACKS AND WHITES." Simulation and Games 2 (March): 95-97.

Schneier, C. E. (1976) "An Empirical Investigation of the Relationship Between Individual Characteristics and Interpersonal Style of Participants and their Success in Simulation-Based Learning Environments." Presented at the 15th Annual Conference of the North American Simulation and Gaming Association, Raleigh, N.C.

Schutz, A. (1962) "On Multiple Realities," pp. 207-259 in Collected Papers: The Problem of Social Reality. The Hague, Netherlands: Martinus Nijhoff.

Segal, R., and B. O'Neal (1978) "Simulation of a National Computer Network in a Gaming Environment." Educom Bulletin (Fall): 2-8.

Seginer, Rachel (1980) "Game Ability and Academic Ability: Dependence on SES and Psychological Mediators." Simulation and Games 11 (December): 403-421.

Seibold, David R., and Thomas M. Steinfatt (1979) "The Creative Alternative Game: Exploring Interpersonal Influence Processes." Simulation and Games 10 (December): 429-457.

Seidner, Constance J., and Richard L. Dukes (1976) "Simulation in Social-Psychological Research: A Methodological Approach to the Study of Attitudes and Behavior." Simulation and Games 7 (March): 3-20.

Shade, W., and J. Paine (1975) "Simulation in the Classroom: A Reevaluation of its Effects." Teaching Political Science 3: 83-89.

Shaftel, F. R., and G. Shaftel (1976) Role Playing for Social Values: Decision-Making in the Social Studies. Englewood Cliffs, NJ: Prentice-Hall.

Sharan, Shlomo, and Chaya Colodner (1976) "COUNSELOR: A Simulation Game for Vocational Decision-Making." Simulation and Games 7 (June): 193-208. n. 2, June.

Sherif, M., O. J. Harvey, and B. J. White (1955) "Status in Experimentally Produced Groups." American Journal of Sociology 60: 370-379.

_____ W. R. Hood, and C. W. Sherif (1961) Intergroup Conflict and Cooperation—The Robbers Cave Experiment. Norman: University of Oklahoma Book Exchange.

Shim, Jae K. (1977) "A Conversational Executive Game." Simulation and Games 8 (December): 461-468.

Shirts, R. Garry (1970) "Games Students Play." Saturday Review 53 (May 16): 81-82.

_____ (1975) "Notes on Defining 'Simulation'," pp. 75-81 in C. S. Greenblat and R. D. Duke (eds.) Gaming-Simulation. New York: Halsted.

_____ (1976a) "Ten 'Mistakes' Made by Persons Designing Educational Simulations and Games." Simulation-Gaming-News 3 (May): 25ff.

_____ (1976b) "Simulation Games: An Analysis of the Last Decade." Programmed Learning and Educational Technology (Journal of APLET) 13: 37-41.

Shubik, Martin (1959) A Short Bibliography of Simulation, Gaming, and Allied Topics. New York: General Electric Company Operations Research and Synthesis Consultations Service.

_____ (1964) Game Theory and Related Approaches to Social Behavior. New York: John Wiley.

_____ (1971a) On Gaming and Game Theory. Technical Report P-4609. Santa Monica: Rand Corporation.

_____ (1971b) On the Scope of Gaming. Report P-4608. Santa Monica: Rand Corporation.

_____ (1975a) Games for Society, Business and War: Towards a Theory of Gaming. New York: Elsevier.

_____ (1975b) The Uses and Methods of Gaming. New York: Elsevier.

_____ (1978) "Opinions on How to Play Some Simple Games." Simulation and Games 9

(March): 67-88.

Shubik, M., and Garry D. Brewer (1972) Reviews of Selected Books and Articles on Gaming and Simulation. Santa Monica: Rand Corporation.

———— (1972) "Models, Simulations, and Games—A Survey." Report for Advanced Research Projects Agency.

Shubik, M., G. Brewer, and E. Savage (1972) "The Literature of Gaming, Simulation, and Model Building: Index and Critical Abstracts." Report prepared for Advanced Research Projects Agency.

Shure, Gerald H., Neil Malamuth, and Shawn A. Johnston (1975) "A Computer Simulation of Group Risky Shift for Teaching Undergraduate Research Methods." Simulation and Games 6 (June): 202-210.

Silber, K., and G. Ewing (1971) Environmental Simulation. Englewood Cliffs, NJ: Educational Technology Publications, Inc.

Sims, Henry P., Jr., and Herbert H. Hand (1975) "Performance Tradeoffs in Management Games." Simulation and Games 6 (March): 61-72.

Smit, P. (1979) "The Structure of Gaming Models With More than One Level of Aggregation." Presented at the 10th Annual ISAGA Conference, Leeuwarden, Netherlands, August 8-11.

Smith, R. M. (1972) Communication Variables Appropriate to Gaming and Simulation. Bethesda, MD: ERIC Document Reproduction Service.

Smoker, Paul (1969) "Social Research for Social Anticipation." American Behavioral Scientist 12 (July-August): 7-13.

Sokolov, V., and I. Zimin (1975) "Gaming Model to Study the Problem of Sharing Natural Resources." (memo)

Spelvin, G. (1979) "Directed Discovery in Debriefing." Simages 1 (Fall): 17-21.

Sprague, Hall (n.d.) "Using Simulations to Teach International Relations." La Jolla, CA: Simile II, Western Behavioral Sciences Institute. (mimeo)

Sprague, H., and R. Garry Shirts (1966) "Exploring Uses of Classroom Simulation." La Jolla, CA: Simile II, Western Behavioral Sciences Institute. (mimeo)

Stadsklev, Ron (1969) "A Comparative Study of Simulation Gaming and Lecture Discussion Methods." M.A. Thesis, Northern State College (ERIC ED 065-405).

———— (1974) Handbook of Simulation Gaming in Social Education—Part I: Textbook. University: University of Alabama.

———— (1979) Handbook of Simulation Gaming in Social Education—Part II. University: University of Alabama.

Stanford, G., and B. Stanford (1969) Learning Discussion Skills Through Games. New York: Citation Press.

Starbuck, W. A., and J. M. Dutton [eds.] (1970) Computer Simulation in Human Behavior. New York: John Wiley.

Steinwachs, Barbara (1971) "The Urbanarium: A Museum Responds." The Museologist 121 (December): 5-9.

Stembler, William A. (1975) "Cognitive Effects of a Programmed Simulation." Simulation and Games 6 (December): 392-403.

Stewart, Edward C. (1967) "The Simulation of Cross-Cultural Communication." Washington, DC: Human Resources Research Office.

Stoll, C. S. (1969) "Player Characteristics and Interaction in Parent-Child Interaction Game." Sociometry 32 (September): 259-272.

Stoll, C. S. and M. Inbar (1970) "Games and Socialization: An Exploratory Study of Race Differences." Sociological Quarterly 2 (Summer): 374-380.

———— (1972) Simulation and Gaming in Social Science. New York: Free Press.

Strategy and Tactics Magazine (1977) Wargame Design: The History, Production, and Use of

Conflict Simulation Games. New York: Simulations Publications.

Straus, Murray A. (1970) "Methodology of a Laboratory Experimental Study of Families in Three Societies," pp. 552-557 in Reuben Hill and Rene Konig (eds.) Families in East and West. Paris: Mouton.

Suits, Bernard (1967) "What is a Game?" Philosophy of Science 34 (June): 148-156.

_____ (1978) The Grasshopper: Games, Life and Utopia. Toronto: University of Toronto Press.

Sussman, M.B., and W.B. Weil (1960) "An Experimental Study of the Effects of Group Interaction upon the Behavior of Diabetic Children." International Journal of Social Psychiatry 6: 120-125.

Sylvan, Donald A., and Charles F. Hermann (1979) "Simulating U.S. National Security Decision-Making." Simulation and Games 10 (September): 227-256.

Szafran, Robert F., and Ann F. Mandolini (1980) "Test Performance and Concept Recognition: The Effect of a Simulation Game on Two Types of Cognitive Knowledge." Simulation and Games 11 (September): 326-335.

Tafoya, Dennis W. (1979) "The Motivation Game: Effecting Social Behavior in Small Groups." Simulation and Games (December): 403-418.

Tansey, P.J. (1970) "Simulation Techniques in the Training of Teachers." Simulation and Games 1 (September): 281-303.

_____ (1971) Educational Aspects of Simulation. New York: McGraw-Hill.

Tansey, P.J. and D. Unwin (1969) Simulation and Gaming in Education. New York: Barnes and Noble.

Tapon, Francis (1978) "Electric Public Utilities in the United States: A Simulation Model of the Process of Rate of Return Setting by State Regulatory Commissions." Simulation and Games 9 (September): 289-300. September.

Targ, H. (1967) "Impacts of an Elementary School Inter-Nation Simulation on Developing Orientations to International Politics." Ph.D. dissertation, Northwestern University.

Taylor, John L. (1971) Instructional Planning Systems. Cambridge: Cambridge University Press.

Taylor, J., and K.R. Carter (1967) "Instructional Simulation of Urban Development: A Preliminary Report." Journal of Town Planning Institute 53 (December): 443-447.

Taylor, J.L., and R.N. Madison (1958) "A Land Use Gaming Simulation." Urban Affairs Quarterly (June): 37-51.

Taylor, J.L., and R. Walford (1972) Simulation in the Classroom. New York: Viking.

_____ (1978) Learning and the Simulation Game. Beverly Hills: Sage.

Tedeschi, J.T., B. Schenker, and T. Bonoma (1973) Conflict, Power and Games: The Experimental Study of Interpersonal Relations. Chicago: Aldine.

Terhune, K.W., and J.H. Firestone (1970) "Global War, Limited War, and Peace: Hypotheses from Three Experimental Worlds." International Studies Quarterly 14 (June): 195-218.

Thiagarajan, S. [ed.] (1973) Current Trends in Simulation-Gaming, Bloomington: Bulletin of the School of Education, Indiana University.

Thiagarajan, S., and Harold D. Stolovitch (1979) "Frame Games: An Evaluation." Simulation and Games 10 (September): 287-314.

Thomas, Clayton J., and Walter L. Deemer, Jr. (1957) "The Role of Operational Gaming in Operations Research." Operations Research 5 (February): 1-27.

Thomas, W.I. (1928) The Child in America. New York: Knopf.

Thompson, John (1977) "Voting Games and Belief Reorganization." Simulation and Games 8 (March): 121-131.

Thornton, Barbara (1971) Gaming Techniques for City Planning: A Bibliography. Exchange Bibliography 181, Monticello, IL: Council for Planning Libraries.

Tiene, D. (1981) "BAFA and After: Exposing Teacher Trainees to the World of Simulation Games." Simages 3 (Spring).

Toffler, A. (1970) Future Shock. New York: Random House.

Tonnies, Ferdinand (1940) "Gemeinschaft and Gesellschaft," in Charles Loomis (ed.) Fundamental Concepts of Society. New York: Random House.

Treadway, Roy C. (1978) "Experience in Using POPSIM in a Family Planning Experiment." Simulation and Games 9 (June): 159-172.

Tumin, Melvin (1958) "Some Social Requirements for Effective Community Development." Community Development Review 11 (December).

Twelker, Paul A. [ed.] (1969) Instructional Simulation: A Research Development and Dissemination Activity. Corvallis, OR: Teaching Research.

———— (1969a) "Designing Simulation Systems." Educational Technology (October): 64-70.

———— (1969b) Instructional Simulation Systems: An Annotated Bibliography. Corvallis, OR: Continuing Education Publications, Teaching Research.

———— (1972) "Some Reflections on Instructional Simulation and Gaming." Simulation and Games 3 (June): 147-153.

Urban Regional Research Institute (1966) METRO: A Gaming Simulation. Report on Phase I. East Lansing, MI: Author.

Uretsky, M. (1973) "The Management Game: An Experiment in Reality." Simulation and Games 4 (June): 221-240.

Van Geen, V. (1980) "The Subjective Value of Games." Presented at ISAGA, Geneva, August.

Van Maanen, J. (1979) "Breaking in: Socialization to Work," in R. Dubin (ed.) The Handbook of Work, Organization and Society. Chicago: Rand McNally.

Van Oosten, R. C. H. (1980) "The Management Game at the University of Groningen, The Netherlands." Simulation and Games 11 (December): 423-439.

Van Oudenhoven, Nico (1980) "Play, Development Education and Games." Presented at ISAGA Annual Conference, Geneva, August.

Van Sickle, R. L. (1978) "Designing Simulation Games to Teach Decision-Making Skills." Simulation and Games 9 (December): 413-428.

Vance, C., and C. F. Gray (1967) "Use of Performance Evaluation Model for Research in Business Gaming." Academy of Management Journal 1: 27-37.

Vargiu, James G. (1977) "Education and Psychosynthesis: An Application to Teacher Training." Simulation and Games 8 (March): 133-148.

Verba, S. (1964) "Simulation, Reality and Theory in International Relations." World Politics 16 (April): 491-519.

Vinacke, W. E. (1959) "Sex Roles in the Three-Person Game." Sociometry 22: 343-360.

Vogel, R. (1973) "The Effect of a Simulation Game on the Attitude of Political Efficacy." Simulation and Games 4 (March): 71-79.

Von Bertalanffy, L. (1968) "General Systems Theory: A Critical Review," in W. Buckley (ed.) Modern Systems Research for the Behavioral Scientist. Chicago: Aldine.

Walford, R. (1969) Games in Geography. London: Longmans.

Walters, C., and F. Bunnell (1971) "A Computer Management Game of Land-Use in British Colombia." Journal of Wildlife Management 35 (October): 644-657.

Warren, J., E. Jansen, and A. Knight (n.d.) "The Blackberry Falls Town Government Game: A Computer-Assisted Gaming Simulation about the Decision-Making Process in the Town Government Framework of a Small Town." (programmed in Basic)

Watson, Hugh J. (1978) "An Empirical Investigation of the Use of Simulation." Simulation and Games 9, (December): 477-482.

Watson, Hugh J., and Carl D. McDevitt (1977) "A Probabilistic, Noninteractive Management Game for Probability Encoding Studies." Simulation and Games 8 (December): 493-504.

Watt, Kenneth F. (1977) "Why Won't Anyone Believe Us?" Simulation (January).

Weigel, R. H., P. L. Wiser, and S. W. Cook (1975) "The Impact of Cooperative Learning Experiences on Cross-Ethnic Relations and Attitudes." Journal of Social Issues 31: 219-243.

Werner, Roland, and Joan T. Werner (1969) Bibliography of Simulations: Social Systems and Education. La Jolla, CA: Western Behavioral Science Institute.

Whithead, M. (1972) "FEDERA SIM: A Prototype Water Resources Management Simulation Game." Presented at the 3rd International ISAGA Conference, Birmingham, England, July 6-9.

Wilcoxson, Georgeann (1971) "Some Useful Games," in Simulation, Gaming and the Church. (Presbyterian Church U.S.), Leadership Edition, (November 15).

Williams, Robert H. (1980) "Attitude Change and Simulation Games: The Ability of a Simulation Game to Change Attitudes When Structured in Accordance with Either the Cognitive Dissonance or Incentive Models of Attitude Change." Simulation and Games 11 (June): 177-196.

Wilson, James Q. (1968) "Planning and Politics: Citizen Participation in Urban Renewal," in Bernard J. Frieden and Robert Morris (eds.) Urban Planning and Social Policy. New York: Basic Books.

Wing, R. (1968) "Two Computer-Based Economics Games for Sixth Graders," pp. 155-165 in S. S. Boocock and E. O. Schild (eds.) Simulation Games in Learning. Beverly Hills: Sage.

Wolfe, Joseph, and Thomas I. Chacko (1980) "Cognitive Structures of Business Game Players: Relationships Between an Individual's Cognitive Processing Equipment and Business Game Performance and Play." Simulation and Games 11 (December): 461-476.

Zachet, M. (1975) Simulation Teaching of Library Administration. New York: R. R. Bowker Co.

Zey, M. (1979) The N.Y.U. MANAGEMENT GAME: Attitude Change in a Simulated Environment. Ph.D. dissertation, Rutgers University.

Zieler, Richard (n.d.) Games for School Use: An Annotated List. Yorktown Heights, NY: Board of Cooperative Educational Services.

Zif, Jehiel J. (1976) "Optional Versus Fixed Information System in a Simulation Game." Simulation and Games 7 (March): 35-52.

Zuckerman, David W., and Robert E. Horn (1973) The Guide to Simulation Games for Education and Training. Cambridge, MA: Information Resources, Inc.

Games-Simulation Index

AT-ISSUE! Designed by Richard D. Duke and Cathy S. Greenblat. Published in *Game-Generating Games: A Trilogy of Issue-Oriented Games for Community and Classroom*. Sage Publications, 275 South Beverly Drive, Beverly Hills, CA 90212.

BAFA BAFA. Designed by R. Garry Shirts. Published by Simile II, P.O. Box 910, Del Mar, CA 92014.

BALDICER. Designed by Georgeann Wilcoxson. Published by John Knox s, Press, 341 Ponce de Leon Avenue, N. E., Atlanta, GA 30308.

BLACKS AND WHITES. Designed by Robert Sommer and Judy Tart. Published by Psychology Today Games, Clinton, IA.

BLOOD MONEY. Designed by Cathy S. Greenblat and John H. Gagnon. Published by National Heart, Lung and Blood Institute, OPCE, Bethesda, MD.

CLUG (Community Land Use Game). Designed by Allan G. Feldt. Published by the Free Press, Department F, Riverside, NJ 08075.

COMMUNITY DISPUTES. Designed by Armand Lauffer. Published by Gamed Simulations, Inc., Suite 4H, 10 West 66th Street, New York, NY 10023.

CONCEPTUAL MAPPING GAME. Designed by Richard D. Duke and Cathy S. Greenblat. Published in *Game-Generating Games: A Trilogy of Issue-Oriented Games for Community and Classroom*. Sage Publications, 275 South Beverly Drive, Beverly Hills, CA 90212.

DOCTOR'S GAME (TERMINEX). Designed by Sister Miriam Jude Doogan, Leah Rowbathan, Diane Walker, Judy Foster Karshmer, and Jerry Wallhauser, with assistance from Cathy S. Greenblat and Shirley Smoyak. Published by Department of Psychiatric Nursing, Rutgers University Medical School, New Brunswick, NJ.

END OF THE LINE. Designed by Frederick L. Goodman. Published by Institute of Higher Education Research and Services, Box 6293, University, AL 35486.

EQUATIONS. Designed by Layman Allen. Published by WFF 'N PROOF, 1490-TZ South Boulevard, Ann Arbor, MI 48104.

... ET ALIA ... Designed by R. H. R. Armstrong, Margaret Hobson, and Jim Hunter. Published by Institute for Local Government Studies, University of Birmingham, Birmingham, England.

FUTURE STATE OF THE UNION. Designed by Olaf Helmar. Published by Institute for the Future, Santa Monica, CA.

FUTURES. Designed by Olaf Helmar. Published by Kaiser Aluminum and Chemical Corporation.

GHETTO. Designed by Dave Toll. Published by Bobbs-Merrill Company, Educational Division, 4300 West 62nd Street, Indianapolis, IN 46268.

HORATIO ALGER (A Welfare Simulation Game). Designed by Ann Kraemer, Bob Preuss, and Helen Howe. Published by Citizens for Welfare Reform, 305 Michigan Avenue, Detroit, MI 48226.

IMPASSE? Designed by Richard D. Duke and Cathy S. Greenblat. Published in *Game-Generating Games: A Trilogy of Issue-Oriented Games for Community and Classroom.* Sage Publications, 275 South Beverly Drive, Beverly Hills, CA 90212.

MARBLES (or THEY SHOOT MARBLES, DON'T THEY?). Designed by Frederick L. Goodman. Published by Institute of Higher Education Research and Services, Box 6293, University, AL 35486.

THE MARRIAGE GAME: Understanding Marital Decision-Making. Designed by Cathy S. Greenblat, Peter J. Stein, and Norman F. Washburne. Published by Random House, Inc., The College Department, 457 Hahn Road, Westminster, MD 21157.

METRO-APEX. Designed by Richard D. Duke. Published by Environmental Simulation Laboratory, University of Michigan, Ann Arbor, MI 48109.

METROPOLIS: The Urban Systems Game. Designed by Richard D. Duke. (3 volumes) Published by Gamed Simulations, Inc., 10 West 66th Street, New York, NY 10023.

METROPOLITICS. Designed by R. Garry Shirts. Published by Simile II, P.O. Box 910, Del Mar, CA 92014.

NEXUS. Designed by R. H. R. Armstrong and Margaret Hobson. Published by Institute for Local Government Studies, University of Birmingham, Birmingham, England.

ON-WORDS. Designed by Layman Allen, Fred Goodman, Doris Humphrey, and Joan K. Ross. Published by WFF 'N PROOF, 1490-TZ South Boulevard, Ann Arbor, MI 48104.

POLICY NEGOTIATIONS. Designed by Frederick L. Goodman. Published by Institute of Higher Education Research and Services, Box 6293, University, AL 35486.

POLIS NETWORK. Designed by Robert C. Noel. Published by POLIS Laboratory, Department of Political Science, University of California, Santa Barbara, CA 93106.

SIMSOC. Designed by William A. Gamson. Published by the Free Press, 866 Third Avenue, New York, NY 10022.

SITTE. Designed by R. Garry Shirts. Published by Simile II, P.O. Box 910, Del Mar, CA 92014.

STARPOWER. Designed by R. Garry Shirts. Published by Simile II, P.O. Box 910, Del Mar, CA 92014.

VALUE GAME. Designed by Thomas Linehan and William S. Irving. Published by Seabury Press, 815 Second Avenue, New York, NY 10017.

WALRUS (Water and Land Resource Utilization Simulation). Designed by Allan G. Feldt and David Moses. Published by Sea Grant Advisory Services, University of Michigan, 1101 N. University, Ann Arbor, MI 48104.

WFF 'N PROOF. Designed by Layman Allen. Published by WFF 'N PROOF, 1490-TZ South Boulevard, Ann Arbor, MI 48104.

WOMEN'S LIBERATION. Designed by David J. Boin and Robert Sillman. Published by Edu-Game, P.O. Box 1144, Sun Valley, CA 91352.

About the Authors

Cathy Stein Greenblat is Professor of Sociology at Rutgers University. She has published numerous books, monographs, and articles dealing with simulations, games, and issues of the family. Among the most recent works she has co-authored are *Getting Married; Game-Generating Games: A Trilogy of Issue-Oriented Games for Community and Classroom;* and *Gaming-Simulation: Rationale, Design, and Applications.* Her text, *Introduction to Sociology,* was published by Random House in 1981. Among the games she has designed are THE MARRIAGE GAME, BLOOD MONEY, and POMP AND CIRCUMSTANCE. She has served as Editor of the journal *Simulation & Games* since 1979. Dr. Greenblat received her Ph.D. from Columbia University.

Richard D. Duke is Professor of Urban and Regional Planning and Chairman of the Urban Planning Program at the University of Michigan. He has served as a Fellow at the Netherlands Institute for Advanced Studies in the Humanities and Social Sciences in Wassenaar. Dr. Duke has developed several urban game simulations, including METROPOLIS, METRO-APEX, and ODECAS, and has served as a consultant on the design and use of games in a variety of situations here and abroad. He has designed over 3 dozen simulations for clients in the last decade. His publications include *Gaming: The Future's Language.*